Fund Custody
and Administration

T0319279

Fund Custody
and Administration

David Loader

Director, Consultancy and Training
The DSC Portfolio Ltd
Managing Director, Loader Associates Ltd

AMSTERDAM • BOSTON • HEIDELBERG • LONDON
NEW YORK • OXFORD • PARIS • SAN DIEGO
SAN FRANCISCO • SINGAPORE • SYDNEY • TOKYO
Academic Press is an imprint of Elsevier

Academic Press is an imprint of Elsevier
125 London Wall, London EC2Y 5AS, United Kingdom
525 B Street, Suite 1800, San Diego, CA 92101-4495, United States
50 Hampshire Street, 5th Floor, Cambridge, MA 02139, United States
The Boulevard, Langford Lane, Kidlington, Oxford OX5 1GB, United Kingdom

Library of Congress Cataloging-in-Publication Data
A catalog record for this book is available from the Library of Congress

British Library Cataloguing-in-Publication Data
A catalogue record for this book is available from the British Library

ISBN: 978-0-12-804400-1

For information on all Academic Press publications
visit our website at https://www.elsevier.com/

  Working together
to grow libraries in
developing countries

ELSEVIER   Book Aid International

www.elsevier.com • www.bookaid.org

Publisher: Nikki Levy
Acquisition Editor: Scott Bentley
Editorial Project Manager: Susan Ikeda
Production Project Manager: Jason Mitchell
Designer: Matthew Limbert

Typeset by Thomson Digital

Contents

3. The Day-to-Day Operation of a Fund

4. Risk

About the Author

David has worked in the financial markets since leaving college. Initially involved in the debt and equity markets, he then spent a considerable time in the evolving derivatives markets. David rose through various roles including working with fund management and externally in various industry committees to senior management where as a Director with key responsibility for operations he oversaw much change and development in the processes, procedures, and risk management profiles of the firms he was associated with.

This wealth of experience has enabled David to author over 12 titles on subjects including areas such as operations management, derivatives, clearing, settlement and custody, fund administration, and operational risk.

He also works closely with CLT International and Manchester University Business School on their Advanced Certificate & Diploma in Fund Administration. He also provides consultancy services on a wide range of topics.

David is a highly regarded and sought after trainer who works internally with a wide range of major organizations in the UK and internationally, as well as leading public training programs for major training companies. He has frequently been asked to speak at major conferences across the world.

Married with a wife, daughter, and three grown up grandchildren, David enjoys, when time permits, boating on canals and rivers, cooking, and politics. He also lists football, cricket, and gardening among his favorite pastimes.

David is a member of the Institute of Directors and the Chartered Institute for Securities and Investment.

Preface

The workflow that personnel in the custody and administration teams deal with and their role in providing operational support to investment funds is a constantly changing and challenging environment.

Over the years there has been, as has happened across the financial and other markets, a significant move into automated processes and at the same time growth in the globalization of activity in these markets.

There has been many developments that have seen more and more centralizing of the clearing and settlement process, for example, clearing houses for securities transactions, CLS Bank in foreign exchange and more recently the central clearing of over the counter (OTC) derivatives.

Most changes relate to the efficiency and risk management both of which are fundamentally important to any fund and indeed the investors in the fund.

Naturally, they are also important to the regulators and a significant amount of recent change has been prompted by new legislation and regulation in the wake of the market crash of the 2007–08 period.

Subprime mortgages in the United States are widely blamed for precipitating the biggest market falls in modern times and yet while the explosion in this type of lending was heralded as one of the benefits of a long and unprecedented period of growth some thought otherwise.

While many saw great prosperity as the subprime market began to explode, others began to see red flags and potential danger for the economy. Bob Prechter, founder of Elliot Wave International, consistently argued that the out-of-control mortgage market was a threat to the US economy as the whole industry was dependent on ever-increasing property values. (The Fall Of The Market In The Fall Of 2008 http://www.investopedia.com/articles/economics/09/subprime-market-2008.asp#ixzz3n1aHnVmz)

The extent of the impact of the crash was however far from anything that was predicted. Fuelled by the collapse in value of products like collateralized mortgage obligations that had been sold to financial institutions including banks worldwide but especially in Europe, bank after bank, institution after institution needed government bailout or the prospect of going out of business.

More importantly the interbank lending virtually stopped as the collapse of Lehman Brothers sent a message that banks were not "too big to fail" and as a result a credit crunch compounded the market collapse.

Central banks reduced interest rates to near zero, quantitative easing became essential to try to stimulate lending to businesses and to kick start economies. (Definition: An unconventional monetary policy in which a central bank purchases government securities or other securities from the market in order to lower interest rates and increase the money supply. Source: Investopedia)

The crash was certainly without precedence in terms of its size and reach.

How did it all affect the fund administrators and custodians?

The answer is simple—massively!

In the first instance both were faced with a massive increase in workflow as managers tried to adjust portfolios and also meet unprecedented levels of redemptions as investors exited the funds either because they needed cash or just out of disillusionment with the huge drop in value of their investment that many experienced or out of fear.

Sales of assets were high even though most were being made at rock bottom prices and so the processing of both asset transactions and, mostly, redemptions kept both the administrators including the transfer agency and the custodian busy (The part of the administration service that deals with the investors).

Of course, not all investors could exit the funds as some types of fund like property and private equity funds had built into the offering documents restrictions and prohibition on redemptions, unlike retail funds which under the regulatory environment they operate in are usually required to have redemption on demand or certainly frequently.

Valuations of portfolios also came under intense pressure both from the general illiquid markets to questions about how values had been arrived at and the independence and robustness of the process (many funds saw dramatic falls in value with at least some questions as to whether they had been "overvalued" pre the crash).

The location of and certainty of the assets of the fund also came under intense scrutiny with many issues arising about assets that had been lent under securities lending or utilized in repurchase (repo) agreements and assets that had been used as collateral.

As one of the key roles of the custodian is the safekeeping of assets, they faced significant workload in verifying, validating, and reporting of asset positions.

Those custodians involved in operating securities lending and borrowing pools faced several issues including clients withdrawing assets from the pool and also the revaluation of collateral held against the value of the securities lent. Securities lending pools allow lenders and borrowers of securities to operate via a centralised process often managed by custodians, securities depositories and prime brokers.

Post 2008 collateral management became a major industry hot topic as regulators and risk managers placed much greater emphasis on managing exposures and counterparty risk as well due diligence on the type of investments being made. This particularly focused on investment into other funds. Today the results of a raft of new legislation and regulation, different attitudes to risk, loss of trust etc. has changed the financial markets and investment extensively presenting challenges for investment managers, fund promoters, and service suppliers to funds like custodians and fund administration.

The change and challenges show little sign of abating and so the future for administrators and custodians is a fluid situation.

An article in Funds Europe published in Oct. 2015 suggests the future of some service providers like sub-custodians may not be encouraging.

Indeed the whole infrastructure in the financial markets may be in for further radical change with new technology developments like block chain as well as initiatives like Target 2 Securities (T2S) perhaps replacing long established institutions and methodology in the trading and settlement of securities.

Meanwhile the whole cost structure of fund support is concerning fund promoters and investors and is something that administrators, depositaries, and custodians will need to address.

It is also something that regulators must take into account.

David Loader
June 2016

Introduction—What Is Fund Administration and Custody

Fund administration and custody are generic processes that all funds whether retail products available to all investors or what have become referred to as alternative investment funds (AIFs) which are restricted in terms of the type of investor.

There are many tasks and functions that will be carried out by teams under the services of administration and custody.

Some will be common across funds and others will be quite bespoke to particular types of fund.

Common tasks and functions will include for the administrator areas such as

1. Fund set up
2. Fund records
3. Pricing and valuation of assets
4. Compilation of the fund accounting records
5. Production of the audit file
6. Calculation of the Net Asset Value (NAV) of the fund
7. Dealing with investors subscriptions and redemptions
8. Communication with investors
9. Secretarial services
10. Reporting

The precise workflow will be very much dependent on the fund and is determined by things such as the investment products and strategies used in the investment process. In addition the regulatory requirements will affect the work the administrator is involved in and the level of work will vary from lightly (relatively) regulated funds like AIFS to the heavily regulated retail funds. Of course, there are also unregulated funds, which have very little associated work.

Custodians will have common services they provide to funds in particular the following:

1. Safekeeping of assets
2. Managing the asset settlement process with the market infrastructure
3. Managing activity in securities lending and borrowing
4. Managing activity in corporate actions
5. Dealing with withholding tax (WHT) reclaims

In terms of the bespoke services that the administrator and custodian offer this is perhaps more prevalent in the context of the alternative Investment funds which in general terms comprises Hedge Funds, Private Equity Funds, and Property Funds as well as perhaps Commodity funds and those investing in specific alternatives.

The administrator is in effect, the management of the Fund in virtually all aspects of the day-to-day operations of the Fund, except the actual investment of the assets, which is the responsibility of the investment manager.

As a result, the administrator is always answerable to the Board of Directors, General Partner or Trustee and does not have any actual senior management control. In simple terms, an administrator is responsible for ensuring the efficient operation of a fund leaving the investment manager free to concentrate on the portfolio of investments.

Some funds are listed on exchanges and if this is the case, the administrator will ensure that the company and the directors comply with the ongoing obligations of the relevant stock exchange.

AGREEMENTS

Both administrators and custodians will sign an agreement with the Fund that will cover the relevant topics listed earlier.

Depending on the terms of its agreement, the administrator may also be responsible for ensuring that the Fund complies with the terms of its offering documents such as Offering or Placement Memorandum, Prospectus, Scheme Particulars etc.

ADVANTAGES OF 3RD PARTY ADMINISTRATORS AND CUSTODIANS

The market crash and aftermath left investors disillusioned and destroyed the trust between the Fund and the investor. Regulators and investors both see comfort in having key operational aspects of the fund carried out independently.

This includes pricing and valuations of the assets and the safekeeping of the fund's assets.

It is important of course to recognize that the majority of directors and general partners of funds maintained complete and accurate records and the value of the fund was likewise accurate.

Assets were recorded and safely kept in the records of the custodians, however as noted in the Preface, the environment today is one of caution and prudent management of risk and so independence and transparency are key issues.

The size as well as the activity and complexity of the assets and strategies employed by the investment manager will have a significant impact on the workload and difficulty of the task for both administrator and custodian.

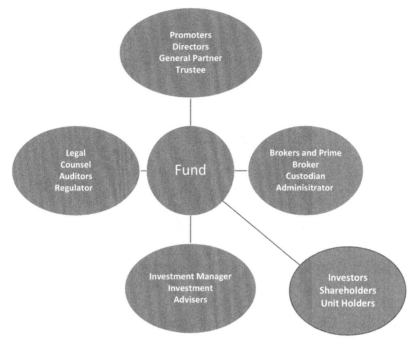

DIAGRAM 1   Fund structure. *(Source: The DSC Portfolio Ltd.)*

Retail funds can have billions of dollars or pounds or euros under management whereas many AIFS can be far less than 500 million.

Also retail funds are mostly open-ended meaning that subscriptions and redemptions take place frequently, possibly daily whereas a lot of non-retail funds are closed with less activity in this area. Naturally, the frequency of subscription and redemption affects cash flow and therefore portfolio activity.

FUND RELATIONSHIP STRUCTURE

There are several key parties in the fund structure as the Diagram 1 shows.

They range from the parties who own the fund and have governance responsibilities to institutions, which provide access to markets and services.

Also of course, there are the investors in the fund providing capital as shareholders or unit holders. Unit Trusts have unit holders whereas companies and partnerships have shareholders.

ADMINISTRATION STRUCTURE

A full service administrator will involve the three key areas shown above and can often include the services of the fund Secretary, provision of Directors and assistance with risk management and compliance (Diagram 2).

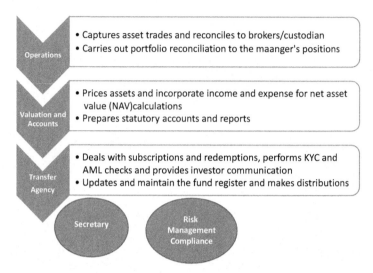

DIAGRAM 2   Administration workflow. *(Source: The DSC Portfolio Ltd.)*

Comparison With Retail/Mutual Funds

The term Mutual funds is widely used globally whereas in Europe the term Retail Fund also used. In the rest of this book, we will mainly use the terms Retail and Alternative Investment Funds. There are a number of areas in which the administration of alternative investment funds like Hedge Funds differs from the administration of the more traditional Retail/Mutual Funds or Unit Trusts. These include the range of investment instruments in the portfolio; and the strategies used to exploit these instruments; the ability to go short; leverage; fee structures, including incentive or performance fees; and equalization. A process that seeks to ensure each investor pays the correct amount of any performance fee due to the investment manager. The traditional Mutual Funds or Unit Trusts are, for the most part, retail funds with quite restrictive investment policies, which include:

- very broad diversification;
- no short selling;
- no leverage; and
- derivative trading limited to Efficient Portfolio Management, which is a term that refers to hedging risk

Hedge Fund strategies can utilise a vast range of derivative instruments, which can introduce pricing problems for the administrator as many of these products have bespoke bilaterally negotiated terms with no independently published value unlike listed products. These instruments range from the relatively straightforward exchange traded commodities, financial futures and options contracts, to highly complex derivative products, which include swaps and swaptions, as well as contracts for difference (CFDs), currency forward contracts and a wide variety of customised instruments created by major banks and financial institutions and sold on the Over the Counter or OTC market. We will become familiar with many of these instruments as the book progresses. Hedge Fund portfolios, which have these "exotic" investments in the portfolio, are not inherently difficult to administer or account for, providing, and this is the key, the Administrator is able to obtain a reliable and verifiable price for the investments, upon which that Administrator can base the NAV calculation. Funds that operate in these bespoke OTC products must have a clear valuation policy that is disclosed in the offering document. Where possible, an independent price source must be used. If that is not possible, for some reason, a reasonable, practical pricing formula must be agreed between the Investment Manager, the Administrator, and preferably the Auditor, before the Fund is launched and incorporated in the pricing policy and the offering documents.

FUND SET UP

Many administrators offer services related to setting up a fund in a jurisdiction.

This is of particular value for a promoter setting up a fund in an offshore jurisdiction. Here the knowledge of the local regulatory environment enables the administrator to compose and file the necessary application forms, provide the reference and provisional appointments for the key support services etc.

CUSTODY AND DEPOSITARY SERVICES

Custody services are either on a direct basis between the fund and a custodian in various jurisdictions that the fund may transact asset activity or on a Global Custody basis whereby the fund appoints a single custodian who will manage the services across various markets centrally.

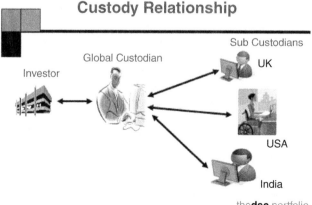

The way in which the custodian operates in the market infrastructure is shown below:

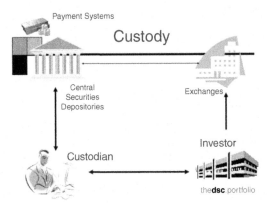

WHAT IS THE ROLE OF A DEPOSITARY?

A depositary is required under the regulations for some types of fund.

In Europe this relates to retail and non-retail structures under the UCITS and AIFMD.

Depositaries have specific roles including those related to the oversight of cash management process, the safekeeping and verification of assets and the valuation of assets, all of which are also services that a traditional custodian offers.

We will look at this role more closely in Part 2 of the book.

TYPES OF FUND

Administration and custody will vary across different types of fund.

Traditional retail or mutual funds will generally have high levels of activity in both assets and subscriptions and redemptions whereas AIFs such as hedge funds, private equity funds and property funds will have often much less activity in both areas. Valuation, reporting, and fund records are of course common across all funds but the degree of difficulty and challenge for the administrator will again vary depending on the assets and strategies employed by the investment manager.

In this book, we will be looking at both retail funds and AIFs.

SUMMARY

The fund support process can be extensive, occasionally complicated and involves a high degree of effective communication, knowledge and system capability in its provision.

Above all the administrator has a very significant relationship with the investment manager, the senior management of the fund and through the transfer agency services, the investors in the fund.

In this book, we will look at how the fund operates and how the administrator and custodian play a major role in that operation.

Part 1

Introduction to Investment

INVESTMENT ENVIRONMENT

The process of investment is a concept that has been around for a long, long time. For the purposes of this book we will be considering the investment industry from the 1900s onward.

It is always interesting to ponder the question of what is gambling and what is investment?

Is the pursuit of profit greed or a structured contingency against future requirements, for example, a pension?

In the 1800s canal and railway mania in the UK created and lost fortunes so was this gambling, speculation, or structured investment?

Certainly for the lucky ones it was a foundation for enormous wealth that has sustained the family through generations. Others lost all their money and often ended in debtors jails with families broken and living in terrible deprivation. This was not a UK phenomenon but spread across the globe as the industrialization and growth of economies, often on the back of colonization and empires captured the imagination of entrepreneurs, businessmen, and of course speculators.

In the United States, which originally was what we would call today an emerging market, an example would be the gold rush and this was also in evidence in Australia and New Zealand, Africa, and other countries. In Asia and the Caribbean, the spice trade was heavily "invested in" and of course at the other end of the spectrum slavery was another "investment" that generated huge fortunes for individuals and families.

Today we can look back at this "market" and recognize that most fortunes were built on exploitation, often brutal and uncaring, of people, often children like in mining and industry, and the natural resources of other countries with little or no benefit to the people of that country.

Traders, merchants, and speculators were totally dominant and profit and returns came before all.

Ironically, today we have some disturbingly similar parallels with investment (or some will say exploitation) in "emerging markets" where the wages, working and living condition of workers is appalling, particularly compared to the standards found in the mature markets of the United States and Western Europe.

The kind of highly speculative investment found in the 1800s underwent an evolution and to all intent a purpose became the forerunner of the investment industry we are familiar with today, as those with insufficient capital to take a reasonable stake in an enterprise joined together to create "collective investment" often in the form of syndicates and partnerships.

Earlier "investors" were exposed to some extraordinary risks, often without being aware of such risks, and their general naivety left them vulnerable to scams and frauds.

Today investment is a structured process with collective investment schemes (CIS) created in the form of investment funds, many of which are regulated. In many jurisdictions around the world investors, especially those with limited knowledge of finance and awareness of risk are offered high levels of protection.

Those investors with greater knowledge and awareness can opt to invest their capital in more lightly regulated products and even products that are unregulated.

The need for the regulation of investment and the adoption of change can be found in numerous case studies, some a long time ago but also some more recent.

Case Study 1—Bearer Securities

The main form of asset that investors typically have exposure to are equities and debt instruments or generically known as securities.

For many years a significant number of these securities were in bearer format meaning that they were physical or paper securities that did not carry the name of the owner of the securities (hence the term bearer—whoever had possession of the instrument was the owner).

This created problems and risks, not least loss through theft or destruction.

It became clear that these types of securities needed safekeeping and so the concept of the "custody and safekeeping" was born to reduce the risk of loss of assets.

The first custodian banks surfaced in the United States in the 1930s as simple safekeepers of paper assets holding them in a vault on behalf of the owner. Today the role of the custodian is far more diverse and has undergone huge changes as we will see later in the book.

Case Study 2—Bernie Madoff

The market crash of 2008 and the subsequent recession and economic problems of the United States and Europe created cash flow issues for almost everybody from government, through corporate companies to individuals and not surprisingly many investors looked to exit investment funds to raise much needed capital.

The market crash of 2008 preceded by the demise of Bear Stearns and precipitated by the collapse of the sub-prime mortgage market and Lehman Brothers bank in the United States led to a global credit crisis, the collapse of banks and massive government bailouts followed by severe austerity measures in many countries. From an investment point of view, this was the worst possible time to exit funds as many assets were at all-time lows, but needs must as they say.

Bernie Madoff was a highly respected and influential individual in the US capital markets. He had held high positions of responsibility, was hugely experienced and had set up an investment fund, which naturally attracted many investors around the world who implicitly trusted him and believed in his skills and talents. As a well-respected financier, Madoff convinced thousands of investors to hand over their savings, falsely promising consistent profits in return. He was caught in Dec. 2008 and charged with 11 counts of fraud, money laundering, perjury, and theft.

Sadly for those investors Mr Madoff was not operating an investment fund. Instead he was operating a Ponzi scheme.

Definition—A Ponzi scheme is a fraudulent investing scam promising high rates of return with little risk to investors. The Ponzi scheme generates returns for older investors by acquiring new investors. This scam actually yields the promised returns to earlier investors, as long as there are more new investors.

So what purported to be and was assumed by investors to be an investment fund that had assets and was performing extremely well had actually defrauded investors and left most with a complete loss of capital.

Just over six years ago Bernie Madoff was sentenced to 150 years in prison for running the biggest fraudulent scheme in United States history. Even now, only a few of his victims have since regained all of their losses.

Had the market crash not put pressure on investor's finances and thus led to redemption requests that could not be met, his scam could still be working today with no one any the wiser.

Readers can find further details of how a Ponzi scheme operates and Madoff's downfall at http://www.businessinsider.com/how-bernie-madoffs-ponzi-scheme-worked-2014-7.

Fund management became an enormously important component of what was rapidly becoming a key part of the capital markets as the increasing wealth of individuals sought returns and the capital needs of growing companies and indeed economies had to be financed.

Diagram 1.1 shows the general structure of the capital markets broken into sectors. Purists may consider commodities and other assets as being outside the scope of capital markets.

Investor's pooled capital in a CIS became a prime source of the capital flow. Their capital was either passively managed, which meant it was placed in a fixed, unchanging portfolio of assets or one that tracks a benchmark like an equity index, or is actively managed, which means that an investment manager creates and manages the portfolio seeking to generate a return higher than a benchmark. We will consider this again shortly.

DIAGRAM 1.1 The markets. *(Source: The DSC Portfolio Ltd.)*

In the capital markets, financial instruments are created and offered to investors by originators such as corporate companies, governments, and sometimes intermediaries. These offerings can be in the form of a public offering or a placement. An offering of securities or financial instruments can be in the form of, for example, an initial public offering (IPO) or can be placed with financial institutions by investment banks.

As the globalization of investment grew and more and more issues arose, regulation increased. Regulatory authorities were established in onshore jurisdictions and also offshore fund centers, where the regulatory environments were suitable for those investors needing less protection and where the regulation was less onerous and costly for the fund promoter. Onshore and offshore refers to the domicile of the investor and the domicile of the fund, for example, a UK investor who has invested in a Jersey domiciled fund (offshore) or a UK investor who has invested in a UK domiciled fund (onshore).

By the latter part of the last century, regulation became focused on funds that would be sold to general investors generically called "retail" funds and those that were designed for more experienced individuals and institutions which became generically called "alternative," "nonretail" or "qualifying funds."

The crash of 2008 exposed huge gaps in the levels and efficiency of the regulatory structures.

As a result huge changes took place post the crash.

As noted earlier, the investment is structured and fund management is part of that structure as illustrated in Diagram 1.2.

The process of investment needs support and this is provided by parties that fall under the title of fund services.

The kind of workflow they deal with would be based on:

1. Settlement of acquisition and disposal of assets and the correct portfolio records.
2. Subscription and redemption requests, receipts, and proceeds being managed.
3. Accruals, income, benefits, entitlements, and expenses being processed and recorded in the fund's records.

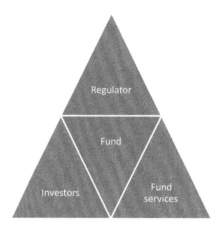

DIAGRAM 1.2   Fund relationships. *(Source: The DSC Portfolio Ltd.)*

4. Accurate calculation of the value of the fund. Many funds publish a Net Asset Value (NAV) of the fund either daily or periodically and this may be used as the subscription or redemption price of the fund's shares or units.
5. Distribution of income where applicable. Some funds distribute income to investors periodically while other reinvest income to create growth in the fund's value.
6. Statutory accounts, management, and investor information regulatory reports must all be compiled and distributed.

In addition performance must be monitored and above all the fund must comply with any applicable regulation, have strong governance and control of risk.

ISLAMIC INVESTMENT FUNDS

So far we have been describing investment as found in the conventional markets of Europe, the United States, and Canada etc.

The investment process including the investment funds are operated under commercial Law, for example, Partnership, Trust, or Company Law and the legislation and regulation applicable to the markets in which the assets are traded.

However Islamic funds are part of the Islamic finance environment, which operates under quite different circumstances.

What is Islamic finance?

- A faith based proposition
- Underpinned by beliefs, values, and principles
- Not solely for Muslims as core principles can be embraced by many sections of society

Why does this impact on investment fund products?

- The teachings of Islam encompass all aspects of life
- Islam is an Arabic term which means "submission to Gods will"
- Islam is dynamically involved in public affairs unlike typical Western religions
- Islamic faith has clear principles and guidelines for business and financial dealings

An excellent example of the difference between how a fund is invested involves interest or *riba*. A key feature of Islamic finance is that paying or receiving interest is forbidden. The Muslim holy book the *Qur'an* warns against this in the strongest terms.

Conventional finance is very often based on the concept of interest and yet the Holy Bible says:

"Do not take interest of any kind from him, but fear your God, so that your countryman may continue to live among you." (Leviticus 25:36)

and

"If you lend money to one of my people among you who is needy, do not be like a moneylender; charge him no interest" (Exodus 22:25)

and

"Do not charge your brother interest, whether on money or food or anything else that may earn interest." (Deuteronomy 23:19)

However, the dynamic nature of Islam means that although both Holy Books condemn interest, only Islam enforces a prohibition on it.

Conventional funds therefore can invest in bonds and other financial instruments and arrangements that involve payment of interest but Islamic funds cannot.

The rules and guidelines that Islamic finance operates under is referred to as Sharia which is a framework of rules, principles, and guidance derived from Islamic teachings. It can be referred to as Islamic Law and financial products used by individuals, corporates, and other institutions like investment funds can be referred to as *sharia*-compliant.

Other concepts in conventional financial markets and products like profit, income from dividends and rentals, as well as instruments and assets like equities, property etc. are also found in Islamic finance.

Islamic investment funds have grown substantially.

In a recent study by Thomson Reuters and their subsidiary Lipper, it was found that Islamic mutual funds globally now hold $53.2 billion of assets under management, recovering from a low of $25.7 billion in 2008, and that the total numbers of Islamic mutual funds established reached 943 in 2014, up from 828 a year earlier, and double the number in 2008 (May 2015—full article can be found at http://www.reuters.com/article/2015/05/19/islam-financing-funds-idUSL5N0YA04I20150519).

We will return to Islamic funds later.

As markets and the investment industry have changed it has placed more and more pressure on funds and their administrators.

We can summarize the investment industry today as:

It is still recovering from market crash and ongoing liquidity problems as well as more current situations like Greek debt issues, migrants flooding into Europe, and what seems to be a slowing Chinese economy.

Investors, both private and institutional, are wary of issues like strength of control, oversight, and reconciliation over the assets of a fund (Madoff), large and sudden drop in Net Asset Value (NAV) of some funds (suggesting unrealistic valuation of assets) and a general negative view of participants in the financial markets (short selling, high performance fees, bank rip offs, lack of control etc.).

Alternative investments have become popular with some investors, for example, buying gold, art, antiques, stamps etc.

There has been a significant amount of regulation and new legislation introduced including the Alternative Investment Fund Managers Directive (AIFMD), The European Markets Infrastructure Regulation (EMIR), UCITS V, and the Markets in Financial Instruments Directive II (MiFID) in Europe as well as Dodd-Frank (United States) with greater emphasis on transparency and reporting (Full title—the Dodd-Frank Wall St Reform Act).

There is also increasing legislation aimed at tax avoidance like the US Foreign Account Tax Compliance Act (FATCA) although if the following comment is anything to go by it is not always perceived as successful.

America's controversial global tax law, FATCA, has been slammed as "a masterclass in fiscal imperialism and the law of unintended consequences," by the boss of one of the world's largest independent financial advisory organizations.

The comments from Nigel Green, deVere Group CEO and founder, come as it is shown that, despite FATCA, America is increasingly secret in matters of financial data; and because of FATCA, a growing number of US citizens are giving up their American citizenship.

Under the Foreign Account Tax Compliance Act, which came into effect in July 2014, all non-US financial institutions are required to report the financial information of American clients who have accounts holding more than US$50,000 directly to the IRS (Full article can be found at http://www.globalcustody.net/n8163)."

We look more at regulation in Part 2 of this book.

What we do know is that the main drivers behind what is happening in the investment industry today are simply regulation and investor pressures.

Investment Objectives

There are many reasons for investing and a wide variety of expectations by investors, some more realistic than others.

Logically one expectation of investment is that the value of capital is maintained or increased. So the investment return must at least be equal to the inflation rate and the cost of investing, that is, management fees.

Another expectation is to provide a form of income such as a pension or to top up other income sources like salary and other savings.

All kinds of quaint expressions have been spawned over the years like "saving for a rainy day" or "look after the pennies and the pounds will take care of themselves" or "don't put all your eggs in one basket."

The reality of investment is that *return* and *risk* are intrinsically linked.

The higher the return expected the greater the risk in achieving that return.

Time is another huge factor in delivering the objective of a fund with more risk likely to happen in achieving short-term returns.

The objectives of the fund are contained in the offering documents.

These can be called prospectuses, offering or placement memorandums, scheme particulars etc.

With each term relating to a type of fund, for example, an investment company, a unit trust etc. which we will look at in more detail in the next section, but which are designed to provide all the relevant information that an investor needs to decide on whether to place their capital in the fund.

For example, the UK Financial conduct Authority (FCA) has in its conduct of business source book the following in respect of offering documents under the AIFMD.

The Meaning of an Offering or Placement
PERG 8.37.5G22/07/2013

1. *The terms "offering" or "placement" are not defined in the AIFMD UK regulation but, in our view, an offering or placement takes place for the purposes of the AIFMD UK regulation when a person seeks to raise capital by making a unit of share of an AIF available for purchase by a potential investor. This includes situations which constitute a contractual offer that can be accepted by a potential investor in order to make the investment and form a binding contract, and situations which constitute an invitation to the investor to make an offer to subscribe for the investment.*

2. *An "offering" includes situations where the units or shares of an AIF are made available to the general public and a "placement" includes situations where the units or shares of an AIF are only made available to a more limited group of potential investors.*

3. *However, an "offering" or "placement" does not include secondary trading in the units or shares of an AIF, because this does not relate to the capital raising in that AIF, except in situations where there is an indirect offering or placement (see PERG 8.37.7 G). Similarly, the listing of the units or shares of an AIF on the official list maintained by the FCA in accordance with section 74(1) of the Act will not in and of itself constitute an offering or placement, although it may be accompanied by such an offering or placement.*

Source: https://www.handbook.fca.org.uk/handbook/PERG/8/37.html

It is also worth at this point looking at the following again from the FCS sourcebook and in relation to what is a share or unit in an AIF and the meaning of investor:

The Meaning of a Unit or Share of an AIF

PERG 8.37.8G22/07/2013

The terms "unit" and "share" in the AIFMD UK regulation are generic and can be interpreted as encompassing all forms of equity of, or other rights in, an AIF. As such, the terms are not limited to AIFs, which are structured as companies or unitized funds and may include other forms of collective investment undertakings, such as partnerships or nonunitized trusts.

The Meaning of Investor

PERG 8.37.9G22/07/2013

1. *The reference to "investor" in the AIFMD UK regulation should be regarded as a reference to the person who will make the decision to invest in the AIF. Where that person acts on its own behalf and subscribes directly to an AIF, the investor should be considered to be the person who subscribes to the unit or share of the AIF.*
2. *However, where that person engages another person to subscribe to the AIF on its behalf, including, for example, where:*

    a. *a nominee company will subscribe as bare trustee for an underlying beneficiary; or*

    b. *a custodian will subscribe on behalf of an underlying investor, the AIFM or investment firm that is marketing the AIF should "look through" the subscriber to find the underlying investor who will make the decision to invest in the AIF and that person should be regarded as the investor.*
3. *Where a discretionary manager subscribes, or arranges for another person to subscribe, on behalf of an underlying investor to the AIF and the discretionary manager makes the decision to invest in the AIF on that investor's behalf without reference to the investor, it is not necessary to "look through" the structure and the discretionary manager should be considered to be the investor for the purposes of the AIFMD UK regulation.*

In respect of a prospectus, often used for retail funds we have the following from the FCA:

PR 2.3 Minimum Information to be Included in a Prospectus

Minimum information

PR 2.3.1EU27/09/2013

Articles 3 to 23 of the *PD Regulation* provide for the minimum information to be included in a *prospectus*:

Note: the Annexes (including *schedules* and *building blocks*) referred to in these articles are set out for information in *PR App 3*.

Article 3
Minimum information to be included in a prospectus:

A prospectus shall be drawn up by using one or a combination of the schedules and building blocks set out in this Regulation.

A prospectus shall contain the information items required in Annexes I to XVII and Annexes XX to XXX depending on the type of issuer or issues and securities involved (See https://www.handbook.fca.org.uk/handbook/PR/App/3/#D1). Subject to Article 4a(1), a competent authority shall not require that a prospectus contains information items which are not included in Annexes I to XVII or Annexes XX to XXX.

In order to ensure conformity with the obligation referred to in Article 5(1) of Directive 2003/71/EC, the competent authority of the home Member State, when approving a prospectus in accordance with Article 13 of that Directive, may, on a case by case basis, require the information provided by the issuer, the offeror, or the person asking for admission to trading on a regulated market to be completed, for each of the information items.

Where the issuer, the offeror, or the person asking for the admission to trading on a regulated market is required to include a summary in a prospectus, in accordance with Article 5(2) of Directive 2003/71/EC, the competent authority of the home Member State, when approving the prospectus in accordance with Article 13 of that Directive, may, on a case by case basis, require certain information provided in the prospectus, to be included in the summary.

Part of the content of the offering documents will relate to risk and return.

As far as risk and return are concerned, we have investments that are very low risk like, for example, US Treasury Bonds or higher risk like Corporate Bonds and listed equities or very high risks like High Yield bonds and private equity.

However, the investment process may also incorporate hedging against some risks and so the use of derivative instruments may also occur (Derivatives are explained in more detail in Part 5 of the book).

Highly speculative investment can utilize derivatives as well but they may also include structured products, illiquid assets, and complex strategies in the portfolios.

That said we must put investment risk into context and while the value of investments can go down as well as up, the complete and total loss of capital is not a common occurrence.

To summarize;

Investment—revolves around key concepts

These are:

1. Risk and return are related
2. Time to realize the return is important—long, medium, short
3. Risk appetite:
   a. Low-conservative—diversified across many assets, no use of derivatives (except for currency risk management) and other "risky" assets, no

borrowing (gearing/leverage created liabilities), no risky strategies, for example, short selling, foreign exchange risk removed through forward contracts, often benchmarked or tracker type funds (passive).

b. Medium—diversified portfolio of assets, some use of derivatives mainly to hedge risk, limited gearing and exposures, major part of the portfolio in low risk assets like G7 government bonds, blue chip equities, rest in more volatile assets, for example, high yield bonds, speculative equities—example split 80–20% or 70–30%, often actively managed.

c. High-low diversification—wide use of derivatives and structured products, use illiquid assets like private equity and property (real estate) gearing/leverage common, unlikely to distribute income, use high risk strategies like short selling, skewed exposures, mainly absolute return funds.

However, investors have to be careful when considering the amount of return they expect as many jurisdictions levy tax on both income and capital gain.

Investment is often made into financial instruments like those found in the equity and debt offerings, which in turn are part of the capital markets. Financial instruments are created and offered by corporate companies, local authorities and governments and purchased by investors. See Diagram 1.3.

However investment funds are rarely members of the institutions in the capital market infrastructure and utilize the services offered by banks and brokers.

This will include research services that the investment manager will combine with their own "inhouse" research before deciding on the asset allocation of the portfolio.

The fund could invest in new securities that are being issued for the first time in what is called the primary market, for example, an initial public offering (IPO) of securities or they could buy and sell securities in the secondary market.

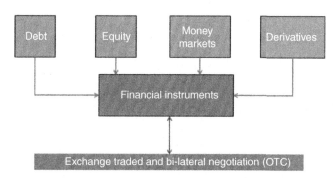

DIAGRAM 1.3   Capital markets Overview. (*Source: The DSC Portfolio*)

Alternatively, a fund may acquire securities from a placement by an investment bank. A placement is where the investment bank "places" the shares with their institutional clients like investment funds rather than offering them to the public.

Some funds will also invest in the shares or units of other funds and as noted earlier could be using instruments like derivatives, for example, to manage risk. (see Part 5)

Funds can be capital *growth* or *income* (or combination of the two, eg, balanced fund). The higher the need or expectation of growth will involve the fund taking more risk.

Hedge funds tend to focus on growth and therefore often take more risk, for example, selling short and leveraging the portfolio through borrowing cash. Performance is measured via the absolute return of the fund. Absolute return is the return from every asset irrespective of whether the market rises or falls.

Retail funds are more low risk, that is, have no liabilities and have higher diversification. They tend to invest in high income stocks which pay dividends/interest income and liquid securities. Liquid securities are those usually listed on an exchange that can be bought and sold easily. Performance is measured against a benchmark.

Investment objectives are met via an investment *strategy*. Strategies can broadly be split into:

Top Down Style—Focus is initially at the macro economic level before deciding on the specific industries and stocks to purchase.

Bottom Up style—Seek out individual companies worth investing in.

Management style can also be classified as either *passive* or *active*.

Passive—Investment manager does not exist as there is a constant composition of the portfolio, for example, tracker funds.

Active—Investment manager may make frequent changes to the composition of the fund in order to take advantage of opportunities when they arise.

Collective Investment Schemes (CIS) and the Investment Management Process

There are many types of CIS and they fall into types of fund entity of which there are three main structures which are listed here with their oversight responsibility.

Investment company—board of directors—established under company law in the jurisdiction.

Unit Trust—trustee—established under trust law of a jurisdiction.

Partnership—general partner—established under partnership law of a jurisdiction.

There can also be funds with no legal personality often called *Common funds* operated by a management company or broker.

As noted previously, we have *Retail* funds which can be sold to anyone, have a high level of regulatory protection for the investors, usually have to have transferability (investor can enter/exit fund on demand), have diversity in the portfolio and does not have liabilities like cash borrowing or short sales in the portfolio.

We then have funds that carry a title such as *Qualifying Investor, Expert, or Market Professional funds, as well as Fund of Funds and Exempt funds* all of which have a restricted investor base [market professionals, institutions, high net worth individuals (circa. $1 or 2 million in cash) as determined by the regulator and or Laws in the jurisdiction and therefore need to have less regulatory protection].

In Europe especially these funds are generically called "alternative investment funds" (AIFs) and may take the form of hedge funds, private equity funds, and property funds. In Europe specific legislation, the Alternative Investment Fund Managers Directive (AIFMD) is in place for the management of these type of funds.

We also know that funds are either passively or actively managed however they can also be open-ended or closed. *Open-ended funds* can increase or reduce the number of shares or units issued so have variable capital and their name often clearly relates to this, that is, *Open-ended Investment Company* (OEIC), *Investment Company with Variable Capital* (ICVC), or *Société d'Investissement à Capital Variable*(SICAV). Many European retail funds are open-ended funds to comply with the redemption requirements of the Undertaking for Collective Investment in Transferable Securities (UCITS) Directive. The UCITS Directive requires funds to allow an investor to sell their shares or units without restriction.

In the United States, we find *Mutual funds* which are open ended and on sale to retail customers.

Each jurisdiction will have specific regulation linked to what type of investment funds can be established. This will include retail and alternative investment funds. The following is an example of the Jersey Expert Fund requirements:

Expert Funds

Where a fund is to be regulated as a collective investment fund, which means an unlimited number of offers can be made to an unlimited number of investors, then a regulatory light touch is still possible providing all the investors qualify as expert investors and expressly acknowledge an investment warning, which allows a fund to qualify as an "expert fund" under the JFSC Expert Fund Guide. Expert investors include among other tests that any person investing at least $100,000 or currency equivalent. The approval process for seeking a permit for the fund is streamlined and allows for the establishment of a fund within as little as three days of the formal filing of the application.

The investment manager must be regulated in a state being an OECD member or subject to a memorandum of undertaking with the JFSC or otherwise approved by the JFSC.

An expert fund is available only to expert investors.

The offer document for an expert fund must comply with certain content requirements.

The fund company, general partner, or trustee requires at least two Jersey resident directors and the fund itself must be a Jersey company, or have a Jersey general partner (if a limited partnership), or a Jersey trustee (if a unit trust).

An expert fund must have a Jersey "monitoring functionary" being either an administrator or a manager in Jersey.

Source: Jersey Fund Association.

For details of the full Jersey Investment Funds—regulatory options, please see Appendix 1.

UNREGULATED FUNDS

Many jurisdictions have unregulated funds, which are designed for specific types of investors and often have a limited number of investors in the fund.

For example, in Jersey we find the following fund structure type:

Unregulated funds are exempted from regulation as collective investment funds by virtue of an exemption order, which specifies schemes or arrangements, which have been established as either:

An unregulated exchange-traded fund, being a scheme or arrangement established in Jersey, which is a closed-ended fund and which is listed on a stock exchange or market or which is applying for its shares or units to be granted such a listing; or

An unregulated eligible investor fund, being a scheme or arrangement established in Jersey and in which only eligible investors may invest, being either an investor who makes a minimum initial investment of US$1 million or the currency equivalent (whether through the initial offering or by subsequent acquisition) or, alternatively, institutional investors or professional investors, as defined in the order. An unregulated eligible investor fund may be open or closed and transfers of interests are only possible to other eligible investors. Stock exchange listings for unregulated eligible investor funds will be possible subject to transfer restrictions, as referred earlier, still applying.

Either type of unregulated fund may take any form recognized under the laws of Jersey as being a Jersey company (including a cell structure), a Jersey limited partnership having at least one Jersey corporate general partner, or a unit trust having a Jersey corporate trustee or manager.

Subject to the structure complying with the order, there is no regulatory review or oversight of the terms or conduct of such an unregulated fund and, therefore, processes for their establishment will depend only on being carried out in accordance with the exemption order.

The offer and /or listing document of an unregulated fund must contain a prominent statement that the fund is unregulated, together with a prescribed form of investment warning.

In order to claim exemption as an unregulated fund, a completed notice needs to be filed with the Jersey registrar of companies.

For details of the full Jersey Investment Funds—regulatory options, see Appendix 1.

Note: An unregulated fund must still maintain full and proper records related to the fund and there will be legal responsibilities associated with the directors, general partner, or trustee of such funds. Also, the unregulated fund may still need to be registered with the regulator and only authorized or licensed personnel and service providers can operate the fund.

A *closed fund* has a fixed investment capital and does not issue or cancel shares however this does not necessarily mean that shares or units cannot be transferred between parties.

In the first part of this section, we saw that the funds have offering documents and so the detail of whether the fund is open-ended or closed will be found there along with other crucially important information.

The Prospectus/Offering Memorandum/Scheme Particulars will contain all the relevant information and disclosures about the fund including:

- Investment objectives.
- Risk profile including products invested in.
- Functionaries (including investment manager, management company, trustee, directors, general partner, administrator, custodian/depositary, auditors, secretary).
- Subscription and redemption details.
- Investor constraints.
- Taxation issues.
- Legal details—company, trust, partnership, or common fund.
- Valuation of the fund and the NAV publication.
- Regulator or statement that the fund is not regulated.
- Fees and charges applicable to the fund including any performance fee payable to the investment managers if targets are met.
- Rights of the shareholders in an investment company, or unit holders in a trust, or the limited partners in a partnership.
- Conflicts of interest.

The information will be used by financial advisers and investors but the fund support teams generically called fund administration and custody as well as the investment manager will also use these documents for guidance and to plan the necessary procedures and processes for the operation of the fund.

The investment process itself depends on the type of fund so a passive fund which tracks a benchmark will invest the capital into the assets in the weighting that makes up the benchmark. There is no decision making and no investment manager.

In an actively managed fund, the investment process will involve portfolio management including asset allocation and selection, which we will look at in later sections.

Active investment management is usually carried out either by an *investment manager* who operates under a Discretionary Investment Management Agreement (IMA or DIMA), which details what the manager can and cannot invest in, strategies that can and cannot be used etc. plus the expected performance, remuneration including performance fees. In addition the manager must comply with applicable regulation or by an investment committee and investment advisers.

Investment advisers research potential investments and recommend them to, for example, the investment committee who will decide on the final composition of the portfolio. The advisers earn fees and possibly a share of the return the portfolio generates.

By way of example, the manager structure is common in retail funds and the latter structure in private equity and property funds.

While there will always be variances, the investment process looks like that shown in Diagram 1.4.

The boys and girls in the administration and custody teams must be fully conversant with this flow so that they can identify the key sources of data, critical action points, primary reconciliations, and the potential operational risk areas.

A failure to do this would leave the fund vulnerable to costly errors, noncompliance with investment mandates, internal policies and agreements, possible breaches of regulation, and even fraud.

Other fund structures:

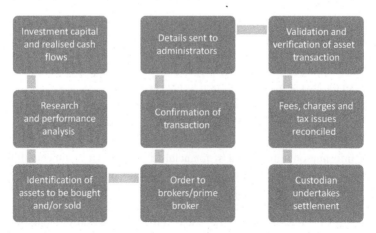

DIAGRAM 1.4 The investment process. *(Source: The DSC Portfolio Ltd.)*

There are many possible structures for funds such as Fund of Funds, Multi-Manager Funds, Master/Feeder Funds etc. and Diagram 1.5–1.7 illustrate these.

Each of these will have different characteristics and therefore pose different challenges for the administrator and custodian. For example, the fund of fund structure means that the valuation of the fund is going to be based on the value of the funds invested in rather than a portfolio of assets. A multi manager fund has potentially a series of administrators allied to the individual management and a master/feeder structure has individual funds established in different

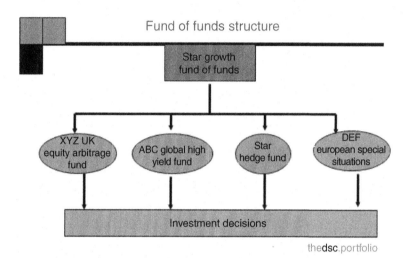

DIAGRAM 1.5   *(Source: The DSC Portfolio/one Study Training)*

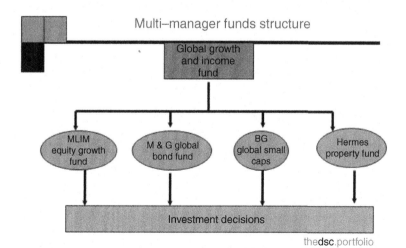

DIAGRAM 1.6   *(Source: The DSC Portfolio/one Study Training)*

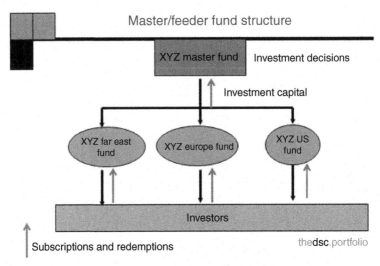

Master/feeder fund structure

XYZ master fund   Investment decisions

Investment capital

XYZ far east fund   XYZ europe fund   XYZ US fund

Investors

Subscriptions and redemptions   thedsc.portfolio

DIAGRAM 1.7   *(Source: The DSC Portfolio/one Study Training)*

jurisdictions that investors subscribe capital to. In turn the funds subscribe to a master fund. So the workflow for the administrator of the master fund is mostly to do with investments and the portfolio while the administrators of the feeder funds are mainly dealing with the investors.

As always the regulatory environment and offering documents together with internal procedures and controls determine exactly what work will be involved.

To summarize:

Different fund locations have developed around the world in response to the growth of investment funds both retail and nonretail. For example, Luxembourg and Dublin are home to many UCITS and other structures as well as hedge funds and other alternative investment funds like property and private equity. Other fund centers like Cayman are home to many hedge funds although the administration of these funds may be done elsewhere, for example, Dublin. Each center will have the ability to provide the fund functionaries like lawyers, accountants, administrators, custody services, as well as potentially sourcing directors and trustees. The Channel Isles and Isle of Man offer mature and extensive services and are home to many types of funds. So too are Singapore, Malta, Gibraltar, and Mauritius with the latter servicing many Indian funds. Each center will have its own types of fund structures, which are basically one or more of companies, trusts, and partnerships depending on the Law in that jurisdiction. Common funds, UCITS compliant funds, SICAVs, OEICS, ICVCs, protected cell companies, expert funds, qualifying funds, market professional funds are all examples of the type of fund structures that different centers have created. Developing centers, for example, Cyprus need to build the same kind of strong set of services and to look to attract fund promoters from inside and outside the EU.

One common thing in all successful fund centers is to have strong, workable regulation of investment funds that will give investors comfort. Having advantageous tax arrangements can also be important but expertise and comprehensive services is also very important.

The level of due diligence that prospective investors now carry out means that a good reputation for a fund center the fund promoter plans to use is essential.

The investment process is about assets, strategies, and portfolio management so let us now look at all of these.

Asset Classes—Securities, Derivatives, Alternatives

When the investment capital is utilized and the portfolio is managed, the manager will select the assets to be purchased and sold.

Clearly, this is driven by the objectives of the fund in terms of return and must be compliant with any mandates, agreements, and any regulatory constraints.

The process of constructing the portfolio is referred to as "asset allocation." The portfolio will reflect the fund's involvement in different types of assets and in the UK, the Investment Association has categorized funds into different sectors making it easier for investors and financial advisers to identify suitable funds to meet their objectives. The categorization is shown in Appendix 1.

As the assets are allocated to the portfolio under the asset allocation process the manager will be looking at different "asset classes."

Asset classes are typically:

- Equity
- Debt
- Cash (Will include money market instruments as well as cash deposits and currency)
- Property (Will include residential and commercial property as well as land)
- Alternatives (Will include commodities, antiques and collectibles, art, and other funds)

To illustrate the amount of investment in these asset classes we can look at some statistics.

Appendix 2 shows the data from the Investment Association for UK Managed assets while in the US, mutual funds are defined by just three asset classes, equity, debt, and money market. Within this however there are defined funds like equity growth, specialty, balanced etc.

The Investment Association refers to around 3000 UK funds while according to Investopedia there are around 10,000 US funds (http://www.investopedia.com/university/mutualfunds/mutualfunds1.asp).

Another key source of data is the Investment Company Institute (ICI) who have defined Mutual Fund Investment Objective Definitions as follows

(Classifications are made by reviewing mutual fund prospectuses for language included in these definitions):

- To reflect changes in the marketplace, ICI has modernized its investment objective classifications for open-end mutual funds. At the macro level, our categories—domestic equity, world equity, taxable bond, municipal bond, hybrid, taxable money market, and tax-exempt money market funds—will remain the same. The changes will occur at a more detailed level, affecting the data at the composite investment objective and investment objective levels.
- To help members, the media, analysts, and the public understand trends in mutual fund investing, ICI reports data on open-end mutual funds at several levels. From the broadest to the most detailed, those are:
  - *Level 1*: Long-term funds and money market funds.
  - *Level 2*: Equity, hybrid, bond, and money market funds.
  - *Level 3*: Domestic equity, world equity, hybrid, taxable bond, municipal bond, taxable money market funds, and tax-exempt money market funds.
  - *Level 4*: Thirteen composite investment objectives (eg, capital appreciation, world equity, hybrid, and investment grade bond).
  - *Level 5*: Forty-two investment objectives (eg, growth, alternative strategies, global equity, flexible portfolio, and investment grade: short-term) (The full data can be found at https://www.ici.org/research/stats/iob_update/iob_definitions).

Within each fund, the composition of the portfolio will be about different assets. Traditional assets are considered to be equities and bonds but today the portfolios could contain a variety of debt and equity products or instruments as well as property, commodities, and alternative investments. They may well also use derivatives to manage risk or as alternative forms of instruments.

INVESTMENT STRATEGIES

The process of investment follows a generic life cycle starting with research and investment decisions, followed by the execution of trades resulting in the settlement of purchases and sales and onto the custody and safekeeping of the assets including cash.

This activity is reconciled and then recorded in the records and accounts of the fund by the administrator who will also be involved in the calculation and publication of the NAV etc.

The assets the investment manager can utilize have characteristics that will determine the potential return from those assets, for example:

Equities offer growth (capital increase) and income (dividends).

Debt offers income (risk based and possibly some capital gain).

Money market instruments offer income over a short time.

The instruments used in these assets can be highly liquid or very illiquid and this will impact on the strategies employed by the manager.

Property or Real Estate is a medium to long term investment either direct into retail (apartments, houses) or commercial properties (offices, shopping malls, warehouses) or through shares in property company and construction company shares, land and land company shares etc. In general terms, property is an illiquid asset as the time to complete a purchase or sale can be significant. In Europe UCITS funds are usually prohibited from investing in physical property because of the liquidity issue. However the asset offers both growth and income through the possible rental generation from the properties.

Commodities are based on softs like agricultural products and also on metals, energy etc. that can offer high volatility and therefore capital gain potential.

Alternative investments are assets like antiques, wine, art etc. and like commodities and property, these will need specialist skills and knowledge at both investment and support level.

However earlier we looked at Islamic finance and saw that conventional interest paying bonds are not Sharia compliant however in Islamic finance, we do have a term Sukuk.

A sukuk can be described as Islamic bonds but of course riba is prohibited. Instead sukuk holders receive return based of participation, for example, a manager creates a SPV that holds the sukuk for investors and pays a return based on the investment or participation that the sukuk holder's capital has been placed in. Naturally, the investment must be Sharia compliant.

It is also clear that an administrator and custodian that provide services to Islamic funds must have the knowledge of Sharia and understand Islamic finance.

USING DERIVATIVES

A fund manager may be permitted to use derivatives either with restrictions, for example, only for hedging risk or maybe able to use the instruments for more strategies like gearing.

We can look at an example of this here:

A hedge fund, which can assume far greater risk than an authorized unit trust, can "gear" or "leverage" the portfolio's exposure by using products like derivatives, where it can acquire a much greater exposure for the money invested than a unit trust can by investing the same amount in shares.

Note: derivatives' positions may be "margined", a process that requires the deposit of collateral with the prime broker or counterparty while the position is open, to protect against a failure to meet the obligations of the transaction.

Example

A hedge fund has £50,000 to invest in BP shares, which are currently trading at £5. The manager wants to gear the exposure so, instead of buying 10,000 shares, he or she looks at the BP options listed on the exchange and sees that the price of the BP July 550 call options is 50p. Each option contract is based on 1000 shares with a delivery price if the option is exercised of 550p. The cost of one contract is therefore £500 (1000 × 50p). The hedge fund manager buys 100 contracts for a total of £50,000. However, the exposure to the shares is actually 100 × 1000 = 100,000 shares. (This is a long position and does not carry any margin call as the premium is settled straight away).

The mutual fund manager cannot gear the fund so the investment he or she can make is restricted to buying 10,000 shares in the market.

Let us assume that BP's share price jumps to £6 and the price or premium of the BP 550 call options increases to £1 per option. The mutual fund manager has made a healthy £10,000 profit (10,000 × £1).

The hedge fund manager can sell the options at £1 and has gained 50p per option contract (100,000 shares × 50p = £50,000) profit for

exactly the same outlay as the mutual fund manager and without any of the costs associated with buying shares like stamp duty!!

Of course, there is a good reason why the mutual fund investor is protected against gearing the exposure. Suppose BP's shares fell to £4. By expiry, the options are worthless, as no one will pay £5.50 for shares that are only worth £4. The hedge fund has lost £50,000.

Now let us assume that the mutual fund has lost £10,000 as the shares have fallen by £1 in price. However, the mutual fund owns the shares and can wait until they rise in price. The mutual fund will also receive any dividend BP may pay, while the hedge fund has no dividend income, as it owns options not shares.

It is important to understand the restrictions and guidelines that fund managers must follow because there are so many possibilities in terms of products and strategies in the markets that a fund manager could use, as is shown in the illustration earlier.

It is also important to remember that there may be restrictions on how much exposure a fund can have to a type of product, issuer, security etc. While a manager may be able to buy shares in a company, the fund may be restricted to holding no more than, say, 10 or 15% of the fund's total value in any one share.

UCITS are funds that are established under and comply with the EU Directive on UCITS, currently UCITS IV/V. One of the features of these funds is the restrictions imposed. The following are examples of some of the areas where UCITS IV imposes restrictions:

- Eligible assets,
- Techniques and instruments relating to eligible assets (strategies),
- Diversification,
- Borrowing, and
- Risk management process relating to financial derivatives instruments (FDI) (securities/derivatives).

Source: CLT Advanced Certificate in Fund Administration/the DSC Portfolio.

PORTFOLIO MANAGEMENT

Portfolio management is about the asset allocation and stock selection process set against the objectives of the fund set out in the offering documents and the mandate/investment management agreement.

This process will require the investment manager(s) to comply with any constraints imposed by either regulation or internal policies such as exposure limits, diversification, use of strategies etc.

As mentioned earlier, most investment management processes include research, which can be done inhouse and/or bought in from external analysts, for example, the prime broker.

As well as seeking capital gain from increasing value of the assets and income from, for example, dividends and interest, the investment manager may also seek to generate income from activities like securities lending as well as where permitted, the writing of options to generate premium (the fee the buyer of the option pays to secure the right).

The structure of the portfolio, use of assets, and the strategies employed will generate the workflows that the custodian and the administrator will process.

Assets are allocated into asset classes like equity or debt or commodities and then geographically and finally by sector.

Portfolios can have static or virtually static assets like for instance a tracker fund or be managed so that changes take place to the component parts of the portfolio when targets are realized or market conditions prompt change.

In general terms, we can say that portfolio management involves:

- Portfolio structure and objectives
- Constraints
- Research
- Asset choice and asset allocation
- Generating additional income
- Administration flows
- Measuring performance

The administrator and custodian will be involved in the workflow associated with the portfolio.

The custodian will be dealing with the settlement of the securities asset trades and potentially other forms of assets as well as dealing with servicing the assets in respect of, for example, corporate actions. Derivatives, commodities etc. may be electronic positions or physically may settle and be held by a clearing broker.

For funds with a depositary, the depositary will be responsible for oversight of the cash management process related to the purchases and sales and associated income or expense items. A depositary under the AIFMD is defined as having duties related to safekeeping of assets, cash management and oversight of leverage, risk management, and regulatory reporting.

The administrator will have a key or primary reconciliation to undertake between the records of the investment manager and those of the custodian and the prime broker or other agents like derivatives brokers and counterparties.

In addition the administrator will need to make sure that any entitlements for and changes to assets as a result of corporate actions have been correctly updated in the fund records.

Finally, the administrator may be involved in monitoring activity in the portfolio to ensure compliance with any regulatory requirements, offering document or policy restrictions, and constraints.

INVESTMENT PERFORMANCE

Portfolios are designed to deliver the return set out in the offering documents of the fund. Some funds look at providing income, some growth, and some a mix of both. Performance is often measured against a benchmark or based on generating maximum return on assets whichever way a market moves. The latter are mainly AIFs as they need to be able to adopt strategies such as selling short which "long" only retail funds cannot use or are very restricted in the use. Risk is dependent on many things like country, economic, political, currency, time, and liquidity. Retail funds reduce this risk by diversifying the assets in the portfolio and not undertaking any liabilities. Assets themselves carry risk so a US Treasury bond is considered risk free whereas a small lowly credit rated corporate bond would be much higher risk as there may be questions about whether the issuer can repay the debt or the interest or both. Strategies also affect the risk level so that leverage and gearing through borrowing capital over and above the investment capital creates liabilities and risk, but also offer potential high returns.

The whole basis of investment performance can be described simply as:

RISK VERSUS REWARD

So what does the investment manager look for in an investment universe?

The investment universe might be described as in Diagram 1.8:

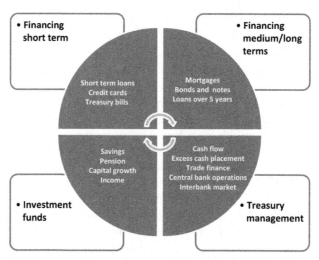

DIAGRAM 1.8 Investment universe. *(Source: The DSC Portfolio.)*

Within this universe the investment managers analyze the instruments available, the risk and return of the instruments, and the cost of buying and selling the instrument plus expenses such as brokerage commission.

The fund's performance will be based either on the index of benchmark it tracks or on the success of the asset allocation in an actively managed fund.

We can summarize the investment performance as being a combination of the following items in relation to the portfolio and operational costs of the fund:

- Acquisition and disposal costs of assets—cost, commissions, accruals, tax etc.
- Growth of asset values—increase in the price of the asset.
- Income generated from assets—dividends, interest, benefits and entitlements.
- Management fees—annual management fee and performance fees, initial and exit fees.
- Service provider fees—custodian, administrator, auditor, legal, bank charges etc.
- Returns versus risks.
- Performance fees—equalization.
- Tax—capital and income, withholding tax.

For the investor a key performance indicator is the net asset value of the fund which is derived from the following:

- *Value of the assets minus any liabilities*
- *Income minus Expenses*
- Which includes realized and unrealized gains, income, and expense.

Note: only realized gains and income can be distributed to investors.

The way in which a fund's performance is analyzed through the use of what is called contribution calculation and also using ratios.

Measuring performance is therefore about

1. Return against targets
2. Return against competitors
3. *Total Expense Ratio* (TER): The TER of a fund is a measure of the total costs associated with managing and operating the fund which consist primarily of management fees plus additional expenses and other operational expenses. The total cost of the fund is divided by the fund's total assets to arrive at a percentage amount, which represents TER = Total Fund Costs/Total Fund Assets. Source: http://www.investopedia.com/terms/t/ter. asp#ixzz3zZnYpICm
4. Return against benchmarks and risk
   a. Alpha ratio
   b. Beta ratio
   c. Sharpe ratio
   d. Treynor ratio

TABLE 1.1 The Benchmark of a Fund

Asset class	Strategic asset allocation (%)	Benchmark
Equities	60	FT All Share
Bonds	30	FT Gilt Index
Cash	10	Merrill Lynch Index

Source: The DSC Portfolio Ltd.

Let us look at an example in Table 1.1.

The investment manager is permitted to use tactical asset allocation and so the end performance of the fund is as shown in Table 1.2.

So the fund has outperformed the benchmark by 0.10% however it is important to know how this outperformance was achieved so we look at the contribution the TAA made in Table 1.3.

This table shows us that actually each of the revised positions in the asset classes achieved a *minus* contribution which therefore begs the question how was a 0.10% outperformance achieved?

The answer is that the individual stock selections were outstanding and still managed to deliver a higher return despite the TAA.

The performance of a fund is obviously vitally important to the investor but also to the manager as they may be participating in a performance fee arrangement.

This is a method that rewards the investment manager for generating a return for the fund.

It is included in the investment management agreement and details are also contained in the offering documents of the fund.

TABLE 1.2 Performance Versus Benchmark

	Portfolio			Benchmark		
Asset class	Weight (%)	Return (%)	Weighted return	Weight (%)	Return (%)	Weighted return
Equities	50	5	2.50%	60	4	2.40%
Bonds	35	2	0.70%	30	2.50	0.75%
Cash	15	1	0.15%	10	1	0.10%
Total	100		3.35%			3.25%
			A×B			E×F

thedsc.portfolio

TABLE 1.3 Asset Allocation Performance

			Asset allocation			
Asset class	Portfolio (%)	Bench-mark (%)	Over/Under weight	Return (%)	Asset class return-benchmark	Contribution
Equities	50	60	(10)	4	0.75	−0.0750
Bonds	35	30	5	2.50	−0.75	−0.0375
Cash	15	10	5	1	−2.25	−0.1125
Total	100			3.25		−0.2250
					D—3.25	C×E

the**dsc**.portfolio

Criteria exist such as "high water mark" and "hurdle rate," which must be met before any performance fee becomes due.

The administrator will be involved in the calculations to determine if a fee is due and to then make the payment and adjust the fund records accordingly. The payment of a fee will have the impact of reducing the NAV of the fund and so the administrator may also be involved in a process called equalization, which attempts to ensure that each investor irrespective of when they entered the fund pays the right share of any performance fee. An excellent article by Dermot Butler explains this process and can be found at http://www.customhousegroup. com/speech/equalization-why-is-it-necessary-how-it-works/.

There are many useful websites that offer comparison of fund performance such as; http://funds.ft.com/uk/.

PERFORMANCE RATIOS

Various ratios can be used to ascertain how the fund's performance has been achieved. Examples of these include:

Alpha Ratio

If an investor is trying to see whether a mutual fund has beaten the performance of its relative index, he should look at the alpha ratio. If the index is the MSCI World Index, he would look to see whether the fund has beaten this index and, if so, by how much.

For example, say the alpha ratio for a growth fund for the last 5 years is 0.46. If this number is greater than 0, then it has a "positive alpha." In this case, over the last five years, the growth fund has been able to outperform the relevant index. The higher the number, the greater the out-performance (as it is referred to) achieved.

Beta Ratio

While the alpha ratio looks at excess returns over the index, the beta ratio looks at excess risk over the index. If the growth fund has outperformed the index in the last five years, the beta ratio asks how much risk did it take to do so?

Say the beta for a growth fund is 0.61 and the benchmark for the beta measure is 1. If the fund had a beta of 1, it would have the same risk as the market. With a beta of 0.61, it has approximately 61% of the risk of the market.

Betas and alphas go hand in hand. Ideally, an investor would probably want a fund with a low beta and a high alpha. This means that the investor has a fund that has outperformed the index while posing less risk than the index.

Sharpe Ratio

The Sharpe ratio measures the return of a mutual fund compared to the risk-free rate of return, for example, the US 91-day T Bill rate. This should be similar to money market returns so this ratio is used to determine if a mutual fund is able to beat the money market. For example, a growth fund has a Sharpe ratio over the last 5 years of 0.57 and the recent range of Sharpe ratios for global equity funds has gone from a low of −1.11 to a high of 0.94. A positive Sharpe ratio means the fund did better on a risk-adjusted basis than the 91-day T Bill rate. In other words, the higher the Sharpe ratio, the better.

The Sharpe ratio tells an investor about history but it does not tell him anything about the future. Just because a fund has had a positive Sharpe ratio for the last 5 years does not mean it will outperform money market instruments for the next 5 years.

Treynor Ratio

The Treynor ratio is similar to the Sharpe ratio but instead of comparing the fund's risk-adjusted performance to the risk-free return, it compares the fund's risk-adjusted performance to the relative index.

For example, a growth fund could have a Treynor ratio of 11.52 and the range of ratios for global equity funds has recently ranged from a low of −20.91 to a high of 32.00. Just like the rule for interpreting the Sharpe ratio, the higher the number the better.

Source: CLT Advanced Certificate in Fund Administration/DSC Portfolio Ltd.

INVESTMENT MANAGEMENT FEES AND COSTS

Investment advisers and/or managers usually charge an annual management fee based on the value of the assets under management. A performance-related fee, based on the level of growth achieved, may be added to this.

In addition, there may be initial fees and exit fees (in the United States and elsewhere known as "front-" and "back-end loads").

Let us look at the different fees in more detail.

Annual Management Fees

The level of the fee will depend on the type of fund. A tracker or passive fund will tend to have lower fees than an actively managed fund as less time is spent on managing the portfolio, utilizing expertise and trying to outperform a benchmark. As a result, the charges may vary from, say, 0.25–3%.

Performance Fees

We have already mentioned that in some funds the investment manager is rewarded with an additional remuneration in the form of a performance fee.

Performance fees are common in hedge funds and private equity funds. They reward the managers' performance on the basis of high watermarks and/or hurdle rates. The manager will be entitled to receive a performance fee if the fund's NAV has increased by a minimum amount (hurdle rate) and/or is higher than the previous high value (the high watermark).

Some funds also incorporate claw back fees when performance falls below a certain level.

In hedge funds, the average performance fee level is around 20% but some very high performing funds charge more. Retail funds that have performance fees tend to set these at much lower rates, perhaps 1 or 2%, reflecting the incentives given to the manager to maintain the fund's performance.

Initial and Exit Fees

These fees are charged on the entry to and exit from a fund and cover items such as administration costs and commission to sales agents. Initial fees can be around 4–5% but are often offered at a discount and sometimes waived by the manager.

Exit fees are usually only charged for a set period of time. For example, an exit fee may have a 5 year limit, with a 5% fee in year 1, falling as each year passes, so that, if the investor leaves the fund after 5 years, there is no exit fee at all.

SUMMARY

In this part of the book, we have begun to look the investment environment and also at the types of investment funds and the investment process including asset classes, basic strategies, portfolio management, and performance.

It is essential that anyone working in administration, custody or fund support understands the investment environment.

To assist with the learning process you may like to look at the questions relevant to this part of the book, which can be found at the end.

In the next Part of the book, we look at the regulatory environment for funds and also at fund structures in more detail.

Part 2

Regulation and Fund Structures

In this part, we will consider the regulatory environment that some investment funds will fall under. Not all funds are regulated although they may need to be registered with a regulator in the jurisdiction.

The amount of change that has taken place in the regulation of funds has been a massive challenge, and a significant cost, to both promoters and administrators as well as custodians and depositaries.

OVERVIEW OF REGULATION

Each country will have its regulatory authority or authorities that will have the responsibility for authorizing and monitoring participants, their activities, and their relationships with customers and other parties. For example, in the UK the regulatory authorities are the Financial Conduct Authority (FCA) and the Prudential Regulatory Authority (PRA). In the United States we have the Securities Exchange Commission (SEC) and the Commodity Futures Trading Commission (CFTC).

In the Far East we have the Monetary Authority of Singapore (MAS), in Japan we have the Financial Services Agency (FSA) and the Securities and Exchange Surveillance Commission (SESC), in Hong Kong we have the Hong Kong Monetary Authority (HKMA), and in Australia we have the Australian Securities and Investment Commission (ASIC). (Appendix 4) (http:// asic.gov.au/).

In China the regulator is China Securities Regulatory Commission (CSRC). (Appendix 7)

There has been significant legislation enacted in both Europe and the United States in the years, since the market crash of 2008.

Some of the regulation is aimed at the financial markets in general and some is specific to investment and investment funds.

REGULATION AND DIRECTIVES

In the United States, a key piece of legislation introduced post 2008 was the Dodd–Frank act.

Investopedia defines the Act as:

"--a compendium of federal regulations, primarily affecting financial institutions and their customers, which the Obama administration passed in 2010 in an attempt to prevent the recurrence of events that caused the 2008 financial crisis" (http://www.investopedia.com/terms/d/dodd-frank-financial-regulatory-reform-bill.asp).

The Dodd-Frank Wall Street Reform and Consumer Protection Act, commonly referred to as simply "Dodd-Frank," is designed to lower risk in various parts of the US financial system including the investment industry. It is named after US Senator Christopher J. Dodd and US Representative Barney Frank because of their significant involvement in the formulation and passage of the act.

A key part of the Act is the Volcker Rule, which restricts the ways banks can invest and regulates trading in the derivatives.

In Europe, post the crash the regulatory landscape changed as within the EU, the European Securities Market Association (ESMA) was created to oversee the European Market Infrastructure Regulation (EMIR).

A key piece of new legislation introduced in Europe was the Alternative Investment Managers Directive (AIFMD), which sets out the regulation that will be applicable to the managers of alternative investment funds (AIFs) (Appendix 6).

AIFMD AND AIFMs

The following is a brief explanation of AIFs and the Alternative Investment Fund Manager (AIFMs).

The scope of the AIFMD is broad and, with a few exceptions, covers the management, administration, and marketing of AIFs. Its focus is on regulating the AIFM rather than the AIF.

The following gives the FCA definition of some of the meanings:

Meaning of "AIFM," "managing an AIF," "external AIFM," and "internal AIFM."

1. "AIFM" means a legal person, the regular business of which is managing one or more AIFs.
2. Managing an AIF means performing at least risk management or portfolio management for the AIF.
3. The AIFM of an AIF may be either—
   a. another person appointed by or on behalf of the AIF and which through that appointment is responsible for managing the AIF ("external AIFM"); or
   b. where the legal form of the AIF permits internal management and where the AIF's governing body chooses not to appoint an external AIFM, the AIF itself ("internal AIFM").
4. None of the following entities is an AIFM—
   a. An institution for occupational retirement provision which falls within the scope of Directive 2003/41/EC of the European Parliament and of the Council of 3 Jun. 2003 on the activities and supervision of institutions

for occupational retirement provision(**a**), including, where applicable, the authorized entities responsible for managing such institutions and acting on their behalf referred to in Article 2.1 of that directive, or the investment managers appointed pursuant to Article 19.1 of that directive, in so far as they do not manage AIFs;

b. The European Central Bank, the European Investment Bank, the European Investment Fund, a bilateral development bank, the World Bank, the International Monetary Fund, any other supranational institution or similar international organization, or a European Development Finance Institution, in the event that such institution or organization manages AIFs and in so far as those AIFs act in the public interest;

c. A national central bank;

d. A national, regional, or local government or body or other institution which manages funds supporting social security and pension systems;

e. A holding company;

f. An employee participation scheme or employee savings scheme;

g. A securitization special purpose entity.

An AIF is a "collective investment undertaking" that is not subject to the UCITS regime, and includes hedge funds, private equity funds, retail investment funds, investment companies, and real estate funds, among others. The AIFMD establishes an EU-wide harmonized framework for monitoring and supervising risks posed by AIFMs and the AIFs they manage, and for strengthening the internal market in alternative funds. The Directive also includes new requirements for firms acting as a depositary for an AIF.

Some of the main changes are that:

- A number of fund managers in the UK hold a permission to manage investments. It is likely that some of these firms, dependent on business models, needed to be reauthorized under the AIFMD to operate as AIF managers. These included:
    - MiFID firms carrying out portfolio management and/or risk management for EEA funds that are not UCITS funds or funds located offshore in third-country jurisdictions, such as the United States and Cayman Islands; and
    - Operators of collective investment schemes that are not UCITS funds carrying out portfolio management and/or risk management inhouse.
- The AIFMD meant certain fund managers are being regulated for the first time. For example, investment companies that do not employ an external manager will need to be authorized or registered with the FCA under the AIFMD.
- Depositaries of AIFs have to comply with new requirements.
- The AIFMD brought in significant changes to the management/administration of AIFs in the EU and introduced new EU-wide passports for authorized full-scope AIFMs to market and manage AIFs from 22 July 2013.

- Marketing and management passports are not be available to non-EEA managers of AIFs or to EEA managers in respect of their non-EEA AIFs (this may be adopted from 2015 subject to ESMA reports and Commission delegated acts). Marketing of such funds to professional investors is allowed under national private placement (NPP) regimes. Note: It is envisaged that existing NPP regimes will be phased out after the non-EEA passport regime becomes operational, although not before 2018.

EEA Firms

- AIFM authorized in their EEA home Member State ("EEA AIFM"), are able to exercise management and marketing passport rights in the UK in relation to certain types of EEA AIF, on a services and/or establishment basis, from 22 July 2013 onward.
- In order to exercise these rights, the EEA AIFM's home Member State competent authority will need to send the relevant notification forms, in accordance with the requirements of the AIFMD, to the Financial Conduct Authority, the UK's competent authority for these purposes.

Source: http://www.fca.org.uk/firms/markets/international-markets/aifmd/uk-aifms#Authorisations.

RETAIL FUNDS

In Europe, retail funds are often established under the Undertaking for Collective Investments in Securities Directive (UCITS).

UCITS DIRECTIVE

Created as long ago as 1985, UCITS has become a global benchmark structure with popularity in the Far East and Latin America.

As a single market within the EU, UCITS allow asset managers to offer funds across the region after authorization from one of the Member States.

UCITS IV is now being superseded by UCITS V, however the new version is designed to enhance and supplement UCITS IV so that following the introduction of the AIFMD which gives greater protection to investors in AIFS, investors in UCITS funds will have a similar level of protection. For example, UCITS V aligns the rules governing asset managers' remuneration and duties of depositaries with the corresponding provisions of AIFMD. It also strengthens the protection of UCITS investors in relation to asset managers and depositaries by focusing on three main areas. These are:

1. Rules governing remuneration of asset managers
2. The depositary's eligibility, obligations, and liabilities
3. The sanctions regime

Other important changes cover areas such as the disclosure of information to UCITS investors and conditions for the appointment of a UCITS depositary.

In these and some other cases UCITS V rules exceed those within AIFMD, for example:

1. Specific independence requirements of the depositary from the asset manager.
2. Insolvency protection when the safekeeping has been delegated by the depositary.

The new directive was published in the Official Journal on 28 August 2014 and entered into application on 18 March 2016. Some aspects of UCITS V are dependent on information being published, for example, the Level 2 Text (due late 2015) and the ESMA recommendations on managers remuneration also due end 2015.

In the book, we will be referring many of the existing and new key UCITS requirements like diversification, salability, limited exposure to liabilities and illiquid assets as well as strategies that involve the borrowing of cash or assets and may be considered to have an unacceptable level of risk.

MONEY LAUNDERING

No fund wants their reputation tarnished by being found to be assisting money launderers. Antimoney laundering (AML) regulations exist in most jurisdictions and must be rigorously enforced and any suspicion reported to the relevant person. A regulated administrator may lose their authorization if they are found guilty of lax controls and non-implementing of AML processes and procedures.

Subscription and redemption applications via intermediaries are an issue as it must be clearly established that the AML checks have been done.

In the UK the Financial Conduct Authority states:

> All firms who are subject to the Money Laundering Regulations 2007 must put in place systems and controls to prevent and detect money laundering. Money laundering is the process by which the proceeds of crime are converted into assets, which appear to have a legitimate origin. Many authorized firms also have an additional regulatory obligation to put in place and maintain policies and procedures to mitigate their money laundering risk.
>
> Source for further reference: https://www.fca.org.uk/firms/being-regulated/meeting-your-obligations/firm-guides/systems/aml

However some regulation and directives in the EU are causing issues with associations representing fund management.

For example, in an article published in Funds Europe, the investment management industry has called on Brussels to delay and change the updated Markets in Financial Instruments Directive (MiFID II), which is due to be implemented just over a year from now.

The European Fund and Asset Management Association (EFAMA), which represents national industry bodies, want a delay partly over fears the directive will be implemented unevenly between countries (http://www.funds-europe.com/home/news/16841-efama-calls-for-mifid-ii-delay).

PRINCIPLES AND RECOMMENDATIONS

The regulators in many jurisdictions issue guidelines, principles, and recommendations, which funds must follow and which the administrator and custodians must be aware of.

For example, the Association of the Luxembourg Funds Industry (ALFI) published in 2013 an updated Code of Conduct for Luxembourg Funds.

ALFI stresses that these are "Principles" not Rules and are designed to establish the best practice framework for Luxembourg funds and management companies, whether listed or unlisted.

Although we have talked about the regulation of UCITS and AIFs, it is important to remember that there is a great deal of commonality between the two.

For example, AIFMD and UCITS V are similar in the following:

- Remuneration policy—UCITS V introduces remuneration provisions that are similar to AIFMD.
- Conflicts of interest—UCITS V broadly consistent with AIFMD.
- Liquidity policy—UCITS V broadly consistent with AIFMD.
- Risk management policy—UCITS V broadly consistent with AIFMD.
- Authorization and delegation—UCITS V broadly consistent with AIFMD.
- Valuation policy—UCITS V contains no explicit requirement for a valuation policy, but it remains standard industry practice in some jurisdictions.
- Calculation of leverage—UCITS V broadly consistent with AIFMD.
- Calculation of AUM—Explicit AIFMD obligation but no equivalent in UCITS V.
- Minimum capital—UCITS V ongoing obligations broadly consistent with AIFMD.
- Regulatory report—New Annex IV requirement in AIFMD.
- Annual financial report—UCITS and AIFMD ongoing obligations broadly consistent.
- Disclosure to investors—Similarly to AIFMD, UCITS V requires disclosure to investors in relation to management remuneration and conflicts of interest.
- Depositary operations—A single depositary must be appointed for each UCITS and AIF (unless acting as depo-lite). AIFMs of non-EEA AIFs do not need to comply with AIFMD Article 21 (Depositaries). However, if a non-EEA AIF is marketed to European investors via "National Private Placement" rules, as opposed to reliance on passive marketing/reverse solicitation, an AIFM needs to comply with Article 36. This requires the AIFM to "ensure that one or more entities are appointed to carry out" the depositary duties of (1) safe custody; (2) cash flow monitoring; and (3) oversight. Strict liability does not apply. This has therefore been dubbed the "depositary lite"

model. Source: http://www.thehedgefundjournal.com/node/8459#sthash.
TnSUwiNh.dpuf.

- Asset safekeeping—Assets to be entrusted to the depositary for safekeeping, with new requirements on delegate and reuse of assets.
- Cash monitoring—Depositary must monitor cash flows and ensure cash booked to the correct account (delegation of oversight and cash).
- Investment compliance—UCITS V broadly consistent with AIFMD.
- Depositary oversight—UCITS V broadly consistent with AIFMD.
- Insolvency protection—New to UCITS V, assets held in custody are not available to general creditors on the insolvency of the depositary or its delegate if they are located in the EU.
- Location—A depositary must have its registered office or established in the home state of the UCITS.
- Discharge of liability—No option for depositary to discharge liability under UCITS V.

Source: Northern Trust—readers should access the Convergence Checklist at –
https://www.northerntrust.com\l
We can now look at different fund structures:

Fund Structures—Companies, Trusts, Partnerships, Common Funds

In the Introduction and Part 1, we looked at the possible structures we can find in funds. Let us now continue this. A general structure of a fund is shown in diagram 2.1.

The management company deals with the day-to-day process of the fund operation.

Investment management is done by managers and/or advisers in conjunction with investment management agreement, investment committee etc. and through brokers, the prime broker for securities, commodities and derivatives, agents for property, advisers/agents/directors of private equity firms for opportunities for PE funds etc.

The administrator manages the day-to-day processing of the activity of the fund and the custodian holds the assets and deals with settlement of the asset transaction (Diagram 2.1).

There are many different types of funds and the way in which the fund is structured and operate will determine the work, the administrator and custodian will be involved in.

As we have already seen specific structures can apply to some funds.

FUND OF FUNDS

Fund of funds are a structure where the fund invests in the shares or units of other funds rather than in assets directly. The investment management process is to research and select the best performing funds in a sector and then to allocate the funds to the portfolio on the basis of the asset allocation (Diagram 2.2).

DIAGRAM 2.1 *(Source: The DSC Portfolio Ltd.)*

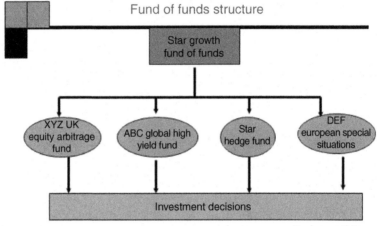

DIAGRAM 2.2

As shown, the XYZ Equity Arbitrage Fund may be 10% of the total portfolio.

For the administrator the main issue is the valuation of the portfolio as they will be using the NAV of the funds in the portfolio rather than valuing assets.

MULTIMANAGER FUNDS

Multimanager funds are structures where the investment management process is outsourced to other investment managers under a mandate or an agreement (Diagram 2.3).

In the example, it is shown that Hermes will manage the property asset class and M & G the bond asset class. The administration could also be outsourced but if not, the administrator will receive details of the assets held by each manager and will then value the portfolio as well as reconciling to the custody accounts.

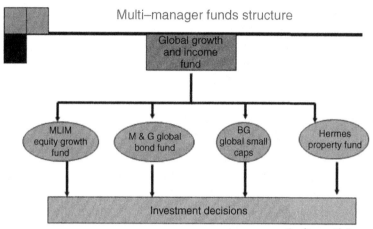

DIAGRAM 2.3

OTHER STRUCTURES

Other structures include *master/feeder funds* where funds are set up to meet regulatory and investor requirements but all the subscription capital is then passed to (invested in) a master fund where the portfolio will be managed. Each feeder fund will have an administrator as will the master fund (Diagram 2.4).

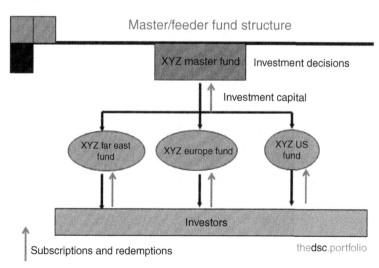

DIAGRAM 2.4

The structure of a fund like a master feeder can be used to manage the potential investor base. For example, as shown in the diagram, Fund A is set up under European regulation and Fund B is set up under US regulation. Fund A will have Euros as the base currency and Fund B will have US dollars as the base currency.

The fund promoter has created a structure that appeals to different investor domiciles but has an efficient single investment process.

RETAIL FUNDS

We have already mentioned that retail funds is a generic term for funds that can be marketed and sold to a wide audience of investors who do not need to have any particular knowledge of finance or risks associated with investment.

We saw earlier in this part of the book that in the EU these funds are often UCITS compliant funds.

The main characteristics of retail funds are:

- Authorized and regulated.
- Open-ended to allow constant subscription and redemption.
- Promoters are usually Investment Management/Asset Management Companies.
- Designed to provide income or growth and some funds will have two classes of shares, one growth and one income.
- Established as either companies or unit trusts.
- Minimum subscription is usually 1 share or unit.
- Net Asset Value is calculated and published.
- Marketed and sold via third parties like financial advisers, banks etc.
- Mainly securities funds but some property funds like Real Estate Investment Trusts (REITs).
- Funds can focus investment on domestic or international assets (or both).
- Many are "passive" funds, that is, ETFs or benchmark/tracker funds.
- Most are long only funds.

Alternative Investment Funds

Although there are potentially many types of AIFs and the term alternative investments can mean nontraditional assets such as wine, antiques, vintage cars etc. However in many types of context AIFs means "nonretail" structures such as hedge funds, private equity and property funds.

We can look at some of the features of these funds here.

Private Equity (Often referred to as the "waterfall")—drawdown capital, growth, and then distribution periods, fund has a projected life (5–10 years). Distribution pays off in order:

a. The initial capital of the investors.
b. The preference return to the investors.
c. The carried interest of the general partner.

d. Remaining return distributed across investors/general partner.
e. Fund is charged fees throughout the life of the fund so initially investors have a negative situation.

The basic structure of a private equity fund is shown in Diagrams 2.5 and 2.6:

HEDGE FUNDS

Hedge funds have their origins back in the 1950s, in the United States, there are many types of hedge funds including long-short funds but very wide range of hedge fund strategies including distressed stocks.

Private equity and venture capital valuation

- By nature data about PE and venture capital is confidential
- Valuation is made using the international private equity and venture capital valuation guidelines

PE structure

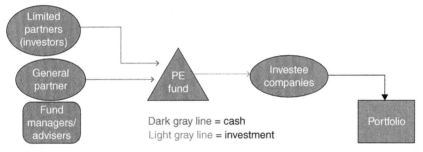

DIAGRAM 2.5

Returns

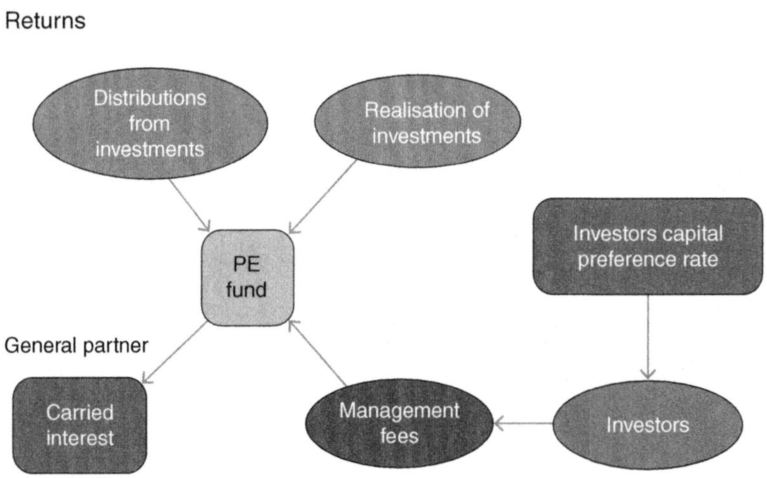

DIAGRAM 2.6 *(Source: The DSC Portfolio Ltd and Onestudy Training.)*

Widely considered as AIFs, hedge funds are also popular investment for other funds including some retail funds that are permitted to invest part of their portfolio in other funds.

Fund of hedge funds are often the vehicle for this type of investment.

Let us look at one of the common hedge fund strategies, long-short.

The basic concept is shown in (Diagram 2.7)

We can see the idea is that by correctly selecting undervalued or strong performers and buying these assets and offsetting these by selling short, selling something we do not own, overvalued or weak performers, the portfolio should make gains irrespective of which way the market moves.

The following two diagrams show (Diagram 2.8):

Here the undervalued/strong assets move ahead strongly if the market rises while the offsetting short positions rise less strongly. As we are short of these

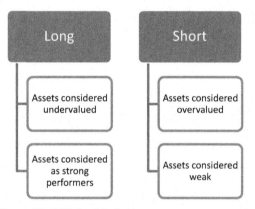

DIAGRAM 2.7   *(Source: The DSC Portfolio Ltd.)*

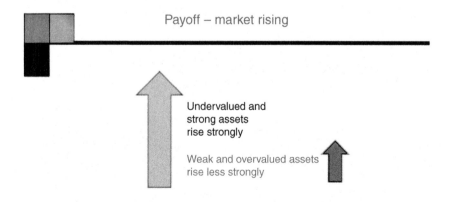

DIAGRAM 2.8

Payoff – market falling

Undervalued and
strong assets
fall modestly

Weak and overvalued assets
fall sharply

the**dsc**.portfolio

DIAGRAM 2.9

assets, the portfolio makes a loss but it will be offset by a much greater profit on the long position (Diagram 2.9).

When the market falls the loss on the long position should be more than off-set by the profit on the short sales, which have dropped sharply and the short position can now be bought back for a much lower cost and therefore large profit.

Whichever way the market moves, if the manager's selections are right the profit will outweigh the losses.

For the administrator and custodian, the key issues in a long-short fund are the short sale of assets, which means the fund will need to borrow securities to enable the settlement of the transaction. The fund records will need to reflect the cost of borrowing these securities and the liability (borrowed shares will have to be returned) plus any collateral that is required by the prime broker or securities lender (see Part 3 of the book).

If the short position is being achieved through the use of derivatives like index futures, by exchange-traded funds, contracts for difference or other non-deliverable products, there will be no borrowing of assets involved.

Open Ended and Closed Funds

As we have already mentioned the open-ended fund is a structure that has variable capital and can therefore issue and cancel shares or units in the fund in response to supply and demand.

A closed fund on the other hand is a fund that has a fixed capital and issues a finite number of shares or units based on the fixed amount of capital.

Open-ended funds are common in retail funds because if you remember retail funds are usually required by the regulator to allow an investor to exit the fund at any time, however they are also found in AIFs like hedge funds and property funds, although there may be dealing periods rather than constant subscription and redemption associated with these funds.

The closed structure is common in funds like private equity and some property and hedge funds.

For the administrator the major difference is the amount of workflow for the transfer agent dealing with the subscriptions and redemptions (see Part 3 of the book).

Fund Jurisdictions

There are numerous jurisdictions that are home to funds, administrators, custodians, and other service providers.

Popular fund centers include:

- The Channel Islands and Isle of Man
- Cayman
- British Virgin Isles
- Bermuda
- Turks and Caicos
- Dublin
- Luxembourg
- Switzerland
- Gibraltar
- Malta
- Singapore
- Hong Kong
- Malaysia

This is only a small sample of fund centers and, as each center is unique in terms of the funds they support and the services available including many more readers should research them all by using journals like Funds Europe as well the Useful Website List at the end of the book.

Key Players in the Operation of a Fund

There are many people and entities involved with most types of fund from promoters, through the managing of investments, the fund administration and custody process, and the fund secretary.

Fund promoters, like the issuers of securities, bring funds to the "market" so that investors can invest their capital. Most investment funds are collective investment schemes where investor monies are pooled together. Promoters can set up large retails funds with a wide base of investors (often run by investment management companies that are part of large banks, or more specialized and sometimes smaller funds with a restricted investor base which can be owned by companies or by individuals.

The fund owners have a fiduciary responsibility to the investors in the fund and whether they are companies or individuals they must ensure the fund is set up and operates correctly. The governance responsibility has been reinforced in regulations' introduced after the market crash of 2008, which includes more transparency and more reporting to the regulators.

The reputation or track record of the fund promoter can also be a key factor, particularly where the owner/promoter is also the investment manager.

The owner/promoter will make money out of the management fees they apply to the fund and which are paid by the investors minus the business expenses that are not rechargeable to the fund itself, for example, premises. Some types of fund like the AIFs will often have a structure where the owner/promoter has a stake in the fund through investing their own capital, sometimes called founders shares and some key investors may provide seed capital to the fund in return for shares that have some rights or advantages over the ordinary investor shares or units. We have seen that a term used in some funds like private equity to describe this type of participation is "carried interest."

The fund promoter will need to decide which investment and support processes to set up internally and which to outsource, although in some cases regulation may be a determining factor.

Prime brokers (PBs) and their services started to appear in the latter part of the last century to service hedge funds. Today PBs provide services to a wide range of fund clients. The PB is often a large investment bank with a wide range of capabilities and services. It forms an integral part of the fund operations sitting between the investment process and the administration process.

The range of services offered can be extensive and may include:

- *Executing portfolio trades* but will "accept" trades executed elsewhere for settlement.
- *Selling shares/units in the fund and possibly direct investment*—using the PBs extensive client base and market position.
- *Research*—providing information and opinion on possible investments.
- *Financing leverage*—lending the fund capital over and above its subscription capital and against collateral (assets of the fund), for example, for strategies that involve "trading on margin."
- *Lending securities*—to facilitate strategies like short selling.
- *Custody Services*—holding physical assets and electronic records of assets of the fund.

The relationship between the fund and the PB is a key one that must be established and operated properly and professionally. It will be covered by:

- *Service Provision*—Covered by a Prime Broker Agreement.

- *Other agreements*—Needed, for example, for OTC derivative transactions and any other intermediaries. OTC transactions are mainly transacted under the International Swaps and Derivatives Association documentation even when the OTC transaction is centrally cleared.
- *Risk*—Fund has a counterparty risk with the PB.

The prime broker may offer custody services.

The role of the custodian is essential in investment funds as they are both the safekeeper of assets that belong to the fund as well as providing key services related to the settlement of asset trades and collection of benefits and entitlements due to the fund on the assets in its portfolio.

The use of a custodian brings potential benefits to the fund operation. By centralizing the settlement and safekeeping processes there are both potential risk management benefits and cost savings.

In addition the fund can benefit from the expertise and market knowledge of the custodian including areas like short selling and securities lending opportunities and regulations.

Post 2008, the *independent* safekeeping of the fund's assets is of prime importance for investor. Remember the earlier case study on Madoff's Ponzi scheme.

Although the custodian is holding the assets in their name, a concept sometimes called the nominee process, the assets belong beneficially to the custodian's client.

In the financial markets, a custodian is any business entity that holds its customer's investment assets for protection. As we have seen typically, a custodian also offers trade settlements, foreign exchange transactions, and tax services. The custody service industry has grown significantly since 1980s and yet its profit margins have been under significant pressure. Smaller companies have, it appears, adapted to the challenge through technological innovation.

RETAIL/MUTUAL FUND CUSTODIAN

Banks often provide custody services to many types of customers, including retail/mutual funds, alternative investment managers, retirement plans, insurance companies, foundations, and agency accounts. A custodian that takes care of its customer's retail, mutual, AIF, hedge fund, property fund, or private equity funds is simply called a "custodian."

A fund custodian can either be a bank or a trust. The fund's assets, for example, its underlying securities, are kept with the third party to reduce the risk of manipulation, fraud, or unauthorized use of the fund assets. The custodian may also keep records for the fund or collate and provide other information as needed.

Custodians act on the instructions from their client and so communicating data between the client and the custodian is critically important.

There are several ways this can happen including proprietary systems operated by the custodian and in many cases via SWIFT messages. The Society for Worldwide Interbank Financial Telecommunication (SWIFT) provides a network that enables financial institutions worldwide to send and receive information about financial transactions in a secure, standardized, and reliable environment. SWIFT also sells software and services to financial institutions, much of it for use on the SWIFTNet Network, and ISO 9362. Business Identifier Codes are popularly known as "SWIFT codes". www.swift.com

The importance for the administrator is to be aware of the custodian's deadlines for receipt of an instruction. These deadlines are partially set by the deadlines imposed by the securities and payment settlement systems in the jurisdiction of the asset trades as well as the settlement conventions for the instruments. For example, in early October 2014, in many jurisdictions the settlement convention for equities became T + 2 and so any asset trades by the fund would have the expected finality of settlement two days after the trade date. The fund must ensure that any instructions related to the settlement are conveyed to the custodian in time for them to meet the obligation on settlement day.

The custodian is dealing primarily with the securities depositaries (where applicable), for example, Euroclear, Clearstream, or DTC and the payment systems, for example, Target 2, Fedwire, BACS as well as the brokers used by the client to settle the transactions in the assets.

They will monitor the situation through the clearing and settlement process for the instrument and update the client account as the finality of the settlement takes place. They will provide status updates to the fund administrator so that the primary reconciliation process can be performed between the fund record and the administrators record taken from the investment managers detail.

Custodians usually divide their services into what are called "core" and "added value" services.

Core services are those related to the safekeeping of assets both physical and the "book entry" electronic record of dematerialized assets plus the settlement, income collection like dividends and interest and managing of corporate action events like rights issues.

The fund administrator needs access to the custodian's records in order to first make sure that the fund records agree with those of the custodian and then to ensure the accounting records of the fund are complete so that NAV, statutory accounts, and reporting can be produced.

In many jurisdictions custodians need to be authorized and are regulated, for example:

Custodians in the United States of America.

The Investment Company Act of 1940 regulates the custody of mutual fund assets. Under the Act, mutual funds and custodians both need to register with the Securities and Exchange Commission.

FUND ADMINISTRATION

Another key player is of course the fund administrator.

Let us look at the high view of fund administration:

1. Fund administration—a service based product that has developed from the independent provision of pricing and valuations of assets and portfolios into a broad based product covering:
   a. Fund operations—asset trade capture and inputs to records, validation and verification of positions (exposure limits/mandate), assets (settlement status and location, eg, custodian), and reconciliations.
   b. Fund accounting and valuations—statutory accounts, general ledger, pricing of assets, posting of actual and accrued income (from assets, eg, dividends, interest from debt instruments, and cash deposits), and expenses (from transactions, eg, broker commissions, services, eg, custody fees, audit fees, licences and registrations, bank charges etc.).
   c. Transfer agency—managing subscriptions and redemptions, client due diligence, AML checks, the fund register, communication with clients.
   d. Secretarial services, risk and compliance management, fund set-ups.
2. Change to the service requirement—driven by the need for funds to show higher degree of control and management over the day-to-day operation of the fund including risk management and compliance—key issue is quality and professionalism.
3. Product characteristics—essential that the administrator understands the structure and characteristics of different products the fund may have in the portfolio, for example, the process of accrued interest on bonds, margin, and collateral associated with derivatives, for example, and the possibility of corporate action events. Also the valuation issues surrounding "easy to value" assets like listed equities and "difficult to value" like property and illiquid assets.
4. Workflow—the ability for the administrator to manage the workflow associated with the process of subscription and redemption, through cash forecast update, asset trades, postings, reconciliation, and finally the pricing and valuation process.
5. Identifying problems—data quality crucial as is the timings and cut offs associated with key processes, for example, asset trade capture from investment manager, receipt of subscription/redemption requests etc. managing situations in a practical way.
6. NAV calculations—pricing policy, tolerances and parameters, exception management, initial reasonableness checks, for example, portfolio change versus a benchmark, correct accruals.
7. Private equity—drawdown capital, growth and then distribution periods, fund has a projected life (5–10 years). Distribution pays off in order:
   a. The initial capital of the investors.
   b. The preference return to the investors.
   c. The carried interest of the general partner.
   d. Remaining return distributed across investors/general partner.
   e. Fund is charged fees throughout the life of the fund so initially investors have a negative situation.

PRIME BROKER/BROKERS

Most investment funds are not members of exchanges and the central securities depositories but instead access markets and assets via agents. These agents are often brokers or banks and the fund pays a commission to the brokers for the transactions they undertake on behalf of the fund.

PB services were originally designed for hedge fund managers but are today widely available to other types of funds.

The PB sits in the overall fund operational structure as shown (Diagram 2.10):

As can be seen, the link from the PB to the administrator is a crucial one in enabling the administrator to carry out primary control reconciliation of the activity by the manager against the records of the broker and custodian.

We will look at these and other key relationships more in Part 3.

Setting up a Fund

The fund administrator may be involved in helping the promoter of a fund to establish the fund in the jurisdiction.

This is very often the case for offshore funds where the expertise that the administrator has of the regulatory environment and available service providers can be highly beneficial.

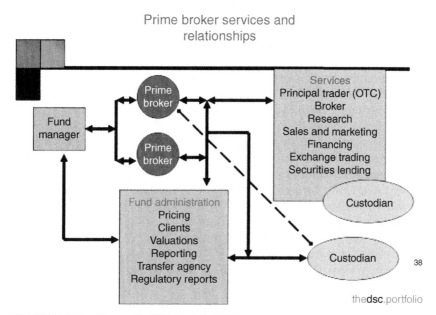

DIAGRAM 2.10 *(Source: The DSC Portfolio Ltd.)*

Detailed below is the kind of questions that need to be addressed in respect of the setting up of a hedge fund.

1. Confirm precise name of the fund.
2. Confirm precise name of overseas management company/distributor if such a structure is to be used. If the structure is just to be a fund with a direct contract down to a UK investment management company, then please confirm this.
3. Confirm full name, registered office address, and date of incorporation of investment manager. Also, confirm whether the investment manager is regulated. If the investment manager is located in the UK, it will normally need to be regulated which can take 3–4 months.
4. Confirm initial minimum subscription for shares and minimum incremental subscription thereafter. Confirm currency of share capital and whether there is one or more currency share classes.
5. Confirm provisional target date for launch of prospectus.
6. Describe the principal investment objectives of the fund and the target rate of return of the fund (this should be in the region of 10–15 lines to enable this wording to be inserted in the "Summary" section of the prospectus).
7. Describe the investment restrictions that will apply with reference to leverage, investment of assets in particular securities or strategies, etc.
8. Confirm identity of the Administrator for the fund and location of that Administrator. Also confirm that they will act as company secretary and whether there will be a Custodian and PB or whether nobody will hold the position of Custodian/PB and a number of brokers will be used.
9. Confirm procedure as to subscriptions and redemptions. It is presumed that subscriptions will be accepted monthly but will redemptions also be accepted monthly or perhaps quarterly? What will be the notice period required for redemptions?
10. Confirm the fees of the fund including the fixed fee based on the net asset value of the fund together with the performance fee and whether or not the performance fee will be charged above a hurdle?
11. Confirm whether US investors will be allowed to participate in the fund and, if so, whether this will just be what are known as US tax exempt investors or whether US retail investors will also be allowed to participate. If US individuals are allowed to participate, one must ascertain the minimum wealth level for such investors to allow for the appropriate wording to be added to the prospectus. Often, US taxable investors will be catered for in another parallel limited partnership structure or will be dealt with through what is known as a master/feeder structure.
12. Confirm the identity of the directors of the fund and provide a couple of descriptive paragraphs (ie, academic background and work experience on each person).
13. Confirm the auditors to the fund.

14. Confirm whether or not there will just be a single share class in the fund with all shareholders having the right to vote, receive dividends, receive distributions in a winding up on a "pari passu" basis or whether there is any advantage in having a second class of shares (often known as "founders shares" or "management shares") which would be held by the promoters/offshore management company and would hold the votes on various key issues such as the appointment and removal of the investment manager and possibly changes to the memorandum and articles of association of the fund.

15. Confirm the appropriate "valuation point" for valuations of the fund. Often this will be the close of business in relevant markets that the fund is active in on the last business day of the month or sometimes the first business day.

16. Provide a fairly detailed description of the investment objective and policies of the fund (perhaps 1–2 pages) together with the investment restrictions (if any) that will apply to the fund and any specific investment risks that need to be referred to.

17. Confirm the identity of the directors of the overseas management company/distributor (if there is to be one) and provide one or two paragraphs on each person.

18. Confirm the identity of the directors of the investment manager and provide one or two paragraphs on each person.

19. Confirm the basis on which the performance fees will work. In outline, there are a number of ways of charging performance fees once agreed, whether the fee will be chargeable on perhaps an annual or quarterly basis. The first of these is just to apply a performance fee (which may be 20%) to the growth in the NAV of the fund itself adjusted for subscriptions and redemptions. This is straightforward but it has the drawback of allowing what is known as a "free ride" to investors who enter the fund at a time when it is below a previous high. The second approach is to use what is known as "equalization accounting" whereby the administrator follows a procedure so that all the investors end up paying a fair performance fee based upon their own individual profits on their shares. The difficulty with this approach is that it is complex and it means the company maintaining what is known as an "equalization reserve." The third approach is the so called "series" approach whereby each investor who subscribes for shares receives a different series of shares. Therefore, if one has in the first year investors entering the fund on six different month ends, then one would have series 1–6 issued. Each of these series would have their own individual NAV per share with the result that there would not be a common NAV for the fund itself. Therefore, this third approach really replicates partnership accounting. Although alternatives two and three both prevent the "free ride" issue, both do give rise to complexity both with reference to stating a global NAV per share for the fund and with reference to investor perception.

20. Will there be a sales charge on subscriptions made to the fund and what will this be?

21. Will there be a redemption fee on redemptions from the fund within say the first 12 months from subscription and if so, what will this be?

22. Will there be a minimum holding period for shares in the fund?

23. A limit is normally stated for the payment of the directors fee from the fund and this needs to be agreed.

24. A limit is also normally stated for the establishment and organizational expenses of the fund with these costs being amortized over perhaps a three year period in the NAV of the fund. Again, this limit needs to be stated.

25. Will the fund publish its NAV in journals such as the Financial Times or the Wall Street Journal? Will the fund or the overseas management company have its own website which investors will be able to access for pricing and reports?

26. It is presumed that the fund will not have any stated distribution policy and its objective will be to maximize capital appreciation without paying dividends on a regular basis. Please confirm this.

27. Please confirm what the appropriate reporting will be to shareholders? It is presumed that the shareholders will be sent annual audited accounts together with unaudited half yearly accounts prepared by the administrator. This is required if the fund is Irish listed but only annual accounts are required, if not. Would it also be reasonable for them to receive a report from the offshore manager on a monthly or quarterly basis?

28. Sometimes, provisions may be included limiting the percentage of the fund which can be redeemed in any one month. Commonly, this could be something like 20% of the total fund NAV with redemption requests in excess of this figure being carried over to the next month. Whether or not a client thinks this is necessary and tends to depend on how liquid their portfolio is.

29. Confirm any special pricing provisions—many hedge funds use mid or last traded price whereas some use bid/ask. This can have reasonably material implications, particularly if leverage is used on both longs and shorts.

30. Confirm whether or not the fund should have a listing on a stock exchange such as the Irish Stock Exchange.

31. In a master/feeder structure, the feeder for US taxable investors is normally a Delaware partnership. Such an entity requires a general partner which again is normally an overseas company. Details again should be provided for such a structure including the name of the partnership and the name of the general partner.

Source: The DSC Portfolio Ltd

These are some of the primary issues to be considered in formulating an offering memorandum for a new fund and once discussed and agreed with the promoter, the administrator will formulate the draft structure providing where necessary the names of potential parties, for example, legal firms secretary and directors.

Finally, the administrator will assist with completing any regulatory applications that are needed as well as compiling the draft offering documents for agreement. These will be needed for the regulatory application for the authorization and licensing of the fund.

Another area of importance in setting up the fund is to complete the agreements with the key counterparties, for example, Custody Agreement, Fund Administration Agreement, Prime Broker Agreement etc. and also Service Level Agreements. (See Part 3)

Outsourcing

The fund will in all probability outsource some or even all of the activities.

In general terms we are talking in principle about:

- The investment process
- Administration
- Custody

Outsourcing represents an operational risk for the fund mainly because of the loss of control over the process and the reliance on the skills and performance of the insourcer.

Sometimes the decision to outsource is done for financial reasons or operational reasons, for example, the cost of technology or human resource with the right skill sets. However in some cases, the fund will have no option but to outsource as it may be a requirement of the regulator in the jurisdiction.

Any outsource arrangement must be covered by an agreement.

DOCUMENTATION AND AGREEMENTS

Funds are likely to be involved in several agreements including those covering the key counterparties already mentioned.

The purpose of the agreement is to establish the terms of the relationship, the legal basis and if a SLA, the workflow, data provision etc. and responsibilities of both parties.

In addition, the fund may have to sign other agreements related to securities financing, derivatives use, collateral etc. and these are mentioned elsewhere in the book.

Examples of agreements can be found in the appendices.

SUMMARY

In this part, we have looked at regulation, fund structures, roles of parties associated with the fund, and some important areas like outsourcing and agreements.

In Part 3, we look at fund operations and the work that various parties in a fund undertake.

Part 3

The Day-to-Day Operation of a Fund

INTRODUCTION

The day to day operation of a fund will be driven by the type of fund. Actively managed and open ended funds will potentially have more workflow than passive and closed funds. Portfolios of illiquid assets will be less active than retail funds operating in liquid assets.

As we have seen earlier, the investment objectives, types of instruments, and products and strategies employed by the manager will also impact on the workflow within the fund operations and support.

Likewise the investment process can involve the fund in a legal agreement with the investment manager and the services offered to the manager by the prime broker will be subject to a prime broker/broker agreement.

The service provision by the custodian and administrator will also be governed by legal agreements that establish the relationship and a service level agreement (SLA), which determines the provision and responsibilities in the service delivery by each party.

Key content of the SLA would include:

1. General scope of the service including types of assets to be processed by the administrator, key contacts for both parties, escalation routes etc.
2. Communication channels for receipt and delivery of data, for example, SWIFT messages, prime broker/broker proprietary systems, email, hard copy etc.
3. Timings and deadlines for provision of data between the parties.
4. Sources of data, for example, asset transactions, prices for valuation, subscriptions and redemptions (if administrator is providing the transfer agent service).
5. Internal and external reporting requirements including regulatory and investor communications.

6. Scope of secretarial services if being provided by the administrator.
7. Accounting policies and requirements.
8. Risk management and Compliance services. The administrator can provide assistance to the fund with risk management and compliance for the fund but the responsibility remains the funds.
9. Benchmarking of the service.
10. Waivers, indemnities etc.

This is clearly a key document and is covered again in Part 4.

Parts of the content of the SLA will be related to the process workflow.

PROCESS WORKFLOW

The process workflow for a fund will fall into three areas:

1. Operations
2. Valuation and accounting
3. Transfer agency

As we have already seen in earlier chapters these areas are linked with the investment activity and the investor activity linked to the valuation and accounting processes.

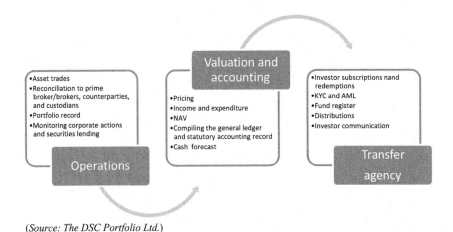

- Asset trades
- Reconciliation to prime broker/brokers, counterparties, and custodians
- Portfolio record
- Monitoring corporate actions and securities lending

Operations

Valuation and accounting
- Pricing
- Income and expenditure
- NAV
- Compiling the general ledger and statutory accounting record
- Cash forecast

- Investor subscriptions nand redemptions
- KYC and AML
- Fund register
- Distributions
- Investor communication

Transfer agency

(*Source: The DSC Portfolio Ltd.*)

Within each area there are specific tasks and functions the team will undertake and we can explore these now.

We saw earlier in the book the following diagram covering the workflow for a securities asset transaction in a fund:

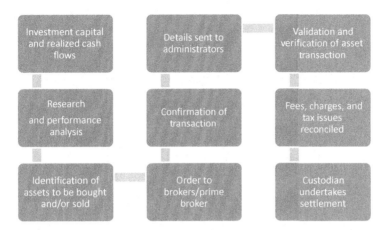

The following provides examples of some of the key process workflow the administrator and/or custodian are involved in during the flow shown earlier.

INVESTMENT CAPITAL

1 Subscription and redemption in the shares and units of the fund

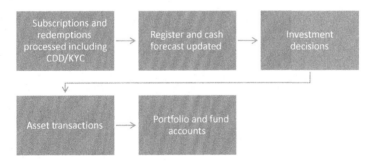

INVESTMENT PROCESS

2 Investment decisions

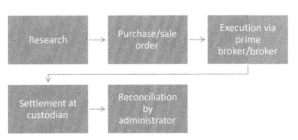

ASSET SERVICING

3 Corporate actions

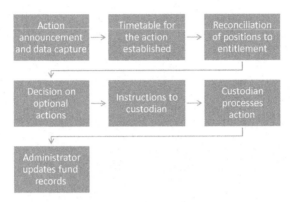

The administrator and custodian will incorporate these high level process blocks into their system capabilities and design procedures to deliver the operational process.

As data is such a key driver in the functions of administration and custody, a strong database capability is essential if the amount of manual process is to be minimized.

As we know generically there are several component parts of what is fund administration as the following diagram shows.

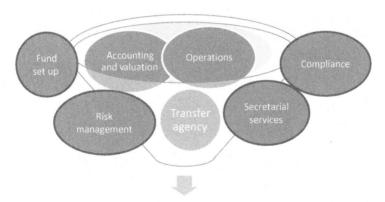

Fund administration

The precise nature of the service that a fund requires and an administrator can offer does of course depend on many factors.

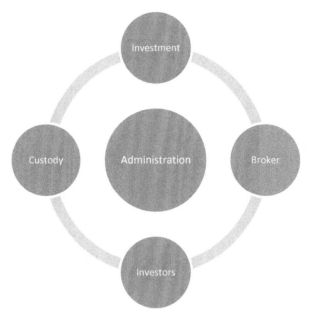

FIGURE 3.1

As we have said this will include the assets the funds invest in, the strategies used, passive or actively managed, form the fund takes in terms of being regulated or unregulated, retail or alternative investment fund, and the requirements of the jurisdiction in which the fund is based. The requirement of the promoter/owner and the investors is also a key component of the relationship that will exist between the fund and its administrator.

Where does fund administration sit in terms of the whole investment process?

Fig. 3.1 shows how the principle relationships are with the investment manager, brokers and prime brokers, custodians/depositaries, and the investors.

The other key parties the administrator may be involved with, include:

- Promoter/owner.
- Nonexecutive directors.
- Risk and compliance managers.
- Auditors.
- Agents and intermediaries—for example, derivative brokers/counterparties as well as property management companies (real estate funds), specialist accountants (private equity funds), and parties involved in the transaction and warehousing of alternatives like art, collectibles, and commodities.
- Banks—that is, custodian banks.

And, possibly, although on probably an infrequent basis,

- Tax advisers
- Lawyers

We will now look at the work flow that each component of the administration service undertakes.

At a high level the possible structure for a full service administrator is as shown in the following diagram.

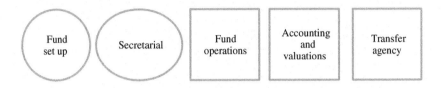

FUND OPERATIONS

The fund operations team will be dealing with the asset transactions, which are made for the portfolio of the fund. The transactions are typically in one of the following:

- Securities—equities, bonds.
- Derivatives—futures, forwards, options, swaps.
- Commodities—agricultural, energy, metals, etc.
- Property—retail (housing) or commercial (offices, warehouses, shops).
- Investment funds—retail funds and alternative investment funds (hedge funds, private equity funds, property funds). Funds like fund of funds and some retail funds are able to invest in the shares or units of other investment funds.
- Alternatives—art, antiques, structured products, infrastructure etc.

In addition we have cash, like deposits (overnight money) and short term money market instruments (Treasury Bills, Certificate of Deposit (CDs), Commercial Paper) as well as trades in currencies (foreign exchange).

The role of the operations team is to interact with the investment manager to obtain the asset trades undertaken and to then reconcile the successful finality of settlement of these transactions. In this book, unless otherwise stated, this means the party involved in the investment process including a manager, committee etc.

As part of this process the administrator will reconcile positions and cash movements in the fund portfolio with the custodian, broker, or counterparty.

Any discrepancies will be immediately relayed to the investment manager for resolution and may need reporting internally to the risk manager and/or senior management depending on the terms of the SLA between the fund and the administrator.

The details of the transaction will be posted into the fund records and accounts.

- *Source*
  - Broker—executed trades
  - Prime Broker—executed trades
  - Manager—placed and completed orders
  - Data received from manager and brokers through statements, confirmations etc.—note this is likely to be an automated process but may also be manual
- *Update portfolio*
  - Validation of manager versus broker data
  - Position/exposure limits check versus mandate/offering document/regulation
  - Transaction details posted to fund records
- *Settlement*
  - Custodian settlement details/ positions in the assets in their account at CSD or clearing house/broker is reconciled to the data for the portfolio—unsettled trades are managed by the custodian but monitored by the administrator and included in the positions and NAV calculations. Note—unmatched transactions cannot proceed to settlement and cannot be included in the funds records and NAV calculations, however pending the resolution by the manager and counterparty they will be provisionally included in the cash forecast.
- *Corporate actions*
  - Managing the outcome of any corporate actions announced on assets held by the fund (fund can lose money or other benefits if this process (carried out by the custodian and monitored by the administrator) is not managed properly.
  - Cash movements resulting from corporate actions will need to be included in the cash forecast.

  Summary of the workflow

- Portfolio trade capture—ensuring that all transactions are properly detailed in the records of the fund.
- Booking into the fund's records—allocating all transactions to the relevant fund.
- Reconciliation to brokers/custodian—primary control for ensuring that the portfolio agrees with the positions from the market/counterparties.
- Portfolio position reports to investment manager—advising the investment manager that the portfolio is reconciled of any discrepancies that the manager needs to resolve/remain unresolved.
- Corporate actions—ensuring that any corporate action has been managed and the outcome updated in the fund's records.
- Mandate checks—ensuring the fund is complying with its offering documents.

- Possibly broker/third-party agreements in conjunction with legal/compliance, that is, ISDA documents for over the counter (OTC) derivatives—ensuring the fund has agreed and signed agreements for services, settlement of products/assets, etc.

VALUATION AND ACCOUNTING

The valuation and accounting team are responsible for maintaining the full accounts of the fund, carrying out valuations of the assets of the fund and incorporating the realized and accruals for income and expenses so that the NAV and if required the NAV per share/unit can be calculated.

The frequency of this NAV calculation will depend on the fund and as we have already seen this could be daily, weekly, monthly, or quarterly. Remember some funds operating in illiquid assets and closed funds with a stated investment period, that is, private equity funds may have a less frequent NAV calculation.

The following are the tasks of the team:

- *General ledger*
  The fund's accounting records will be maintained in the general ledger (G/L) and in most cases the GL will have sub ledgers for the recording of specific items like investments, expenses, income, tax, commissions etc.
  The entries to the GL are usually on a double entry bookkeeping basis.
  The control over and reconciliation of entries to the ledgers is vitally important and is part of the risk management process of the fund and the administrator.
- *Valuing the funds property (investments)*
  This is needed for the measuring of the performance of the fund, contributes to the NAV calculation and may also relate to subscription and redemption values as well as performance fees, where applicable.
- *Income and expenses*
  The team will identify and post realized and accrued income and expenses to the ledgers.
- *Publishing the price of funds*
  This will usually be based on the NAV and shares/units in issue and will be carried out in accordance with the offering documents. The team will need to make sure that the relevant sign offs have been done before publication.
  Usually a senior manager in the administrator will sign off the NAV and pass it to the fund where the investment manager or other designated party will also sign off on the value. The responsibility for the correctness and publication of the NAV lies with the fund.
- *Impact of incorrect pricing of investments*
  Should this situation arise, the regulators and/or offering documents and agreements establish how and when compensation is due on incorrect pricing and the team will need to follow the relevant procedure.

The compensation is due to investors who have subscribed or redeemed their shares or units at an incorrect value. Note—investors that have benefited from the error will be unlikely to have to repay the gain.

On identification of such a mispricing it must be escalated to senior management in the administrator and to the fund manager and governance.

- *Pricing controls and policy*

The fund will need to have clearly laid down controls and policies for the pricing and valuing of assets. This is essential if the risks associated with the valuation process are to be managed and will be followed by the team when calculating the NAV.

It should be compiled by the fund in conjunction with the administrator and any deviation from the policy needs to be logged.

The pricing policy is likely to be linked into an overall valuation policy such as the following:

Extracts on pricing and valuation

The following are extracts from the CLT Advanced Certificate & Diploma in Fund Administration.

Pricing models

Pricing models can be very important but there must also be recognition of their limitations in some cases. Nonetheless, the use of models plus subjective analysis can produce a reasonable and meaningful value.

Models work on data so the access to a data source is critical, but even then a model cannot tell you exactly what will happen to a price unless it is based on all the relevant detail. Pricing models can also be expensive to buy or build and to maintain. Does the fund administrator spend large sums on models only to see a decline in the use of the products the models can now value?

It may also be that the investment manager has developed a pricing model and is not keen to have anyone else access how it works. As part of the pricing policy, accepting a value for pricing purposes from such a model would have to be confirmed as acceptable.

What is a reasonable price or value?

One way of working out what a reasonable value might be for the CMO we have been talking about is to look first at the rate of defaults in sub-prime mortgages of the kind held in the CMO and second at the credit default swaps market for Bear Stearns.

The first should allow a judgement on the likelihood that the tranche will default, while the second could show the probability of a default by Bear Stearns.

Don't forget that hedging the risk will be a cost to the fund and therefore a lower return of interest and or capital than expected if the default occurs.

While a fund that accepts risk might accept the possible default (lower return of interest and/or capital than expected) in favor of the potentially much higher yield, one could still possibly expect to see them hedge part of the counterparty risk, at least, and probably the CMO risk too if things started to happen in the market.

It would be wrong to have the CMO showing in the fund as still valued at $60m, unless the manager and advisers can give a very good reason or can demonstrate that there are offsetting products hedging the exposure.

Would the scenario described above constitute an "easy" or "difficult" position to value? The answer could be that it is easy, if the components and the issuer can be assessed in terms of risk and yield, or difficult, because the precise interpretation of the degree of risk, ability to sell on or novate and the options to hedge out the risk are themselves fairly volatile, for example, the prime broker might agree to novate the position today and refuse or massively increase the discount tomorrow. Likewise, the cost of buying protection through a CDS on Bear Stearns might jump 200 points overnight.

Of course the CMO might be redeemed perfectly OK and all interest paid as expected (assuming the mortgages don't default) because the issuer is taken over by a strong party, as in fact happened when J P Morgan Chase acquired Bear Stearns.

Pricing and value issues

The less transparent the product the greater the degree of caution in valuing it: many highly complex CDOs or so-called toxic assets have a range of value from 0% to 100%. Some may and probably will be near to zero but many may yet deliver much if not all their value.

One possibility is that there will be gradual write-downs and write-ups in value, which are preferable to huge swings in value. The exception to this would be if something highly significant triggers such a change in value, which needs to be reflected immediately.

Accounting rules may also affect how a position is valued and indeed the concept of mark to market and fair value can cause the value to be shown as zero if there is poor liquidity, even though the product in reality does have some potential value.

Valuation in practice

It is important that the process of valuation is thought through carefully on a product-by-product basis.

Valuations of complex products will be based on the issues shown earlier and while this may not be an exact science it should still be possible for auditors and regulators to look for evidence of reasonableness in the interpretation of the "real" value and the "probable" value, taking into account the market situation, hedges, etc. with suitable pricing and valuation then applied. This concept, with some adjustment, should be applicable across private equity and property funds. The issues specific to private equity and property are naturally related to the characteristic of the assets.

Private equity can be venture capital or buy out related.

Venture capital is in turn related to small, medium sized businesses that are start ups or growing entities.

These unlisted companies are in need of capital and this can sometimes be achieved through private equity funds. The PE fund invests in the companies mainly in equity but sometimes in debt instruments.

For the administrator the key issues are how to value the unlisted company and also how income such as dividends or interest is received from the investee company.

For example, dividends could be in the form of shares rather than cash and interest on debt may be paid on maturity and not at regular intervals as would happen with a government bond. Indeed, the interest amount may also be paid in shares rather than cash.

Valuations for PE funds may be done using the IPEV guidelines. The December 2015 edition of the guideline can be found at http://www.privateequityvaluation.com/valuation-guidelines/4588034291.

ON-EXCHANGE PRICING AND VALUATION ISSUES

There are very few issues with the on-exchange products. In the on-exchange markets and products while there can be volatility in prices, because the price is derived from the exchange there is a readily available, independent and robust source of pricing.

VALUATION CHECKLIST

It is always useful for control purposes to have procedures and checklists that can be used operationally and to demonstrate adequate control to auditors and regulators.

Example for Valuation Checklist

Following is an example of such a checklist:

Use of asset and strategy	Meets the mandate/offering documents
Use authorized	Relevant board meeting, committee minutes, etc.
Operational awareness	Check to see that adequately resourced and knowledgeable operational support is in place

Risk awareness	Management controls over exposure and counterparty risk in place
Valuation processes and methodology	Clearly defined, workable pricing policy Designated pricing agent Escalation procedures for issues Documented pricing sources and approved methodologies Approved hedging products and strategies Comparison usage and benchmarks to assess reasonableness of value
"Difficult to value" assets	Identification of types of asset and strategy Documented valuation and pricing policy

Source: CLT International Advanced Certificate in Fund Administration

INCOME AND EXPENSE

The team will need to identify all income and expenses of the fund and post these to the relevant ledgers.

Income can be from a variety of sources, for example, from:

1. Income generating assets like bonds.
2. Distributions of share of profits from dividends.
3. Interest on cash deposits.
4. Fees from securities financing.

Expenses can be generated by the following:

1. Invoices for services from parties such as the custodian, administrator etc.
2. Director's, Trustee, General Partner fees.
3. Commissions and fees associated with assets trades.
4. Fees associated with securities financing.
5. Start-up fees and costs.
6. Performance fees payable.
7. Regulatory fees and costs.

These lists are not exhaustive and unique costs and income might be generated for certain types of funds. For example, withholding tax may occur on income from assets but may be reclaimable. Ledgers will need to reflect this.

MARGIN AND COLLATERAL

Some funds may become involved in margin calls and collateral and this must be reflected in the relevant ledgers in the accounts.

In addition some income and fees will be periodic and some may be one off.

It is vitally important that the Capital and Income elements of the fund are kept separate in the accounts of the fund.

DISTRIBUTIONS

The team will calculate the available amounts for distribution funds over the relevant period.

Once the gross amount is calculated the amount per share or unit is then applied to the investor's holding.

We can look at an example here:

Income for the period calculated incorporating any deductions = £1,000,000
Fund accumulation shares = 50,000
Fund distribution shares = 75,000
Total shares in issue = 125,000
Distribution = £1,000,000/125000 = £8 per share
NAV per share of the fund = £12
Fund accumulation shares receive 1.5 shares
Fund distribution shares receive £8 per share
Impact—accumulation shares now = 75,000
Distribution shares = 75,000

The team may need to seek advice from the tax expert in respect of a deduction of tax, if any.

PERFORMANCE FEE CALCULATION

The team will most likely be involved in the calculation of performance fees where these are payable to the investment manager under the IMA.

The basis for calculation of the fee will be in the offering documents and the administrator will also need to apply any equalization process if this applicable. See Appendices for flows in relation to performance fee and carried interest calculations.

Management Information

The team may need to produce management information for the fund.

This will be contained in the Agreement and the SLA between the fund and the administrator and could include data on:

- Change in NAV
- Commissions and fees paid
- Distributions
- Performance and performance fees
- Errors

Summary of accounting issues and controls
- Key accounting issues.
  - Valuation
  - Profit and loss
  - Cash flows

- Verification
- Disclosure
- Key controls.
- Reconciliation of all cash movements is primary accounting control in any business.
- Independent verification of existence (and value) of assets and liabilities.
- Application of relevant accounting policies and standards.

Regulation and disclosure

- *Capital markets highly regulated*
  - European banking laws & directives (MiFID/MiFID II, Basel II, AIFM)
  - *UK*—FCA/PRA, *Europe*—EMIR/ESMA, United States—SEC, CFTC
  - Industry associations; best practice
  - National accounting standards

Accounting procedures must comply

Summary
- *Consistent valuation policy*
- *Accurate profit and loss measurement*
- *Reconciliation of cash flows*
- *Verification of assets/liabilities*
- *Compliance re disclosure*

TRANSFER AGENCY

The transfer agency team will be involved in several key areas of the operation of the fund.

Naturally a major function is that of dealing with the subscriptions and redemptions by investors in the fund but it is not the only key task.

Other important aspects of the transfer agency role are:

- *The role of the maintaining of the stakeholders register for units or shares:*
  - Issuing acknowledgement
  - Certificated and book entry record to the fund Register
  - Amending records
  - Dividend payments
  - Power of Attorney
- *International transactions*—Ensuring comprehensive KYC and AML checks are carried out, identifying any constraints and ensuring correct share class has been applied.

Subscriptions and Redemptions

The life cycle of the subscription and redemption process can be illustrated by the following:

Subscriptions

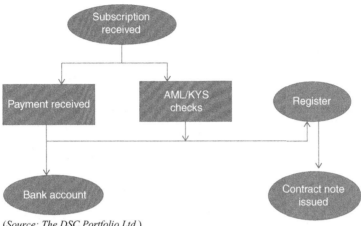

(Source: The DSC Portfolio Ltd.)

This diagram shows the process for the subscription to a fund. This could be via a public offering, placement, advertising, or through an intermediary. The T/A will need to carry out relevant KYC and AML checks. The KYC involves checking that the applicant has the right status for the fund they are applying to invest in, particularly for restricted investor funds and also that the investor is meeting and maximum/minimum application or position and is not for any reason unacceptable to the owners/managers.

AML checks are important and becoming more so, even to the extent of nonregulated funds having to do AML due diligence as matter of law rather than regulation.

If all is in order the cash is received and the register is updated with any acknowledgement, certificate or contract note sent to the investor.

The manager may want to see any significant applications in terms of name and amount as large subscriptions and redemptions can potentially create problems.

Redemptions

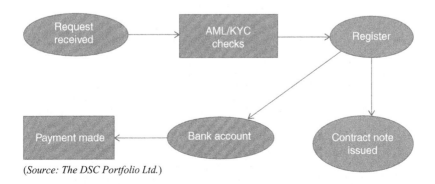

(Source: The DSC Portfolio Ltd.)

Redemptions also require due diligence in terms of who is authorized to request redemption, are the proceeds to go to the same place as the source of incoming capital etc.

Switches are somewhat different as in an umbrella fund the investor may switch between funds without any payment involved but checks are still necessary.

DISTRIBUTIONS

We have seen in the section on the work of the valuation and accounting team that for some classes of shares a fund may be making distributions of income either reinvested for accumulation shares or distributed for distribution shares.

Once the available amount per share has been calculated, the transfer agency will prepare the statement for the investor showing the additional shares now in their name or the amount payable.

On the due date the register will be updated accordingly and payments made where relevant.

The statement will make reference to any tax that may be deductible.

CUSTODY AND DEPOSITARY

Now let us look at the role and work of the custodian.

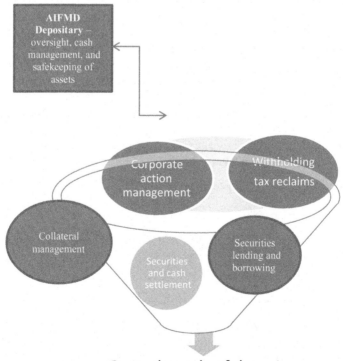

Custody and safekeeping

In the day to day operations of the fund the custodian is performing some key tasks.

The custodian holds and manages, in their name, the assets that belong to the fund. At all times the custodian is holding the title to assets in their name *but* "beneficially" for the client. The custodian has no interest in the assets of the client and they are held segregated away from the assets of the custody firm.

Clients like funds can benefit from having the settlement and postsettlement processes managed by a specialist custodian. The safekeeping of the assets of the fund are a major issue for investors in a fund as loss of the fund's assets through fraud, theft, or uninsured destruction of assets can collapse a fund and lose the investors all their capital.

Typically a custodian has core services and added value services it can offer its fund client.

Core services would potentially comprise:

- Status reporting (matched/unmatched)
- Settlement of trades
- Safekeeping of physical assets
- Income collection
- Managing corporate actions
- Proxy voting
- Withholding tax reclaims

We can see that these services are built around the fact that the custodian is holding the assets of the fund in its name and is therefore well positioned to manage processes like settlement and income selection.

We can see here the detail of what the custodian is doing.

- *Status reporting*
  - As the link between the CSD the custodian can report on the status of the fund's transaction with the market.
- *Settlement of trades*
  - The custodian ensures the receipt and payment of shares or cash in settlement of the transactions the manager has undertaken.
- *Safekeeping of physical assets*
  - Where assets are in paper or physical format the custodian will hold the assets securely in a vault.
  - Where assets are in dematerialized form the custodian holds an electronic record in their books which is reflected in their record with the relevant CSD.
- *Income collection*
  - The custodian can calculate the dividend, interest or other income due from a position and receive and report on the successful receipt of the payment from the source.

- If the payment is not direct, for example, because of a late settlement of a transaction, the custodian will make a claim from the party concerned.
- *Managing corporate actions*
    - The custodian can calculate the outcome of a corporate action and manage the results/adjust the records/make and receive payments etc.
- *Proxy voting*
    - The custodian can vote on behalf of the fund where the regulations permit.
- *Withholding tax reclaims*
    - If investments are in overseas locations where tax is deducted at source, the custodian can, if the fund qualifies and the jurisdiction permits, reclaim the tax paid.

Then there are the added value services that a client of the custodian can opt to use and pay for on the basis of the usage, for example:

- Management, client, and regulatory reporting
- Stock lending and borrowing
- Cash management
- FX services
- Portfolio pricing and valuation
- Derivatives clearing and settlement
- Market information

Custodians have developed these services in order to offer a comprehensive service to clients like funds. For example, some portfolio pricing and valuation are typically part of the services offered by a fund administrator. It therefore follows that a custodian could also be the administrator for some types of fund.

We can see here the detail of these added value services:

- *Management, client, and regulatory reporting*
    - The custodian maintains extensive data and information related to markets, trades, positions, etc. and can provide an extensive suite of reporting to the fund.
- *Stock lending and borrowing*
    - Custodians can manage both the lending and borrowing requirements of securities for the fund, assuming the fund wishes to lend or borrow securities.
- *Cash management*
    - Custodians receive and pay out cash in settlement of transactions or income from dividends etc., and offer management services to ensure funding requirements and excess cash is managed efficiently for the fund.
- *FX services*
    - Custodians can provide foreign exchange services to the fund if required.

- *Portfolio pricing and valuation*
  - The positions held by the fund can be independently valued using the custodian's sources of market prices.
- *Derivatives clearing and settlement*
  - Custodians can provide information, settlement, and position maintenance for many types of derivatives often involving another Group entity.
- *Market information*
  - The custodian is an important source of price information, data on corporate actions, exchange rates etc.

Core services are usually paid for by an assets under management (AUM) formula while added value services are charged on a usage basis.

The fees are negotiated and core service fees will have both a floor (minimum charge) and a tapering charged on high value AUM.

Custody fees are usually accrued in the accounts to avoid a spike affecting the fund's net asset value, which will occur if the total cost of the custodian's invoice hits the fund accounts on a single day.

GLOBAL CUSTODY

A global custodian provides clients with multicurrency custody, settlement, and reporting services, which extend beyond the global custodian's and client's base region and currency; and encompass all classes of financial instruments.

The workflow for an asset transaction is as shown:

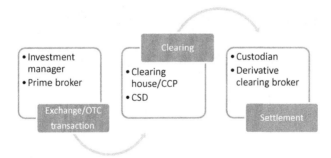

The life cycle of the trade starts with the order being placed by the investment manager to the broker and execution of the trade.

The trade will enter into the clearing phase and is recorded at the CSD and or clearing house/CCP.

This is followed by the data capture and validation process by the fund's administrator and then settlement processing by the custodian of the fund at the CSD.

Key reconciliations will take place at various stages in the process including the primary reconciliation by the administrator of the portfolio positions and those held at the custodian and brokers.

The diagram earlier follows on from the one we saw at the beginning of this section.

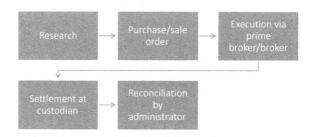

The shown flows are based on securities transactions and yet there will be some important and subtle differences dependent on the actual assets. For example, for a property fund that is operating in physical property, there will be no paper share certificate or dematerialized security but instead there will be the Title Deeds of the property, which will be the evidence of ownership.

We can now look at the life cycle of derivatives transactions.

Life Cycle of Derivatives Transactions

Derivatives are either traded on-exchange or off-exchange OTC and can settle via CCP or directly between parties, although since 2008 regulatory change means that many OTC derivatives now settle via a CCP.

We can look again at the relationships in Fig. 3.2:

Contractual parties to derivative contracts trade as principal; both on-exchange and OTC.

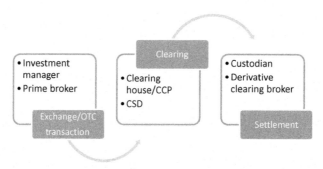

FIGURE 3.2

Exchange traded derivatives (eg, futures) have the benefit of a central clearing house, which greatly reduces counterparty risk exposure within the market by providing multilateral netting among the clearing house members. Today as noted above, many OTC products now also benefit from the central clearing process.

The CCP has various protective procedures in place—especially the margining process and the daily settlement of losses through the variation margin process. Students should study Chapter 5 which explains derivatives further.

Clients or end users as they are known will still have credit risk exposure to their clearing bank or broker.

The life cycle of a derivatives trade follows some of the routing that occurs for some kinds of securities.

Settlement of On-Exchange Derivatives

On-exchange derivatives settle via a CCP/Clearing House and are in the form of a standardized contract. Standardized contracts are designed by the exchange and the product detail is contained in the contract specification issued by the exchange.

Principal on-exchange products are futures and option contracts on a wide range of what is called the underlying such as equities, debt and interest rate instruments, commodities, credit and currencies.

The life cycle of a trade moves through the phases we are by now familiar with so we have execution, trade capture, and then the middle and back office process.

We can see the main processes in the phases in the Fig. 3.3 and we then look at the OTC scenario.

Futures and options margin flows

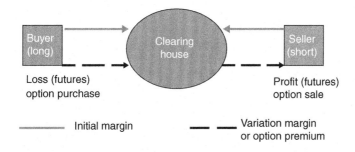

Note: the loss/profit is illustrative and can the other way round

FIGURE 3.3

Daily settlement components

- **Variation margin (paid and received)**

- **Option premium (paid and received)**

- **Change in initial margin requirements**

- **Transaction fees and commissions (paid)**

- **Cash postings (transfers, interest, etc.)**

- **For each currency**

FIGURE 3.4

The post execution phase for futures and options will involve the clearing of the trades and the maintenance of the open positions by the CCP/Clearing House in the name of a clearing member as shown in Fig. 3.3.

For futures contracts there is a daily variation margin calculation (a revaluation process) and the amount generated by the calculation is for settlement.

In addition there is a security deposit that is called initial margin that must be covered by collateral lodged at the CCP/Clearing House until all obligations have been met and the open position closed, delivered, or matured.

The daily settlement components are summarized in Fig. 3.4:

In Fig. 3.4, we see the main settlement processes and to this we can also add monitoring the initial margin and collateral management process.

The daily workflow in this part of the life cycle is illustrated in Fig. 3.5.

As we can see the settlement process is carried out with a convention of T + 1 with the preparatory workflow on trade day.

Operations workflow

- **T+0: In-house data capture:**
  - o Details of all trades executed
  - o Any new contract parameter file data
  - o Relevant exchange closing prices

- **T+1: Reconciliation of broker statements:**
  - o Screen access, data files, paper reports

- **T+1: Payment instructions:**
  - o Margin calls, cash management, etc.

FIGURE 3.5

Operations workflow - 1

- **T+0: In-house system data capture:**
  - o Enter details of all trades executed
  - o Enter any new parameter file data needed
  - o Transfer data to operations & accounts systems

- **T+1: Reconciliation with counterparty:**
  For trades to be settled directly
  - o Send/receive confirmation to/from counterparty
  - o Match trade details; reconcile differences
  - o Sign and return (or acceptance) of confirmation

  For trades to be settled via CCP the same process is used as for on-exchange traded products (see Fig. 3.5)

  Note: a non-centrally cleared derivative trade may need to be reported to a trade repository by the end user or their broker

FIGURE 3.6

This workflow may well involve the same positioning process that we find in securities settlement but related to collateral and payments.

The post settlement phase of on-exchange derivatives involves both the management of the variation and initial margin flows but also the potential exercise, assignment, and tendering for delivery process as well.

The latter can occur on maturity or depending on the contract specification at times during the life of the contract, an example being that American style options can be exercised any busy day by the buyer.

In the appendices, there are diagrams that should be studied carefully as they are related to these exercise, assignment, and tendering for delivery processes.

Life Cycle of the Settlement of OTC Derivatives

As noted earlier many OTC trades are today settled via a CCP rather than directly between the counterparties, for example interest rate and credit default swaps.

Therefore there are two distinct process flows associated with OTC derivatives, one centralized the other not.

We can see the main workflow illustrated in Fig. 3.6.

In Fig. 3.7, we can see that although there may be a variation type process, that is, a mark to market revaluation this may only be for P/L calculations and not a settlement amount.

Operations workflow - 2

- **Daily: Mark-to-market valuation:**
  - o Determine source of prices
  - o Calculate unrealised MTM gain/loss
  - o Initiate collateral movements if applicable

- **Periodic (T+90?): Repeated settlements:**
  - o Calculate settlement amounts due
  - o Issue payment instructions and check actioned

  Examples

  swaps and credit default swaps (CDS)

FIGURE 3.7

Exercise

Now let us do an exercise related to the calculation of variation and initial margins, fees, and change to the cash balance of a series if trades (Fig. 3.8).

You need to calculate the initial and variation margin, commission, and the change to the cash balance at the broker as a result of these trades.

The answer can be found in Part 5 of the book.

SECURITIES LENDING AND BORROWING

Securities Lending

Now let us look at securities lending and explore what it is and the life cycle of what is a very important part of the financial markets.

Exercise: Futures daily settlements

- Day 1
  - Starting cash=£60,000
  - Buy 10 FTSE @5900
  - Eod price = 5907
- Day 2
  - Sell 5 FTSE @5912
  - Fod price = 5915
- Day 3
  - Buy 5 FTSE @5920
  - Sell 10 FTSE @5906

- Parameter data
  - FTSE100 futures contract
    - Value=£10x index
    - Tick size £5 per 0.5
    - IM = £2500/contract

  - Commission & fees
    - £1.50 per lot per side

  Interest rate 1.5%

FIGURE 3.8

Introduction

Securities Lending Defined

Securities lending is the lending of equities and bonds by or on behalf of an investor to counterparties who are authorized to borrow securities in return for a fee.

Securities lending provides liquidity to the market by utilizing securities that would otherwise be "side-lined" by being held in safekeeping thus providing yield enhancement in the form of the fee received.

A major industry organization, The Group of Thirty, recognized the importance of securities lending and made a recommendation which stated that:

Securities lending and borrowing should be encouraged as a method of expediting the settlement of securities transactions. Existing regulatory and taxation barriers that inhibit the practice of lending and borrowing securities should be removed.

The "...expedition of securities transactions" is not the only reason why securities lending and borrowing takes place. Furthermore, not every market or regulatory jurisdiction implements appropriate measures to "...encourage..." the practice. Indeed post the market crash, many regulators and markets had serious concerns that securities lending had contributed to volatility and share price declines primarily associated with short selling strategies used by some hedge funds.

Some regulators introduced prohibitions on short selling and/or securities lending although many have realized that securities lending itself is a crucially important facility in the efficient operation of the markets, particularly, in terms of settlement on due date.

CHARACTERISTICS OF SECURITIES LENDING

Legal title to the securities passes from the lender to the borrower but the benefits of ownership are retained by the lender.

This is important as it means that the lender continues to receive income and retains the right to sell the securities in the stock market although this may be subject to any constraints in respect of the terms of the loan. The lender, however, loses the right to vote.

In terms of the income like dividends or interest this will not be paid direct to the lender as their name will have been removed from the issuer or company's register; instead the income is claimed from and paid by the borrower.

USES OF SECURITIES LENDING

Market participants *borrow* for a variety of reasons, which include to:

- Cover short positions (where participants, for example, some hedge funds and market makers sell securities which they do not hold).
- Support derivatives activities (where participants may be subjected to an option exercise).
- Cover settlement fails (where participants do not have sufficient securities available to settle a delivery).
- Obtain securities that are acceptable as collateral.

Market participants *lend* securities for one purpose; that is, to earn fee income. This has two benefits:

- Fee income enhances the investment performance of the securities portfolio.
- As securities lending decreases the size of the portfolio, there is a corresponding reduction in safekeeping charges, however if the lender is not operating via a lending pool, which we will look at in a moment, they will be taking collateral against the lent securities and may incur custody charges in this respect

Prime brokers and global custodians (often linked) take advantage of securities lending and borrowing by acting as intermediaries or as a conduit in the process by managing the securities lending pool, which utilizes client's assets that are available to lend by providing these securities to the clients wishing to borrow.

The global custodians benefit by:

- Retaining a share of the fee income while running a discretionary lending program (note a custodians client is not obliged to make their securities available for lending) for their client, and/or
- Charging a transaction fee for every movement across their client's securities account where the custodian is unaware of the reasons for the securities movements, that is, they are not moving as part of the settlement of a transaction.

As a global custodian holds sizeable quantities of any particular issue, it is able to play an important role by providing liquidity to the market. Furthermore, lenders and borrowers benefit from increased operational reliability and reduced risk by utilizing the range of the global custodian's services such as:

- Clearance
- Payment
- Settlement
- Pledging (of assets as collateral)
- Valuation (mark-to-market)

SECURITIES LENDING PRECAUTIONS AND CONTROLS

The Risks

The lender is primarily concerned with the safe return of his securities by the borrower and that there are adequate means of recompense in the event that the securities are not returned.

There are four situations each of which could place the lender at a disadvantage:

1. The most serious situation is where a *borrower defaults* with no chance of the lender retrieving the securities.
2. Timing differences between delivery of the loaned securities and the corresponding receipt of sufficient collateral.
3. The late/delayed return of securities due to *settlement and securities liquidity problems* experienced by the borrower.
4. Settlement inefficiencies or a systemic collapse within the local market itself.

Various countermeasures are taken in order to reduce the risk associated with each of the earlier mentioned situations.

BORROWER DEFAULT

Loans of securities are delivered by the lender on a "free of payment" basis to the borrower. For their part, the borrower covers the loan by delivering collateral to the lender.

It is of utmost importance that the collateral should be of such quality and quantity that it must be readily exchangeable into cash in the event that the borrower defaults. This enables the lender to be able to replace the missing securities by using the collateral proceeds to acquire the securities in the market.

To satisfy an adequate collateral requirement, the borrower must deliver collateral with a market value, which exceeds the market value of the loaned securities (the outstanding loans) by a predetermined margin; typically between 5% and 15%.

This margin allows for any variation in the value of the outstanding loans. The securities out on loan are "marked-to-market" (priced at the current market value) at least daily and intraday in volatile markets using the previous business day's closing prices or the current market price. Any resulting shortfall in the amount of collateral is called from and made good by the borrower. Conversely, any excess collateral can be returned to the borrower.

DAY-LIGHT EXPOSURE

Day-light exposure is the intraday settlement risk that loan securities may be delivered before the collateral is received. If the borrower should then default during the intervening period, the lender would be unsecured. The reverse is also true for a loan return.

For example, a lender who delivers securities to the borrower at 10:00 but does not receive the collateral until 15:00 has a day-light exposure of 5 h. There is a particular problem when the parties to a loan transaction and the domicile of the securities are all in different time zones. For example, lender in London, borrower in New York, securities in Tokyo.

Loan transaction for value Wednesday; securities delivered on Wednesday (Tokyo time zone).

Collateral due for delivery value Wednesday: collateral delivered Wednesday (New York time zone).

In the lender's time zone, there is an exposure of at least 14 h, that is, from the time the securities are delivered (before close of business in Tokyo) to the receipt of collateral (after start of business in New York).

SETTLEMENT DELAYS

Delays can be caused by the usual settlement failure types:

- Insufficient securities to satisfy the total delivery.
- Lender or borrower gives late or incorrect delivery/receipt instructions.

MARKET INEFFICIENCIES

Investors will always want to invest in countries where there are opportunities for capital gain and income growth and with scant attention to the efficient operation of the settlements systems.

Effective securities lending does however depend on the ability to deliver securities without delays and complications. For this reason, securities lending is only undertaken in the established markets with reliable and robust settlements.

COLLATERAL

To satisfy the *quality* requirement, the following types of collateral are generally acceptable:

1. Cash

    The lender places the cash out into the money markets and agrees to pay interest (a rebate) to the borrower at a rate lower than the market rate. The difference in rates reflects the lending fee payable to the lender.

    Advantages of accepting cash as collateral:

- Acceptance of cash collateral allows the securities to move on a DVP basis and thus eliminates the risk that the securities delivery and collateral receipt do not occur simultaneously.

- Cash is regarded as the safest form of collateral in domestic markets including the United States of America where it is used in the majority of cases.

Disadvantages of accepting cash as collateral:

- Operational issues—many institutional lenders are not prepared or able to undertake the extra administrative burden of reinvesting the cash.
- The tax and regulatory situations in countries can make the use of cash impractical and or unattractive.
- There can be the added problems of foreign currencies, which require one or two days notice prior to placing funds.
- There is an exposure to adverse exchange rates when using foreign currencies.

SECURITIES

Collateral in the form of other securities can be acceptable however there are issues that need to be considered.

The market value of the collateral must also be monitored and be easily realizable into cash in the event of borrower default.

Other commonly acceptable types of collateral used are:

CERTIFICATES OF DEPOSIT

A popular security type used as collateral is a Certificate of Deposit. CDs are certificates, which give ownership of a deposit at a bank and for which there is an established market.

The advantages of using CDs as collateral:

- Considered to be of high quality and "near-cash" they are guaranteed by the banks on which they are drawn. The lender is able to specify the creditworthiness of the banks by only accepting paper with a rating of, say, "A" or better.
- CDs are straightforward to sell should the need arise.

The disadvantages of CDs as collateral:

- The nominal amount of CDs tends to be in shapes of £1,000,000 or $1,000,000 and this makes it difficult to ensure that the margined collateral value matches the value of outstanding loans.
- CDs have a limited lifespan and borrowers must ensure that CDs are substituted as old CDs mature.

GOVERNMENT BONDS

High-quality securities such as government bonds of the G7 countries, which also benefit from high credit ratings and ease of sale are acceptable.

EQUITIES

Equities are used but the issuer creditworthiness and the high-risk nature mainly volatility of the security type itself are not generally acceptable to lenders. In addition, as some equities can have longer settlement periods (T + 3 or more against T + 1 for say government bonds) can delay the time from borrower default to receipt of the collateral sale proceeds.

IRREVOCABLE LETTERS OF CREDIT (L/Cs)

A once popular method of providing collateral cover, L/Cs are nevertheless under threat as the cost of a L/C during the credit crunch and still today is making borrowing against them unprofitable.

Advantages of taking L/Cs as collateral:

- Lender does not need to reinvest or revalue the L/C.
- Day-light exposure is eliminated if receipt of a L/C is preadvised to the lender before the securities are released to the borrower.
- Face amount of L/C is more than adequate to cover the margined value of the outstanding loans and this results in less collateral movement to maintain the margin levels.

Disadvantages of taking L/Cs as collateral:

- Credit risk of bank that issued the L/C. (Lenders will limit the amount of L/Cs they will accept from one issuer.)
- (For the borrower) the high cost of obtaining a L/C from the bank.

SECURITIES LENDING AGREEMENTS

In order to protect the interests of the lending parties, the borrowing parties and when applicable the intermediaries, agreement forms are drawn up to clearly define the rights, duties, and liabilities of those concerned.

An agreement will contain references to, *inter alia*, the following topics:

- Interpretation definitions of the terms used in the agreement—Rights and title includes reference to the protection of lender's entitlements.
- Collateral—Loans should be secured with collateral.
- Equivalent securities—Securities and collateral should be returned in an equivalent form to the original deliveries.
- Lenders' and borrower's warranties—Statement that both parties are permitted to undertake the lending/borrowing activities.
- Default—Remedies available in the event that one or other party defaults on its obligations.
- Arbitration and Jurisdiction—How and where disputes will be submitted for resolution and under which governing law.

ROLE OF THE PRIME BROKERS/GLOBAL CUSTODIANS

The extent to which the prime brokers/global custodian is involved in securities lending depends on the type of service offered. The global custodian typically operates a lending pool where the whole process of securities lending is managed by the custodian in return for taking a portion of the fee generated. For example, the custodian may receive 50 bps for lending the security but may only pay the owner of the loaned securities 30 bps.

However, some large lending institutions may decide to do direct lending in which case the custodian is only involved in moving assets.

Direct lending will suit the bigger institutions like large investment funds, pension funds etc., who are able to offer portfolios with large and varied holdings to potential borrowers.

They are therefore able to earn larger fees by going direct to the market rather than paying part of the fee earned to the custodian.

The key points are:

- The institution negotiates loan agreements and recalls/returns with the intermediaries or borrowers.
- The institution controls the movement of collateral and ensures that margins are maintained.
- The institution assumes the counterparty risk of the intermediary.
- The global custodian delivers and receives securities on a "free of payment" basis on instructions taken from the institution.

The risks for the institution are:
Investor assumes all risks associated with securities lending including:

- Intraday exposure—They must ensure that securities are not released until adequate margined securities are under their control (directly in-house or indirectly through a global custodian or settlement agent).
- Settlement risk—They must ensure that deliveries of securities for loans are made on time.
- Deliveries of securities "free of payment" demand a higher level of authorization and control than deliveries made on a DVP basis.
- The operations teams must be able to identify in sufficient time situations where securities on loan are required to settle a sale transaction and to initiate timely recalls.
- Market risk—They must ensure collateral is revalued more frequently in volatile markets.
- Legal risk—They are responsible for arranging and monitoring the legal arrangements of the loan, that is, stock-lending agreements, for example, the ISLA Global Master Securities Lending Agreement.

The rewards are:

- Fee income—They will receive the full amount of the fees.
- Exposure—They are able to choose the counterparties they lend to.

NONDISCRETIONARY PROGRAM

Nondiscretionary lending differs from direct lending insofar as the global custodian takes a more active role in the process.

The key points are:

- The custodian seeks approval from the client for each loan request.
- The custodian receives collateral from the borrowers and ensures that the margins/collateral are adequate.
- A fee is charged by the custodian for this service.
- The client assumes the risk of the borrowers.

The extra advantage for the client is:

- The custodian ensures that the collateral is matched to the movement of securities.
- The custodian is better placed to initiate timely loan recalls to cover the sales that their client might make.

The disadvantage is:

That the client's relationship with the intermediaries might suffer now that they approach the custodian for loan requests and returns.

DISCRETIONARY (OR MANAGED) PROGRAM

Discretionary programs tend to suit the small/medium-sized lenders whose individual holdings are not always large and varied enough to attract borrowers.

The stock lending is delegated entirely to the custodian in the following key ways:

- The custodian actively seeks to place securities out on loan with the intermediaries.
- The custodian takes collateral and monitors the margins.
- A portion of the risk of the borrower is transferred from the client to the custodian.
- Depending on the level of risk assumed by the custodian, anything from 50% to 60% of the fee income is retained by the custodian.

The advantages for the lender are:

- The service is totally linked into the custodian's settlement systems thus ensuring that the risk of settlement failure through late recalls is almost eliminated.
- The investor benefits from being a part of substantially larger holdings in the "pool," which may be more attractive to potential borrowers.

The disadvantages for the investor are:

- Depending on the method of loan allocation adopted by the custodian the investor's assets may not be fully utilized.

- The investor receives only a portion of the fee income. However, as noted earlier this may be offset by reductions in transaction charges and safekeeping fees.

OPERATING THE POOL

There is an issue, which affects the ability of a lender to participate in securities lending on an equitable basis. This is the problem of ensuring that loans and fee income are allocated fairly across all participants in the pool. To manage this, the global custodians use sophisticated algorithms to allocate loans and fee accruals fairly.

BENEFITS AND ENTITLEMENTS

As stated in the introduction, the lender loses legal ownership and voting rights of the securities but retains the benefits of ownership.

It is important to appreciate that the lender is treated as if he had not lent the securities; any shortfalls are made good by the borrower who, as is considered the "temporary legal owner" of the securities (in reality the securities will almost certainly have been used for settlement and are not with the borrower), will be considered to have received any benefits. It is the responsibility of the intermediary or global custodian to ensure that the lender is not disadvantaged through securities lending activities.

Any corporate action of a lent security can be an issue but certainly dividends or interest payments create a need for the borrower or intermediary to "make good" the lender.

LENDERS' RIGHTS

Lenders retain the right to participate in all dividends, interest payments, and other benefits on securities that are on loan. The one exception as mentioned earlier is that the lenders lose the right to vote.

MANUFACTURED DIVIDENDS

If securities are on loan over the record date, the issuing company will pay the dividend to the party at the end of the borrowing chain. The lender will therefore be paid an amount of cash in lieu of the actual dividend. In other words, the borrower manufactures a dividend payment in order to make the lender good.

The regulations and tax situation regarding loaned securities where there is a manufactured dividend created must be fully understood. If there is any likelihood of the lender being disadvantaged then the loan needs to be recalled in time for the lender to be on the company register by record date.

There may be issues related to the deduction of the withholding tax (WHT) applicable to the country of issue of the securities.

ROLE OF THE CUSTODIAN OR INTERMEDIARY

The lending intermediary's prime role is to ensure that the lender is "made whole" and this can be achieved in the following ways by:

- Gathering information on actions from numerous sources.
- Comparing information from one source with another to ensure consistency.
- Rearranging the information (including any translations) into a form from which the lender can make a decision.
- Ensuring that all expected instructions are received from the lenders.
- Giving accurate and timely instructions to the correct destination, that is, borrowers agent/custodian.
- Informing the lender of the successful management of the corporate action results.

The need for the intermediaries to receive the lender's instructions in advance of the issuing company's own deadlines can cause problems with the lender. The lender might wish to delay a decision until the last possible moment; sometimes past the intermediary's deadline. Nevertheless the intermediary should, in this situation, attempt to comply with the instructions on a "best efforts" basis.

IMPORTANCE OF ACCURACY AND TIMELINESS

The intermediary is responsible for managing the corporate action event related to the lenders securities (as well as on any collateral held from the borrower).

The way in which the lender receives information depends very much on the nature of the event itself and the manner in which the lender chooses to hold the securities in safekeeping.

All corporate actions have deadlines, especially those which require a decision (the optional events). Unfortunately, differing worldwide standards do not make the task of monitoring corporate actions any easier. For this reason, it is important for the intermediaries and/or their agents to ensure that:

- The information received is accurate.
- Any instructions are given in the form and within the deadlines specified by the company.

Failure to settle situations such as market purchases and sales on time will result in delays and inconvenience. There might be occasions when penalty interest is payable and both counterparties will be exposed to an element of risk while the trade remains unsettled.

However, the obligation to settle the trades remains until such time as the delivery of securities (together with the underlying cash payment) takes place.

With an optional corporate action, however, failure to give and act upon accurate and timely instructions could result in a loss of entitlement to the benefit. The party involved will have to purchase securities (if securities were to be the benefit, for example, a rights issue) in the market and pay the extra costs.

ACTIONS REQUIRED

1. *Voting rights*

   Lenders who wish to exercise their right to vote must arrange for the loans to be recalled in sufficient time to comply with local voting rules. These rules might call for the reregistration of the securities into the lender's (or their appointed nominee's) name or might necessitate the blocking of the shares until the Annual (or Extraordinary) General Meeting has taken place. Sufficient time should be allowed for this to happen.
2. *Corporate actions*

   It is the responsibility of the borrower to ensure that the lender is made whole with respect to corporate actions. The borrower can either unwind the loan returning the securities to the lender or can take up any entitlements on behalf of the lender making any extra cash payments as and when required.

IMPLICATIONS FOR COLLATERAL

There are two points to note with respect to collateral:

The amount of collateral pledged may have to increase or decrease in order to maintain the required (margined) levels of cover. This applies equally to collateral that is taken in the form of cash or other securities (whether in the same currency or different currencies).

If other securities are used, there will be a time when corporate actions will affect the collateral itself. In this case, the collateral can either be substituted or treated in much the same way as the loaned securities.

REPURCHASE AGREEMENT (REPO)

A repo is a purchase or sale of a security now, with an opposite transaction later. The first deal is a purchase or sale of a security for immediate settlement. The second deal is a reversal of the first deal. It is a temporary rather than permanent transfer of securities and cash.

The difference in cash value is the cost of borrowing the cash secured against the security (usually high quality bonds).

SECURITIES LENDING RELATIONSHIP STRUCTURE

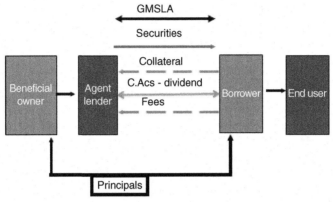

(*Source: The DSC Portfolio Ltd.*)

The loan will be covered by an agreement such as the International Securities Lending Association Global Master Securities Lending Agreement (GMSLA).

Summary

A firm needing to borrow cash that has bonds available will use a repo whereas a fund needing to borrow securities will be involved in a stock or securities loan against either cash or security collateral.

Since the market crash and following subsequent regulatory reviews, there has been the introduction of more reporting of loans and particularly in connection with short selling by hedge funds.

There is some talk of securities lending being subject to reporting to trade repositories and lending is also included in the proposed Financial Transaction Tax.

Finally securities lending is now being centrally cleared through Eurex. Details can be found at http://www.eurexclearing.com/clearing-en/markets-services/securities-lending.

Margin Calls and Collateral Management

As we have seen earlier in this part, a fund may be involved in derivative transactions, which generate margin calls. In addition hedge funds may trade on margin with the prime broker.

In both cases we know it is essential that the accounting team record this correctly in the accounts.

The custodian will be very much involved in the collateral process moving assets that will be collateral and receiving or delivering assets that have been lent and borrowed.

For derivatives we have the variation margin process, which if you recall may involve the payment or receipt of monies with the broker. This must be recorded in the variation margin ledger but also in the cash flow process and the forecast.

Compliance

In Part 2 of the book, we looked at the regulatory environment for funds and the role of the compliance officer is to ensure that the fund complies with external regulation and internal controls and policies.

We can summarize the compliance role in terms of the fund and the administrator/custodian as follows:

- Mandates, scheme particulars, and prospectus.
- Approved clients and antimoney laundering procedures.
- Valuations and pricing.
- Errors and corrections.
- Reporting to clients.
- Interaction with the prime broker.
- Interaction with clients.
- Formal and periodic reporting.
- Process for partial fills.
- Process for reevaluating original order.
- Order reentered or cancelled.
- Procedure for dealing overseas.
- Instructions to the brokers.
- Allocation across funds.
- Execution.
- Reporting completed fills.
- Exposure limits and restrictions.
- Asset allocation policy.
- Use of derivatives policy.
- Monitoring instruments used.
- Monitoring implementation of policy.
- Authorized personnel.

Some of these areas are related to the activity of the investment manager, some to the operational process of the fund and some to the regulatory requirements.

Now we can look at the areas the compliance officer of the administrator/custodian will be responsible for:

- Structure for *administration operation.*
- Creating the *fund administration and service level agreements.*
- Procedures and controls for *fund set up services.*
- Procedures for monitoring fund's—*broker agreements, trustees arrangements, marketing and sales policy.*

- Establishing procedures for *valuations and publishing prices, creation/redemption of shares, client transaction records.*
- Fund transaction records.
- Funding records.
- Asset valuations.
- Distributions.
- Reports to manager.
- Reports to clients.
- Reports to regulator.

Again some of these areas will relate to the services being provided and some will be internal control issues.

In both cases, it is essential that the procedures are set out in the manual and that they are complied with. There must also be an adequate escalation process to senior management when breaches occur.

It must also be reiterated that while the administrator can assist the fund with compliance, the responsibility remains with the fund.

SUMMARY

In this part of the book, we have looked at the operation of the fund and the roles and tasks the teams and parties like custodians and compliance play in the process.

The efficiency with which the teams carry out these tasks will impact on the overall performance of the fund and crucially in some areas the reputation of the fund.

In Part 4, we look at another very important issue for a fund and its support service suppliers and that is risk.

Part 4

Risk

RISKS FACED BY A FUND AND HOW THE ADMINISTRATOR CAN ASSIST THE FUND TO MANAGE THE RISKS

There are many risks associated with funds and fund administration ranging from fiduciary duties to the performance of outsource arrangements as well as the three main risks of market, counterparty, and operational risk.

The following are some high level examples of market risk:

- Liquidity—Ability to buy or sell an asset.
- Tax—Changes to the taxation on capital gain or income.
- Default—Failure of an asset like a bond to repay capital or pay interest.
- Default (2)—Failure of a limited partner in a private equity fund to honor a drawdown.

The following are some high level examples of operational risk:

- Documentation
- Compliance
- Settlement
- Liquidity
- Systems
- People

OPERATIONAL RISK

In general terms we can say that operational risk became high profile following the collapse of Barings Bank. Barings Bank collapsed in Feb. 1995 due to unauthorized trading, poor governance, and failure of the operational control framework in the bank.

Until that time firms operating in financial markets were very much aware of the other two major types of risk, market and counterparty or credit risk. However it was not considered likely that risks associated with operational aspects of a business like settlement, record keeping etc. would, if they were to become a risk event, cause the collapse of a firm.

In this pre Barings era, financial losses caused by errors in the processing and procedures were considered "part" of the business and therefore were absorbed in the profit or loss calculations of the firm.

Following the collapse of Barings and the part that a series of failures in controls, governance, and procedures played in the collapse, the Bank for International Settlement (BIS) established a committee to consider the implications of systemic risk created by the collapse of financial institution because of operational risks.

The committee recognized that there were hitherto unrecognized dangers in a series of linked operational based risk events creating such a significant internal and external systemic risk situation that would threaten not just individual institutions but the markets as a whole.

Regulators, stakeholders, senior management, and investors all began to look at operational risk and its management and today as we have seen earlier in this book, there is comprehensive regulation and risk management in place across the markets and participants.

In any transaction for the fund that involves securities, derivatives or other types of assets, there will be a series of participants during the life cycle of the transaction as well as procedures and processes that take a transaction from origination to finality of settlement and into the post settlement environment.

People and processes are the fundamental structure on which most of the operations environment is based. To that structure we can add knowledge, skills sets, and management.

Operational risks are therefore predominantly related to this structure and indeed the BIS Basle Committee defined operational risk as:

Operational risk is the risk of loss resulting from inadequate or failed internal processes, people, and systems or from external events.

We can then define the management of operational risk as:

Operational risk management is the process of identifying, assessing, monitoring, and controlling/mitigating operational risk.

Operational risks will come in many formats, originate in many varied ways and have very different impacts if they become risk events.

For both the administrator and the custodian operational risks pose a serious threat both financial and reputational.

A significant instance of a risk event could even prove catastrophic and close the business down.

What we also have to remember is that there are *unique risks* that are bespoke to an organization and *generic risks* that affect all organizations within the industry.

Unique risks tend to be associated with people and systems on the basis that no two firms are likely to have the same people or system profile.

Generic risks are those that would impact across many organizations simultaneously like for instance the failure of a country's payment system, a natural disaster, or the failure of a market source of prices preventing the valuation of the funds assets.

Operational risk is rarely static and so the systemic implications both internal and external are significant. "Creeping risk" is where a risk originates in a process or part of a firm but the impact in terms of the risk and resultant risk event would be felt somewhere else.

For example, an error in the processing of a subscription or redemption by the transfer agent causes the NAV per share published by the valuation team to be incorrect.

Another example might be errors in reconciliations process in the custodian are actually caused by poor performance in the transaction processing area rather than the reconciliation team.

Clearly prevention of the operational risk is a major objective in the management of the risk of a fund, its administrator, and custodian.

We have in previous sections of the book also explored the various factors and influences in terms of exactly who the participants will be in a process and to what degree they will be involved.

We have seen that in the context of the operations process in a custodian or administrator, the origin of the transaction and the type of product being transacted are key drivers for the actual operational process that will follow the trade.

Let us remind ourselves of the flows seen earlier in the book:

Portfolio management—Asset purchase/sale flow

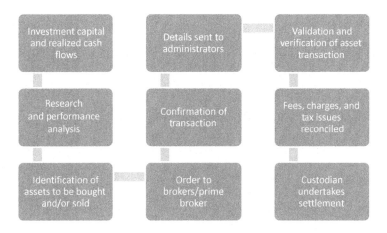

Portfolio transactions and NAV

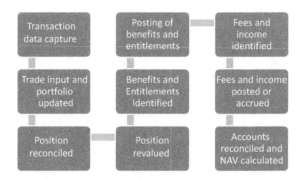

Cash management and collateral (Fig. 4.1)

So operational risk is directly related to the participants in a process and the characteristics of the types of products being processed and the systems being used in that process. However, not all operational risks will have the same profile or the same probability of an event or the same impact should that event actually occur.

TYPES OF RISK

We can say there are three high level types of risk:

- *Killer risks*
- *Key risks*
- *Standard risks*

And these can be illustrated as shown in Fig. 4.2.

Killer risks are so severe that if they occur, the organization's very existence is at risk.

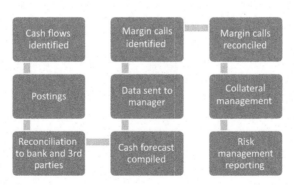

FIGURE 4.1 *(Source: The DSC Portfolio Ltd.)*

FIGURE 4.2   The risk pyramid. *(Source: The DSC Portfolio Ltd.)*

Key risks are risks that would be severely damaging to the firm.

Together they would account for no more than perhaps 20% of the total risk. They would be monitored and often managed by designated risk management teams in conjunction with the business and the operational teams.

The remaining *Standard risks*, around 80% of risks in most firms, are those risks that occur in and are usually managed by the boys and girls in their daily tasks.

It is important to flag at this stage that no firm can eliminate every risk. Many errors can and will occur every day in every process. The key thing is that most of these errors and problems will be identified quickly and resolved. Technically, there is a risk between occurrence, identification, and resolution and a failure to identify the issue or a delay in resolving it is obviously creating a higher risk of an event.

The ability for the custodian and administration teams to recognize when to escalate an issue to management and the risk team is a key requirement for a good risk awareness culture in an organization.

In order to be able to manage these risks successfully it is essential to be able to identify the risks.

We can now look at the risks faced by administrators and custodians.

Risks Faced by an Administrator and Custodian

Typical operational risk that could be faced by an administrator or custodian could be any of those in the following:

- Human error
- Management
- Inadequate technology/systems
- Settlement risk
- Lack of industry awareness
- Poor relationship management
- Counterparty and 3rd party risk (outsource)
- Breaches of guidelines and controls
- Inefficient or ineffective procedures
- Lack of adequate product knowledge and skill sets
- Data errors

- Fraud and money laundering
- Loss of key personnel
- External events

These lists are not every type of risk event category or risk but do show just how diverse and widespread operational risk is.

Let us look at examples under each heading.

1. *Human error*—Perhaps the most commonly perceived operational risk and certainly a human error in a particularly crucial process, for example, validating a subscription or a response to a SWIFT message, could create a major risk event.

2. *Management*—A particularly important source of operational risk as poor and ineffective management will lead to many other types of operational risk situations, for example, poor staff morale leading to poor performance levels.

3. *Inadequate technology/systems*—With so much of the operational process in the financial markets and other highly automated industries, the technology risks are very significant and a major concern would be errors in the accounting systems and control systems. Another major technology risk for the administrator or custodian is inadequate systems for the activity of the fund that is a customer.

4. *Settlement*—This is the risk associated with finality of settlement and can therefore be related to failure to make/receive payment or make/take delivery correctly or even at all. Associated risk would be fraud and default.

5. *Lack of industry awareness*—This risk is about the understanding of the industry in which the business and its management and staff are working, for example, management and staff in a fund administration or custodian firm must be aware of the issues, regulations, and changes happening in the investment fund industry.

6. *Poor relationship management*—A risk that can be related to internal and external scenarios, for example, to the client or prime broker or service provider or inter-team or inter-department internally.

7. *Counterparty and 3rd party*—Related to all risks associated with outsource and insource and any critical service provisions. The performance of a 3rd party can influence the risk profile of a firm and so the risk profile of a fund that outsources to an administrator or custodian is determined by their performance. Likewise an administrator or custodian insourcing from the fund has their risk profile affected by the performance of a fund. This is why having service level agreements in place is crucially important.

8. *Breaches of guidelines and controls*—The failure to follow best practice and a control framework would significantly increase the risk profile of the firm.

9. *Ineffective or inefficient procedures*—This can lead to a wide range of risks, which will have potentially systemic and significant impact outcomes.

The cause could be due to poor management and so it could also be part of that risk.

10. *Lack of adequate knowledge and skill sets*—This relates to competency and capabilities at all levels and is associated with management risk, HR risk, as well as pursuing qualifications for staff and employing qualified staff etc. An example of a related qualification would be the CLT International Advanced Certificate & Diploma in Fund Administration details of which can be found at http://www.cltint.com/course/advanced-certificate-in-fund-administration/.

11. *Data errors*—Linked to systems/technology risk but also to data base management, data security etc.

12. *Fraud and money laundering*—Two key risks and any firm must have strong controls in place to manage these risks.

13. *Loss of key personnel*—Another risk linked to HR but also an operational risk issue for management and team leaders. The recruitment environment can be a major issue particularly in offshore fund centers or where offshoring has been used.

14. *External events*—Risks that are beyond (usually) the control of the firm such as transport disruption, natural disasters etc.

We can see from the above that operational risk is not just about operations or operations risk and that operations risk is one of several that can fall under operational as well as market or credit risk too as shown in the Fig. 4.3.

It is also important to consider operational risk in the context of systemic risk.

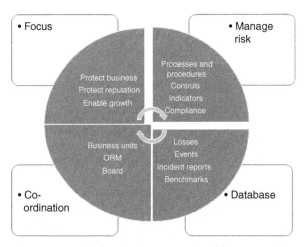

FIGURE 4.3   The operational risk framework. (*Source: The DSC Portfolio Ltd.*)

Cased Studies and Illustrations of Risks and the Management of the Risks

Managing Operational Risk

Operational risk management is the process of identifying, assessing, monitoring, and controlling operational risk.

How? Well depending on the size and nature of the organization, it may be the responsibility of a risk management team. Alternatively there may be oversight of control and procedures by a director or manager. It is possible that the administrator may be asked to assist with the fund's risk management process but cannot have responsibility for the risk management. That will always lie with the fund.

Fig. 4.3 illustrates the components of a risk management strategy:

Risk management structures—Can utilize historical data, self-assessment of the possible risk, and/or likelihood that a risk event will occur.

All entities involved in the fund process need to create an operational risk policy that contains:

- Risks to avoid
- Risks to be contained
- Self assessment process
- Identification of key/killer risks
- Risk monitoring and control processes
- Risk event management
- Risk incident reports

Risk policy will be carried out largely through controls and procedures on a day-to-day basis which will involve the administrator and custodian.

A key element of operational risk management is to benefit from lessons learned and make adjustments where necessary.

Risk Logs/Incident Reports

Logs and incident reports are major tools in the risk management process, however these are not about blame. It is important that they remain factual and focus on the structure of the risk event that has happened from occurrence through to actions taken to close the risk event.

Incident reports should provide the facts and the detail of the actions that were needed to manage the risk event.

Logs provide data that will show trends or the patterns that may be occurring and record the level of financial losses that are being incurred. They can also be associated with the complaints log and can include actual events as well as "near misses." Data in logs needs to be current so that old data about events that happened when the environment and circumstances were different is excluded.

A risk event has a structure as shown in Fig. 4.4:

Understanding a risk event

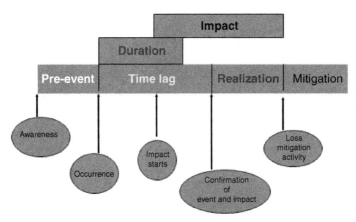

FIGURE 4.4   Structure of a risk event. *(Source: DSC Portfolio Ltd.)*

Subjective versus Quantitative Analyses in Identifying Risks

The process of identifying risks needs to be strong, credible, and realistic and so a mix of quantitative and subjective analysis should be used.

Subjective—Involves self-assessment by the business units within the company and particularly the teams managing the key processes and procedures. The reason for this is that they are dealing with the potential risks all the time and have the greatest knowledge of the processes and procedures as well as the control framework.

Quantitative—Can involve statistical data and comparison, for example:

1. Measuring the levels of financial loss against levels of activity.
2. Complexity of processes or product against the degree of automated processes.
3. Degree of automation versus number of manual processes.
4. Key risk indicators (KRIs).
5. Key performance indicators (KPIs).

KRIs and KPIs will be entity specific but some examples would be:

1. Error rates is key processes.
2. Expected losses versus actual losses.
3. Level of reconciliation breaks.
4. System performance statistics.
5. Level of client related errors, that is, subscription/redemptions.
6. Staff turnover.

SELF-ASSESSMENT AND MEASURING RISK

A major method of identifying risks in a firm is to involve the business units in a process of self-assessment.

The assessment will be based on identifying risks but also assessing the potential for the risk to become an event, that is, to analyze the control framework in place that seeks to manage the risks.

In addition an assessment of the strength of the controls and control framework is undertaken.

We will also look to include some form of assessment of the impact of the event should it occur.

Self-assessment is of course subjective and so we must create a suitable framework for the business unit to work and to achieve consistency across the business with allowance for specific risk issues within each unit.

Part of that framework may well include a review and challenge process undertaken by the risk group whereby the outcomes from the subjective assessment are compared to some form of quantitative analysis perhaps from relevant management information data, and reassessed jointly with the business unit.

This process is crucially important because risks that have been incorrectly assessed and then input to the risk management process will create problems and in fact increase rather than decrease a firm's risk.

Techniques

Many self-assessment techniques utilize the process often used by auditors of scoring or grading. Thus a risk self-assessment by a team would look first at the key procedures, processes, and any controls that are in place, evaluating their potential risk or risks.

An example of what we are talking about could be the illustration shown in Fig. 4.5.

However this process is dependent on the operations managers or process owners having mapped the procedures and processes so that a critical analysis can take place.

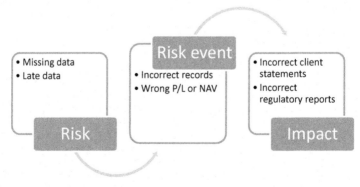

FIGURE 4.5 Risk flow.

If you recall, we looked at the workflows in administration and custody and this will be the foundation on which the risk analysis will take place.

Each stage in that workflow will be analyzed in terms of, for example:

- Manual or automated process
- Straight through processing level
- Complexity of the process
- Context of the process (stand alone or dependency)
- Deadlines
- Workload—activity level, spikes etc.
- Resource level needed and available—people and systems (including competencies, reliability etc.)
- Regulatory risk (reporting requirements, breach context etc.)
- Influences—internal/external

From this data the risk sensitivity can be formulated.

Again it is important to recognize that not every risk will become a risk event. What we are doing at this stage is identifying the principal risks inherent in the process and or procedure. The same self-assessment challenge will also provide us with the probability of the risk becoming a risk event and by creating an internal record or log of risk events we have a quantitative methodology of verifying the self-assessment.

Within the analysis we will also look to identify the critical risk areas, which will be ones that are related to data inflows and outflows, dependencies etc. and or have a systemic risk value.

The picture we create based on the above information shows where the key activity is in the processes and procedures and the degree to which this constitutes a risk.

The content of that picture would include, for example, the following key stages in the securities settlement process:

- Trade capture
- Verification/validation (the clearing process)
- Enrichment
- Instructions
- Settlement fails management
- Settlement
- Valuation and accounting
- Corporate actions
- Reconciliations at every stage

Examples of the identifiable risks would then be:

1. Data unavailability or missing
2. Data incorrect
3. Data not processed

4. Data incorrectly processed
5. Data not distributed or reported incorrectly or late
6. Process failures
7. Action failures, errors, or delays
8. Errors not identified or realized
9. Corrective action incorrect, not made, incomplete
10. Valuation procedures incorrect, incomplete or late

Now if we consider the source of these risks we will see that certainly people and systems including databases are likely to be prime sources of these risks and of possible risk events, for example, incorrect corrective action as illustrated in Figs. 4.6 and 4.7.

Fig. 4.6 shows examples of the risk, possible risk event, and possible impact while Fig. 7 shows the cause, the issue arising and possible remedial action.

Both human error, for example, a dealer may miss data off a deal ticket or may be late in providing the ticket and system error, for example, the incorrect data has been created in the database so the trade information is not complete (or even rejected).

The potential event created could result in financial losses, regulatory action, or loss of reputation.

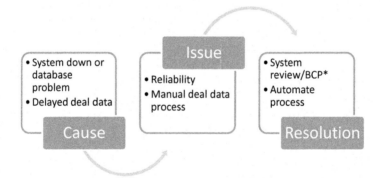

FIGURE 4.6   Risk components. * BCP, business continuity process *(Source: The DSC Portfolio Ltd.)*

Operational risk components

FIGURE 4.7   Stages in a risk event. *(Source: The DSC Portfolio Ltd.)*

Reputation loss is often as damaging and can be even more damaging than possible financial losses as a result of a risk event happening.

For example, an incorrect NAV that is published by an investment fund could result in a regulatory breach, a requirement to compensate investors who may have subscribed or redeemed at the incorrect NAV but above all it may make both regulator and investors concerned about the quality of the processes, procedures, and controls being utilized.

Resolution may look straightforward but on the other hand technology changes are rarely easy and while the changes are happening, a higher level of operational risk will exist. That said adequate BCP capabilities are frequently linked to regulation, to insurance cover, and any risk management information a prospective client or stakeholders may want to see.

All risk events have a structure and the components of that structure can be illustrated as shown in the Fig. 4.7.

The components as we can see are a cause, and event and the effect or impact of that event.

All operational risks have a cause that can become an event that will have an effect on the business that can be negligible, important, or serious.

Understanding what the cause(s) are, what risk event(s) can happen, and what the effect(s) of that will be is crucially important to successful risk management.

There are many ways of successfully addressing this issue but to look at ways of managing the risk process, it is important to consider on a simplistic basis the assessment of a situation.

The following exercise will illustrate this.

RISK SCENARIO ANALYSIS

Identify the possible *causes*, *events*, and *impact* that each of these scenarios has as follows:

1. A new computer system is implemented at the firm but cannot be reconciled to the original system.
2. Increasing information demands from the clients and counterparties has doubled the workload for the operations teams and contains a host of new and alternative procedures and processes.
3. The performance of an outsource arrangement appears to be deteriorating.

Now consider the following scenario and analyze the possible risk issues for the administrator and the custodian.

CONFLICT RESOLUTION EXERCISE

Background

Over the last 24 months, there has been an increasing number of problems occurring between the Process team dealing with trade input, verification, and posting and the Client Support team who deal with corporate actions and provide reports and communications with the internal (dealers, fund managers, business development) and the external client base (fund companies, corporate and private clients).

In particular the following high profile issue occurred:

Error on a Rights Issue

A major client requested to the Client Support team that the one for four rights issue at $5 on a holding of 200,000 shares be taken up.

However the client account was showing only 100,000 shares. When this was queried with the process team the reply was that there were no outstanding transactions.

The Client Support team were reluctant to contact the highly important but quite difficult client and so assumed that the client had made a mistake over the number of shares.

The Client Support team instructed the take up of the rights (25,000 shares) and debited the client account with $125,000.

This left a total of $500,000 on the clients account and a few days later the client called and asked for confirmation of the balance. He was told $500,000 and shortly after placed an order to buy another 80,000 shares at $6.

Later that day, the Process team put through the client's account two trades for 100,000 at $5.50 and 80,000 at $6, total cost $1,030,000. Client Support assumed that these were two new trades and called the client for the balance of $530,000.

The client went mad accusing the firm of utter incompetence and threatened to close the account and report the firm to the regulator.

Client Support asked the Process team what the two trades were and received the reply that there was a purchase for an order of 80,000 shares at $6 placed today and a trade of 100,000 shares at $5.50 that had been placed 7 days ago but had failed to settle in the market until today.

Client Support asked why, when they queried the outstanding trades the previous day they had been told there were none.

The Process team came back and said it was a mistake. When the problem it had caused was pointed out to them, the Process team told the Client Support team it was their fault, as they should have checked with the client.

The client was furious and insisted that as he had acted on the information provided by the firm it was their problem to make good the shortfall in cash and also wanted to know when his additional 25,000 shares from the rights issue would be in his account (remember the client said the rights on 200,000 shares which in fact was his holding)

The firm decided they would need to make the client good and take the loss against the operations department error account.

Exercise

Identify the losses the firm may have to take and the major failings and the risk associated with the mismanagement of this corporate action.

The answers to these exercises can be found in the appendices or at www.dscportfolio.com.

RISK OF FRAUD IN FINANCE

The following is taken from a seminar run by Onestudy Training in Jersey entitled-
Operational risks of fraud in finance—Jersey Nov. 2014
The association between acts of fraud and operational risk may at first seem obvious.

Where there is a lack of and implementation of a control framework with robust procedures and processes, a potential fraudster knows the odds are in their favor.

If we add to this a lack of a risk awareness and culture among management and employees then the possibility of a successful fraud is further increased.

However the ability of operational risk management to prevent and/or detect fraud, or the potential for fraud is not so certain.

The major problem is that no two organizations have identical risk profiles or universes and so by nature the potential for fraud is bespoke. This is not to say that there are not generic operational risks linked to the potential fraud but very often it is a mix of generic and bespoke risks that occur with perhaps the emphasis on bespoke.

Most operational risks have either people or processes/systems as their main source.

Interestingly within the people category, management is a significant source of operational risk. I will come back to this later.

Consider first the typical operational risk universe.

It is likely to be diverse for any type of financial organization and in a sense it is the same with potential fraud.

We may be inclined to assume that institutions dealing with money are the most vulnerable and most likely to be the subject of an attempted fraud and as many surveys suggest banks consider fraud as one of their major potential risks.

However we can also look at other organizations that would have fraud high on their list of risks.

In the investment fund universe, the post 2008 environment has been largely about loss of trust by investors and hugely increased regulation as a result of events like Madoff but also other concerns about where the assets of a fund, and therefore the capital of the investor, actually were.

These issues encompassed the use of assets as collateral, the short selling of securities, and the associated securities borrowing and the buying of assets on margin, common in some types of hedge funds.

In Europe, the regulators introduced new regulation in the form of the Alternative Investment Fund Managers Directive that placed responsibilities for the monitoring and safekeeping of an AIF's assets with the Depositary.

Loss of assets is a major concern of the management of any fund but while loss of assets is perhaps relatively speaking rare, the misuse of assets can be very different.

A scenario that I can give you relates to a broker where two members of staff managing a customer's account noted that they had placed securities as collateral against a written call option. The two staff noted that the client rolled the written position shortly before the expiry of the options series.

A seemingly simple fraud offered itself. If the staff could "borrow" the securities they could carry out several possible actions. One would be to sell the shares safe in the knowledge that the client was unlikely to sell the shares themselves as they had the written option position. Another was to use the shares as collateral against a loan.

The broker was acting as the nominee for the customer and so had custody of the assets.

All that remained to complete the fraud was for the two members of staff to have access to the assets to transfer them and to doctor the internal records so that it appeared the shares were being held against the option position.

The staff were both in key and senior positions and able to collude. There was little awareness of risk in the firm and an almost total lack of a control framework. The two people colluding on the fraud had the responsibility to reconcile assets held for customers, responsibility for instructions to move assets including cash. The data they produced was never questioned.

The fraud was only discovered when the option position was assigned and the securities were needed for delivery. The pair had sold the securities but the price had risen significantly hence the assignment. The pair could not generate the cash needed to buy the securities and the fraud was discovered. It cost the firm a high six figure sum to make good the customer.

Another example is the transfer of assets as collateral to cover margin call.

In this case the assets were held at a third party custodian.

A new recruit working in the operations team received a call from a manager at the custodian requesting authorization to transfer assets to a broker against a margin call for a derivative position.

The new recruit did not know what a derivative was and spoke to their supervisor. The supervisor suggested the young lady concerned spoke to the derivatives operations team who were located on the next desks.

They were pleased to provide the background to derivatives but asked why the interest.

When she said she had received the request they told her not to do anything and to leave it with them.

A few minutes later she received another call from the rather irate manager telling her there would be big trouble if this margin call was not met and the asset transfer not made.

Somewhat distressed she immediately went back to the derivatives operations team.

Reassuring her there was no problem they called the custodian but the manager concerned was apparently at lunch. The situation was escalated and an immediate check on all previous requests to transfer assets from this manager was made.

Two previous instances were found and like the current request there was no derivative margin call that needed collateral.

The previous two that occurred in the past three months were for £5,000 in value and £8,000 in value. The current one was for £900,000 in value.

Internally there was a threshold for automatic authorization set at £1 m with random authorization checks. The first two were not subject to the random authorization checks and so had been processed. The securities were transferred to a fictitious account set up by the manager.

The manager never came back from lunch and the total of £13,000 was never recovered.

Had the young lady not asked about derivatives and the operations team not been suspicious the loss would have been close to a million.

The firm and the custodian negotiated a settlement.

In case one there was no control framework and in case two there was but the threshold was high and so there was a risk that fraudulent payments and or movement of assets could occur.

Clearly the custodian had a much bigger operational risk in terms of internal controls and the manager was able to exploit this.

In a sense the simplicity of the attempts was the key, plus the knowledge that the control framework was nonexistent or weak and this is the key point.

Wherever an organization does not have operational risk awareness and a strong, proven risk management culture then they are vulnerable to fraud and other criminal acts.

The classic case study is of course Nick Leeson at Barings where the bank was subjected to a massive unmanageable exposures through unauthorized and hidden trades because of multiple failures of controls and the incompetence and failures of senior management in the bank as well as elsewhere like the regulator, the Bank of England.

There has been a significant change in the approach to managing operational risk since the collapse of Barings and yet as 2008 showed, risk events still occur and management of risks is still a potential danger for some organizations.

So how can operational risk management be structured to try to deter and prevent fraud?

First we need to understand the sequences in a risk event.

As it is highly unlikely that we can prevent all fraud, although that would be the ultimate objective of the control framework, we need to have a structure that works subsequent to the occurrence of a risk event.

Second we need to consider the way in which to actively manage the potential risk event

Key elements of the structure will be to kill the event to consolidate the loss and then to learn the lessons. For example, did existing controls fail, was this an unforeseeable event, did the one or more internal or external events have significant influence, did the KRIs fail to identify the risk, is the event a systemic risk?

Finally, we will need to have an effective incident report about the event which I will stress needs to be productive and not a "blame document."

To summarize, effective operational risk management can and will play a significant part in managing potential fraud in financial institutions whether that is in banks operations or custodians in the investment fund industry.

Where a potential fraudster believes that there is inadequate risk management and a general disinterest or even hostility to operational risk management they will be comfortable that their fraud has a very good chance of success.

D.A. Loader, The DSC Portfolio Ltd

RISK TERMINOLOGY

Here is a glossary of frequently used risk terms.

GLOSSARY OF RISK TERMINOLOGY

Risk	Description	Associated risk type
Accounting risk	This will occur when a business engages in accounting practices for the products or services that are either not suitable, are deliberately misinterpreted or are implemented incorrectly or do not comply with accepted market principles. The risk can also occur if there is doubt about the acceptable accounting standards or where there is conflict between different standards by the setting organizations.	Audit, regulatory, reporting
Action risk	The risk of an action being implemented erroneously, accidentally, in unsuitable situations or being authorized or undertaken by unqualified personnel. The risks that arise could create losses (costs, fines etc.), reputation damage (outcome and impact) and regulatory problems.	Management, settlement, payment risk Regulatory and financial risk
Audit risk	This is the risk that the audit process and people are unable or do not have the ability to, or do not understand sufficiently the processes and procedures being audited	
Basel directives	Inability to demonstrate compliance with the requirement as set out by the Committee of the Bank for International Settlement	Regulatory
Business risk	A risk that is derived from the specific services and products and are particular to the industry of the firm concerned. These risks are often sub sets of strategic risk and occur or originate from business units.	Operations risk, Technology risk People risk
Business continuity risk	The impact of internal or external events that in some way interrupt or curtail the operation of the business for a significant period of time or in some catastrophic financial or logistical way as to make normal or viable operation of business difficult.	Operations risk Client risk Counterparty/supplier risk
Client risk	The risk of being unable to manage the processes associated with the services provided to clients. Money laundering Fraud Noncompliance with client regulation (Regulatory Conduct of Business Rules etc.)—key areas being suitability (Funds) risk warning distribution, client money/asset segregation.	Operations risk People risk Regulatory (including fines) Reputation—Loss of clients/revenue

Risk	Description	Associated risk type
Competition risk	A complex risk that can arise in a number of ways and is quite different from business risk, which is about internal decisions and actions. Competition risk could arise from the entrance of a new competitor or product into a market with potential loss of market share and or increase in investment/costs to compete. This is particularly the case where new competitors cherry pick profitable market segments, where they have or adapt to new technology and practices quicker, or can respond to changing customer requirements more rapidly. Examples here could be found in e-banking, socially responsible investment products etc. Competition risk can also apply to prolonged declining market share created by inability to change as well as by poorly managed mergers and takeovers resulting in massive loss of customers that in turn renders the strategic aims unobtainable and likely to entail severe losses for some period of time.	
Compliance risk	The inability to adequately comply with external regulations or internal rules and controls. This may be caused by lack of knowledge of certain markets, products and regulatory requirements, and/or oversight of business units involved.	Regulatory Financial
Counterparty risk	This is the risk associated with dealing with or taking services or products from another party. Includes: Ongoing support and enhancement of services, insourcing/outsourcing.	Operations risk
Country risk	Risk of clearing, settlement, and client money regulation not being as strong as in the UK/US Law. Infrastructure. Information distribution may be less transparent and or obtainable. Instability. Tax environment/changes.	Operation risk Legal risk
Credit risk	Risk associated with the default of a counterparty on an obligation.	Financial—Replacement loss
Creeping risk	A risk that starts in one part of a business and then moves across and within the business potentially having a greater impact in other areas (Similar to a computer virus).	
Custody/ depositary risk	The failure to protect assets and any resulting benefits on those assets that are entrusted to the care and safekeeping of the firm.	Reputation, financial, regulatory

(Continued)

Risk	Description	Associated risk type
Data risk	Occurs when data is incorrectly generated, updated, stored, or used. Corrupted or incorrect data in critical systems (including risk systems) can have a devastating impact. Unauthorized access, use or publication of confidential client or business data can have such an impact as to put at risk the very existence of the organization.	Technology, control, fraud
Demand risk (liquidity)	A risk where there is uncertainty about future demand for a product caused by uncontrollable or unforeseen changes in the market, for instance regulatory changes. It also manifests itself in situations where there is greater demand than can be satisfied effectively and efficiently causing delays and penalties to be incurred. Demand risk is relevant in terms of the passing of risk from one business unit to another, that is, the aggressive marketing of a product creating risk for the production team (meeting alterations "sold" by the sales team) or client support teams (delays in delivery, quality etc.).	Strategic, operational, operations
Documentation risk	As well as errors within and the ineffectiveness of legal documentation, there is the risk inherent in the publication of documents to the clients including correctness of information, suitability of the document (KYC and restricted product docs), confidentiality, and frequency requirements (regulatory, agreements etc.).	
Fiduciary risk	Breaching either of the following: 1. A person legally appointed and authorized to hold assets in trust for another person. The fiduciary manages the assets for the benefit of the other person rather than for his or her own profit. 2. A loan made on trust rather than against some security or asset.	
Fraud risk	This is the risk that because of weak controls in respect of payments, asset movements, authorizations, access to systems, and static data in an organization, it is vulnerable to an act of fraud by an individual, group of individuals, or from external sources. E-banking presents potential for fraud if security over access and data is poor.	
H R Risk	See Personnel Risk	

Risk	Description	Associated risk type
Insource Risk	A risk associated with the taking on of additional operational workload with inadequate resource, knowledge, and systems.	Operations risk Financial—compensation for performance Reputation
Key performance indicators (KPI)	Indicators showing a change in performance that may be evidence of increasing or decreasing efficiency and effectiveness of processes and procedures often linked into KRIs.	
Key risk	Identified as risks that could significantly impact on the achievement of the objectives of a business unit. Likely to be proactively managed by Head of Function/Department on a frequent (ie, monthly basis). Typically 15–20% of total risks. Firms develop key risk indicators to measure profile changes of the key risks.	
Key risk indicators (KRI)	The identification of risks and their indicators used in the risk management process. Important that KRIs are monitored for evidence of increasing or decreasing risk levels and also for their continued relevance.	
Killer risk	Identified as risks that could significantly impact on the achievement of firm, divisional and or strategic business unit objectives including a risk that's impact is so severe that it would render the firm incapable of continuing in business or would make the firm so vulnerable that it would subject to takeover or wipe out by competitors. Typically 2–5% of total risks. Managed and tracked through key risk indicators.	
Know your client (KYC)	A risk control measure that demands the organization has adequate and up to date knowledge of the client, its activities, restrictions that apply to the client's actual or potential business, and the suitability of products and services marketed and sold to the client. Also known as *Client due diligence (CDD)*.	Regulatory risk
Legal risk	The risk associated with the business of a firm in a jurisdiction including areas like the Investment Manager Agreement, Prime Broker Agreement, and other outsource agreements. From an operations point of view it would be related to areas such as netting, agreements, claims etc.	Settlement risk
Limit risk	A risk that a control measure is accidentally or deliberately circumvented or is incorrectly set or is not reviewed and amended according to changed circumstances.	

(Continued)

Risk	Description	Associated risk type
Loss database	A database that records incidents where a risk event has created a loss at or above a set threshold plus other statistics related internal and external risk events.	
Management risk	A risk associated with the failure of management to be structured or operate effectively in relation to the business. Poorly trained, under resourced/overworked or ineffective managers and supervisors are a massive operations risk.	Operations risk Reputation Regulatory
Market risk	Risk associated with the transactions undertaken by a firm in a market/product. Mainly about price and liquidity but can also be related to other risk like legal and competition.	
Money laundering risk	A major risk for many organizations that can result in heavy penalties for individuals and loss of authorization to do business for firms for breaches of the regulations. Any organization covered by the Regulations must ensure effective controls over possible money laundering including making sure that employees are adequately trained.	Regulatory risk Financial risk Compliance risk
New market risk	This is the risk of operating in a new market environment where knowledge and experience may initially be low. It is also about the risk that procedures and controls are not immediately at the acceptable standard level of existing market usage. Can also apply to activity that is undertaken in emerging markets where the market infrastructure, practices, and operation is itself untried and tested.	Operations risk Systems risk Settlement risk
New product risk	This risk will manifest itself if the launch or the commencement of trading in a new product or when the launch or use of a new service is undertaken without sufficient infrastructure in place, including controls, systems, knowledge skills etc.), and prior training of personnel.	Operations risk Systems risk Settlement risk Project risk
Operational risk	There are various definitions of operational risk. The Basle Committee define it as "the risk of loss resulting from inadequate or failed internal processes, people and systems or from external events." Most organizations would add in "loss of reputation."	
Operations risk	Part of operational risk it applies to the functions that deal with areas like clearing, settlement, payments, delivery of client services, custody, systems etc. Operations risk is the failure to provide the required process, procedures, and controls for the above.	Operational risk

Risk	Description	Associated risk type
Operational risk management (ORM)	The process of actively managing operational risks in a structure that adds value as well as reduces potential unnecessary losses. Often run by a risk group and usually has one or more operational risk managers in the structure. Likely to include audit and compliance in some capacity.	
Operational risk officers (OROs)	Name given to a person who is part of the group managing risk and is usually closely related to the business so that they can liaise with both the business and the risk managers on risk issues. Can also be called ORCs—operational risk coordinators.	
Outsource risk	A risk associated with the outsourcing of operational functions and processes. *Risk is that you can outsource the function but not the responsibility.*	Operations risk Reputation risk Compliance risk
Payment risk	A risk associated with the erroneous payment of monies. Often but not always associated with fraud it can be nevertheless a risk that is created by poor training, supervision, and procedures for making and or receiving payments.	Fraud Reputation—errors on client accounts
People risk	This is the risk associated with individuals or teams of people and is often about their potential as a source of risk and also their potential to be a significant contributor to managing some risks like operational risk. One obvious people risk is the level of human error in the processes, the knowledge levels both procedural and business, and the ability to work in environments particular to business units, products, services etc.	Operations Financial and reputation risk
Personnel risk	Different from people risk in so much as this may occur because of poor recruitment environments, uncompetitive remuneration, lack of or ineffective training and development etc. Loss of key personal is a major personnel risk. Employment Law is also part of this risk and includes areas such as Diversity in the Workplace Directives and training, unfair dismissal etc.	Operations Financial and reputation risk
Project risk	The failure of a project to be properly managed creating operational problems for the teams/areas of the firm affected plus over run of costs, late delivery of the project, failure to adequately test before roll out, failure to deliver to the project specification.	Financial risk Operational risk Business risk

(Continued)

Risk	Description	Associated risk type
Regulatory risk	The risk of noncompliance with the regulatory environment where the business is operating. Particularly areas such as authorization, marketing and sales, conduct of business, client relationships, client assets etc.	Compliance risk
Risk event	The occurrence of a possible risk situation becoming an actual risk situation with resultant actual impact.	
Standard risk	A risk that is identified and managed as part of the day to day business process by the boys and girls doing their jobs effectively and efficiently. Controls devised and implemented by managers and supervisors in the business. Monitored by risk managers from management information provided by the business but essentially not what the risk managers or OROs should be focusing on.	
Strategic risk	A risk that is associated with decisions and leadership, that is, the adoption of a working practice that is old, untried or ill thought out that results in unnecessary pressure, workloads, costs, and falling performance of people, systems, and the business.	Business risk Project risk
Technology risk	The risk associated with the use of technology in a firm. Most obvious risks are: 1. Lack of knowledge of systems. 2. Inability to manage projects. 3. Lack of support for systems. 4. Lack of awareness of systems capability and scope. 5. Inappropriate systems for the business. 6. Old and outdated technology. 7. Access—hackers and viruses, malicious attack.	Operations risk
Value at risk (VAR)	A technique used to estimate the probability of portfolio losses based on the statistical analysis of historical price trends and volatilities.	
Workflow risk	Risk associated with workflow and processes covering: 1. Variable flow. 2. Under resourcing. 3. Pressure points. 4. Disruption. 5. Lack of knowledge. 6. Unnecessary complex procedures. 7. Poor technology. 8. Lack of STP. 9. Cross border processes. 10. Data sources.	Operations risk

Source: The DSC Portfolio Ltd This Glossary of Terms is compiled from various sources and is believed to be correct although no responsibility can be taken for any errors or omissions. This Glossary of Terms is compiled from various sources and is believed to be correct although no responsibility can be taken for any errors or omissions.

Summary

- Great diversity of risks from internal and external sources can affect administrators, custodians, and the fund itself.
- Risk containment versus risk avoidance parameters must be established as part of the risk policy.
- Recognize and understand the risk exposures that the processes and procedures create.
- Customer service generated risks must be understood and controlled to protect against financial loss and reputation damage.
- Money laundering, fraud, and theft pose real dangers for the fund and in its support process.
- Operational risk is identifiable and can be controlled.
- The organizations people are its greatest control feature.
- If a risk culture exists in the organization it will automatically reduce the risk that organization faces.

Possible Future Changes and Challenges in the Fund Administration and Custody Environment

The investment environment has undergone significant change and this will continue.

The main areas of change will be driven by the evolving regulation, by the economic growth or otherwise in the mature and emerging markets and the innovation within the investment process.

Some of the possible challenges may be related to the list below:

- Greater demand for products from customers who are more and more sophisticated.
- Product complexity increases and so does the associated operational risks.
- Product suitability is an issue and will require greater oversight.
- Competition creates risk pressure.
- Business and process changes are happening and will continue and change is a major operational risk.
- Greater supervision of activities will require accurate and timely record keeping.
- Transparency and market disclosures will increase reporting.
- Greater demands for professional, qualified operational personnel to support more complex products, services, and investment strategies as well as regulatory competence.
- Change management will continue and represents a possible significant operational risk.
- Force fields will need to be managed if projects and change is to take place efficiently and without problem.
- Fluctuating risk levels will pose challenges for the control framework and oversight.

- Firm-wide buy-in across the promoters, managers, administrators, and custodians to support risk management is essential.
- Capital allocation, liquidity ratios and leverage reporting will impact on alternative investment funds under AIFMD.
- Cost of control versus risk must be understood.
- Demonstrating risk competence will be key going forward to meet regulatory requirements and client due diligence.

SUMMARY

Risk is a major concern for both the fund and the administrator and custodian.

With investor confidence and trust still at a low any kind of situation that is related to a risk event will often be magnified out of all proportion.

Potential risk events must be identified and adequate risk management applied however large or small a fund or administrator/custodian might be.

Reputational risk is potentially as damaging as financial losses, maybe more so for suppliers of services to funds.

Agreements may offer some redress possibilities but they do not prevent a risk event happening and so in addition to operational risk, a fund is also exposed to counterparty risk where a third party is used.

Due diligence and oversight become therefore of major importance.

Remember that while a fund can ask the administrator to assist it in managing its operational risks, it cannot outsource the responsibility.

Part 5

Introduction to derivatives

We have seen in the previous parts of the book that more and more use of derivatives by investment funds of all types is being made as investment managers seek to benefit from the hedging and strategy benefits these instruments can offer.

It is therefore important that administrators and custodians understand the products and their characteristics so that relevant processes, procedures, and controls can be established where use is made of derivatives in the portfolio.

Derivatives use will mean that administrators and custodians need to consider several important issues. For example, whether the use of the product has been authorized or is permitted under the regulatory compliance of the fund, for example the UCITS Directive, the accounting entries associated with the use of derivatives and the valuation techniques to be applied.

Further considerations will be possible margins calls, collateral and exercise, assignment and delivery, if the derivative position reaches that stage.

This part of the book will explain the structure of derivatives markets and the characteristics of the common products.

It will also explore the operational issues of derivatives use.

INTRODUCTION

Today, the derivative markets are truly global with both exchange traded futures and options contracts and OTC derivative products based on a wide range of asset classes encompassing currencies, commodities, interest rates, bonds, equities, and credit default insurance.

This vast array of derivative products traded today would seem unbelievable to the farmers and merchants of the Midwest, United States of America in the mid-1800s, who first started trading futures contracts of a form similar to those today.

We have probably read about the problems that certain companies have had with derivatives trading in the past and indeed derivatives were in some people's eyes implicated in the market crash of 2008. However, as you will see from the examples shown in this part of the book, if used properly derivatives are excellent tools for both portfolio and risk management. The problems that have occurred have generally been in situations where derivatives have been misused. In all such cases there has been a lack of appropriate controls and procedures,

119

often coupled with a lack of understanding of the products characteristics, the way in which they can be used, their suitability, and/or the risks involved.

One of the highest profile events was the collapse of Barings Bank in the 1990s as a result of significant misuse. A trader was carrying out unauthorized deals and hiding the resulting exposure the bank was taking. The losses that he was making in his "hidden" account were substantial, yet he was reporting a profit in the bank's accounts. However, the real fault lay with the lack of understanding and control at senior management level that allowed this uncontrolled and unauthorized trading to go on for so long. It was compounded by the fact that the trader was also in charge of the operations function that settled the trades with no additional oversight or segregation of the front/back office functions and controls.

Other examples would be the $ billion+ loss suffered by a hedge fund due to a very large speculative position created in natural gas futures contracts, and the trader at a French bank holding large futures positions that were not reflected in the firm's records and were allegedly unknown to senior management. There are a number of other well documented past "loss events" that provide useful case studies of what can go wrong.

Although there have been well-publicized problems with derivatives, we should also note the fact that millions of contracts are traded quite safely by numerous organizations around the world every single day. These transactions are fulfilling the purpose they were intended for; that is, transferring risk from those that wish to reduce it (hedgers) to those that wish to assume it (speculators); through hedging and trading strategies that enable banks, fund managers, corporations, and private investors to increase or decrease their market exposures efficiently and cost effectively.

EXCHANGE TRADED FUTURES AND OPTIONS

Definitions

A considerable amount of jargon is used in the language of the futures and options industry and, confusingly, often more than one word that has the same meaning. The generic term "*derivatives*" encompasses many different product types and covers more than simply forwards, futures and options, all types of derivative that have been around for hundreds of years.

Derivatives usually indicate something of their meaning in their title; for example:

- "Forwards and futures"—something agreed today in respect of a later (future) event.
- "Options"—something involving a choice of alternatives.
- "Swaps"—the exchange of one thing for something else.

In practice there are many variances on these three basic derivative structures. Let's look at some definitions related to the products

Derivatives

A definition of a *derivative* is:

- *A financial or commodity instrument whose value is dependent on, or derived from, the value of an underlying asset.*

Forwards

A definition of a *forward* contract is:

- *A forward contract is a legally binding obligation to buy or sell an agreed amount of an agreed asset at a certain future time for a certain price agreed today.*

A forward contract is where the buyer and seller enter into a legally binding transaction to buy/sell a fixed amount of an underlying asset (most commonly a physical commodity, energy product, or currency) on a specific future date at an agreed (forward) price.

A forward contract differs from a "spot" transaction to buy/sell an asset now at today's (spot) price. The difference between the spot and forward price is called the "forward premium or discount." Settlement of a forward contract (ie, delivery of the underlying asset from the seller against payment from the buyer) occurs only on the agreed future date of delivery.

Forward contracts are mostly bespoke and nonstandardized with the exact terms being negotiated "over the counter" (ie, outside any exchange) between the two parties. Forward contracts are used extensively by a wide variety of commercial firms in the normal course of their business activities. Currency forwards are quoted on systems as well as being agreed via telephone.

A forward rate agreement (FRA) is a type of forward contract used by borrowers and lenders in respect of interest rate risk management.

Futures Contracts

A definition of a *futures contract* is:

- *An agreement or legally binding obligation to buy or sell a standard amount of a standard asset at a certain specific time in the future for a certain price that is agreed today.*

Futures contracts are standardized versions of forward contracts and are only traded on regulated exchanges. Futures contracts are standardized in respect of the underlying asset type and quality (ie, energy and commodity products, government bonds, stock indices, currencies, or interest rates), unit size, price quotation, settlement terms, and conditions, and offer a limited range of delivery (or maturity) dates. Futures contract specifications are fixed in advance and published by the exchange on which the futures contract is traded.

Exchange traded futures contracts are cleared and settled through a central counterparty clearing house structure and this important feature, together with the standardized nature of futures contracts, makes for a very deep and liquid market in the most commonly traded products.

Futures contracts (and options on futures) are *"marked to market"* every day. This requires the daily receipt of profit or payment of loss against the previous day's settlement (or closing) price and is known as *"variation margin."*

Futures contracts can be bought to create a *"long"* position or sold to create a *"short"* position.

Example

A sale of 20 June. UK Long Gilt* futures contracts @ 107.39 can be traded as an *opening* position, that is, creating a *short* position.

The seller does not need to have an existing long or bought position. As a result of the above transaction the seller would now have a short position. To remove the obligation to deliver cash Gilt securities in June, the seller would need to buy an equal number of June futures contracts to close the position out. Alternatively, they could hold the contract through to the delivery date.

Traded on the NYSE LIFFE exchange (now part of ICE)

Swaps

A definition of a *swap* is:

- *An agreement or legally binding obligation under which two counterparties ("payer" and "receiver") exchange risk exposures and cash flows calculated by reference to an agreed notional principal amount of an agreed asset.*

Measured in terms of notional value, swaps are the most highly traded of all derivative products, in particular interest rate swaps, which represent a significant amount of the total notional value of all OTC derivatives. As well as interest rates, swaps are also traded with reference to underlying energy and commodity products, bonds, shares, equity indices, credit and even property indices.

Swaps are bespoke, nonstandardized transactions, the detailed terms of which are negotiated between the two parties. However, over the last 20 years, many aspects of the swaps market have become relatively standardized; a trend that has been driven by the work of well respected industry bodies such as the International Swaps and Derivatives Association (ISDA).

Since the market crash of 2008, many of these bilaterally negotiated over the counter products have been moved to trading on systems and or being centrally cleared.

Options

A definition of an *option* is:

- *In the case of the option buyer (or holder); it is the right but not the obligation to take ("call") or make ("put") delivery of an underlying asset; and*

- *In the case of the option seller (or writer); it is the obligation to make or take delivery of the underlying asset, if the buyer exercises the option.*

Options have different characteristics from forwards, futures, and swaps.

A *Call/Put* option gives the buyer the right to purchase/sell an agreed amount of a specific underlying asset at a fixed *exercise (strike) price*, on or before a specified future *expiration date*. The buyer chooses whether or not to *exercise* the option.

The seller of the option is obliged to make (call options) or take (put options) delivery of an agreed amount of a specific asset at a fixed exercise (strike) price, on or before a specified future expiration date. In return for accepting this obligation, the seller receives a negotiated *premium* from the option buyer. The premium is also known as the market price for an option.

Options are traded both on exchanges (standardized "exchange traded options") and outside exchanges (over-the-counter "OTC options"). There is often a liquid secondary market for exchange traded options.

As with swaps however regulation is changing the process and so OTC transactions may take place on systems and or be centrally cleared.

Some common terms that are associated with options include:

Expiry date: The last date that an option holder can "*exercise*" their right. After this date an option is deemed to have expired or have been "*abandoned*."

Exercise price: The fixed price, per asset or unit, (also called "*Strike Price*") at which an option conveys the right to the buyer to either call (purchase) or put (sell) the underlying asset or instrument.

Premium or option price: The sum of money paid by the option buyer for acquiring the right of the option. It is the sum of money received by the seller for incurring the obligation, having sold the rights, of the option. Premium is normally paid or received on trade day plus one (T + 1).

In-the-Money

A call option where the exercise price is below the underlying asset price, or a put option where the exercise price is above the underlying asset price. These options are deemed to have "*intrinsic value*" of the in-the-money difference between the exercise price and the underlying asset price.

At-the-Money

An option, whose exercise price is equal, or closest to, the current market price of the underlying asset. This option has no intrinsic value as there is no in-the-money difference between the exercise price and the underlying asset price.

Out-of-the-Money

A call option whose exercise price is above the current underlying asset price, or a put option whose exercise price is below the current underlying asset price. This option has no intrinsic value.

Long and Short Options

As with futures, long and short are terms that describe the position held in the options. When making an opening purchase the buyer of an option becomes known as a position "*holder*" and is said to be "*long*." When making an opening sale the seller of an option becomes known as a position "*writer*" and is said to be "*short*." Option positions can be either long or short. Long or short option positions are closed out by a transaction of the opposite position.

Example

Sale of 100 NYSE.Liffe BT Group plc Dec 400 Calls @ 69

The seller or writer of this option has opened a short position giving the buyer or holder of the option the right to ask for delivery of British Telecom shares at 400 p anytime until expiry of the option in Dec.

For that right the buyer has paid the seller a price (also called a "*premium*") of 69 p. Each contract is for 1000 shares so the seller has received a premium of £69,000 (100,000 × 69 p) but, if this option is exercised by the buyer, the seller must deliver the shares for 400 p irrespective of the price of BT in the market.

Clearly the buyer is expecting the shares to be above 469 p (400 p + 69 p) by Dec. and the seller is expecting the price to be below 469 p, or be willing to sell the shares at this level.

Options on Futures

Options on futures contracts have the same characteristics as the options described above. The difference is that the underlying product is either a long or short futures contract. Premium is not paid or received on T + 1 as these contracts are marked to market each day over the life of the option.

Example

Long 70 NYSE Liffe Long Gilt Dec 107.00 Put options @ 1.06

The buyer has bought the right to a short position of 70 futures at 107 (the seller will therefore be obliged to assume a long position if assigned). For the calculation of variation margin the position is marked to market at 1.06.

If exercised before expiry, this option would provide the buyer with a short position, (because it is a put option), of 70 LIFFE Long Gilt Dec futures at a price of 107.00.

History of Exchange Development and Growth

The development of futures markets can be traced back to the Middle Ages and revolved around the supply and demand of farmers and merchants. The early contracts were for delivery of grains like oats, corn, and wheat.

First Traded Futures Exchange

The Chicago Board of Trade (CBOT) was established in 1848, to standardize the size, quality, and delivery date of these commodity agreements into a contract (CBOT merged with CME in 2007). Once established the standardization enabled contracts to be readily traded. Thus, the forerunner of today's markets was born and farmers or merchants who wanted to hedge against price fluctuations, caused by poor or bumper harvests, bought and sold contracts with traders or market makers who were willing to make a two way price for buying and selling. Speculators, who wanted to gamble on the price going up or down without actually buying or selling the physical grain themselves, were also attracted to the market.

Thus liquidity in the contracts was created. The market maker was able, if he wanted, to lay off the risk he had assumed from buying and selling with the hedgers, by doing the opposite buying and selling with the speculators. The market maker's profit was the difference between buying and selling prices of his contracts. In essence, today's markets do the same job but in hundreds of different products.

In the 1870s, following in CBOT's footsteps, the Chicago Produce Exchange provided a market for perishable agricultural products like butter and eggs. After some upheaval in 1898, certain traders broke away and formed what is now known as the Chicago Mercantile Exchange (CME). In 1919, the CME was authorized to allow futures trading on a variety of commodities including pork bellies, hogs, and cattle. Similarly in the late 19th century, the early versions of futures contracts on precious metals and crude oil were established in New York—the forerunners of the Commodity Exchange (COMEX) and New York Mercantile Exchange (NYMEX), two futures exchanges now both combined as a division of the CME, where futures and options contracts include crude oil, gasoline, heating oil, natural gas, gold, silver, copper, aluminum, and platinum. NYMEX was acquired by the CME Group in 2008.

Emergence of Financial Futures Markets

From the end of World War II until the early 1970s, there was a very stable economic environment in the United States helped by the Bretton Woods Agreement, which kept interest rates in a narrow range. However, when the US dollar was devalued, partly as a consequence of the funding of the Vietnam War and a heavy domestic spending program, uncertainty and fluctuation in interest and currency rates replaced economic stability. Europe and Japan had also recovered in economic terms from the rebuilding effects of World War II and with their economies growing the US dollar came under severe pressure.

The need to be able to hedge (or to protect) against the risk associated with volatile currencies and interest rates became critical for many businesses and industries. Therefore, we saw the birth of the first financial contracts which became the cornerstone of the futures and options industry as we know it today.

In 1972, the CME established a division known as the International Monetary Market (IMM). Its purpose was to enable trading in futures contracts based on foreign currencies. In 1975 the CBOT launched the first futures contract on a financial instrument, the Ginnie Mae Mortgage Bond future, followed by the CME, which listed the Eurodollar (3 month interest rate) contract. Shortly after this, the CBOT listed the Treasury Bond future, which was to become for many years the world's most heavily traded futures contract. In 1983, the CME started trading futures contracts on the S&P500 Stock Index, one of the first futures contract designed for the equity market.

In the United States, prior to 1975, nearly all contracts traded were agricultural. Volume in these contracts was less than 10 million per year. However, by 1994, after the introduction of energy, metal, financial currency, interest rate, and equity index futures, trading volumes had risen to almost 700 million contracts per year.

Since then, the growth in volume of futures and options contracts in the United States and the rest of the world has been phenomenal, as more and more exchanges have opened and a plethora of financial and commodity products have been listed to meet the demands in many different markets for risk hedging mechanisms. Futures and options exchanges are now well established in Brazil, Russia, India, and China and have been increasingly successful in attracting both local and international trading participants.

Futures Exchanges in Europe

The development and growth of futures markets in Europe has mirrored the American experience. The origins of the London Metal Exchange (LME) (LME was acquired by Hong Kong Exchanges & Clearing Ltd in 2012) and the London Commodity Exchange (LCE) can be traced back to the 1600s, with copper and tin trading well established by the 1870s, although more standardized commodity futures contracts (based on coffee, cocoa, and sugar) were not traded until the 1890s. LCE was merged into LIFFE in the 1990s (now owned by ICE). The LME added further metals from the 1920s onward (lead, zinc, and later aluminum). In 1979, the International Petroleum Exchange (IPE)—acquired in 2001 by Intercontinental Exchange Inc (ICE)—was created to trade European Gasoil and Brent Crude. This was followed by the opening of The London International Financial Futures Exchange (LIFFE) (LIFFE was acquired by Euronext in 2002, which merged with NYSE in 2007 and was then acquired by ICE in 2013) in 1982 (listing the first non-US financial futures contract), the Paris based MATIF (MATIF was merged into Euronext in 2000) in 1986, and Germany's DTB in 1990 (DTB was the forerunner of EUREX). Futures trading volumes, especially in respect of interest rate, government bond, and stock index products, grew very rapidly throughout the 1990s.

The expansion of the European market, the introduction of the Euro currency and the shift of trading activity from physical "open outcry" to much cheaper and more efficient electronic trading systems has led directly to a significant consolidation of European futures trading activity and exchange mergers over the last 13 years. The two most liquid futures and options markets in Europe are now EUREX (founded in 1998 from the merger of DTB and Soffex) and Euronext (formed in 2000 from the merger of the Amsterdam, Brussels, and Paris exchanges and later LIFFE in 2002). In 2007 Euronext was acquired by the NYSE, which was itself acquired in 2013 by ICE. The newest European futures exchange is the European Energy Exchange (EEX) in Germany, which started listing derivatives in 2006 and now offers European natural gas, power/ electricity, emission, and coal futures contracts.

Futures Exchanges in Asia

Although futures markets in Asia developed a bit later than in the United States and Europe, growth over the last 20 years has been dramatic. The first Asian commodity futures were traded in the 1950s on the Tokyo Rubber Exchange (TRE) (The Tokyo Rubber, Gold, and Textile exchanges were merged in 1984 to create the Tokyo Commodity Exchange (TCE)) and in 1960s on the Sydney Futures Exchange (SFE) (SFE was merged with the Australian Stock Exchange in 2006 to create ASX), and by 1976 the Hong Kong Futures Exchange (HKFE) had also been established. HKFE was merged into Hong Kong Exchanges & Clearing Ltd (HKEx) in 2000. The first financial futures contracts were trade on the SFE in 1979. The birth of stock index futures in the early 1980s marked the start of a surge in futures trading across Asia and the launch of some of the today's well-known regional benchmark derivative products. The Singapore International Mercantile Exchange (SIMEX) commenced in 1984 and Hang Seng Index futures started trading on the HKFE in 1985. SIMEX became part of the Singapore Exchange (SGX) in 1999. The Tokyo Stock Exchange (TSE) launched Japanese Government Bond futures in 1985 and this was followed by the Osaka Stock Exchange (OSE) Nikkei 225 futures contract in 1988 and the Tokyo Financial Exchange (TFE) Euroyen futures contract in 1989. Originally named Tokyo International Financial Futures Exchange (TIFFE).

Across Asia the geographic spread and growth of new futures exchanges continued into the 1990s. The first Chinese commodity futures exchanges were established from 1993 onward, and the Dalian Commodity Exchange, the Shanghai Futures Exchange, and Zhengzhou Commodity Exchange were all listed in the Futures Industry Top 15 global derivatives exchanges (by contract volume) for 2012. The Korea Exchange (KRX) Kospi 200 Index futures contract (launched in 1996) and the National Stock Exchange of India (NSE) CNX Nifty 50 Index futures (launched in 2000) are now two of the world's most highly traded futures contracts.

First Options Exchanges

As with the futures markets, exchange traded options are now listed on a wide range of financial (currency, interest rate, equity), energy, metals, and commodity products to meet global demand for these risk management instruments. Like futures, the use of options can be traced back to the 18th century, and in certain forms as far back as the Middle Ages. In the 18th century, options were traded in both Europe and the United States of America, but unfortunately due to widespread corrupt practices the markets had a bad name. Indeed, in the 17th century the Dutch economy nearly crashed after the collapse of a market in options on tulip bulbs.

These early forms of option contracts were traded between the buyer and seller and had only two possible outcomes. The option was exercised (ie, the underlying product changed hands at the agreed price) or it expired without the buyer taking up his "option" to exercise the contract for delivery. In other words, there was no "trading" of the option positions, and worse, in the early days there was no guarantee that the seller would honor his obligation to deliver the underlying asset if the buyer exercised his option.

In 1973, the CBOT proposed a new exchange, the Chicago Board Options Exchange (CBOE), to trade stock options in a standardized form and on a recognized market where performance of the option contract on exercise was guaranteed. This was the true birth of "traded options." Several factors also contributed to the growth of traded option markets. First, the ability to calculate a "fair" price for options was made possible with the introduction of a mathematical formula, which was widely accepted by the market. Second, the market maker system was upgraded to insure there was always a two-way (bid and offer) price quoted thus insuring liquidity. Third was the growth of computer processing, which enabled large numbers of trades to be efficiently matched, cleared, and settled. The United States led the way.

Some of the earliest equity option exchanges included the Australian Option Market (now owned by the Australian Stock Exchange), which opened in 1976, the European Options Exchange in Amsterdam (EOE) in 1978 and the London Traded Option Market (LTOM) in 1978, which was originally part of the London Stock Exchange, but merged with LIFFE in 1993. EOE became part of Euronext in 2000, which is now owned by ICE. Equity option and stock index option trading grew rapidly in Asia during the 1990s as more futures and options exchanges opened to offer trading and hedging opportunities on a plethora of newly launched indices.

Futures and Options Exchanges Today

Today, as we have already noted, the derivatives industry is truly global. To illustrate just how big the industry is, we only need to look at the volume of contracts traded on worldwide derivatives exchanges during 2014, which based on activity at 75 worldwide exchanges totaled over 21 billion contracts (Source: The Futures Industry Association).

Although futures and options contract innovation continues to evolve, nearly all the key benchmark financial futures and options contracts (eg, US T Bond, Eurodollar, S&P500 index, Bund, Bob l, Euribor, DAX, Gilt, FTSE index, JGB, Nikkei 225, Euroyen) were first listed in the 1980s. Although some important new futures and options exchanges have been established since then,

particularly in Asia, it is mainly the wider and increased usage by market participants, globalization and the much greater capacity and efficiency of electronic
markets that has driven growth in the last 10 years. Increased volatility and
economic uncertainty in the markets has also led to additional growth in trading
activity as hedgers use derivatives to manage risk. Today there is significant
consolidation taking place with exchanges merging and readers of this book
should access the FIA website at www.fia.org.

Futures and Option Contract Specifications and Diversity

Exchange traded futures and options contracts have standardized terms and
conditions. These contracts are standardized with regard to the unit of trading (contract size), delivery months (contract expiry/ maturity), price quotation,
minimum price fluctuation ("*tick*" size and value), trading hours, last trading
day, and delivery procedures. For each contract type, these headline specifications are supported by a comprehensive legal agreement that sets out all the
detailed contract terms and delivery procedures (if applicable), as designed and
determined by the relevant exchange authority. Contract specification details
can be found on the exchange's website.

Tick Size

The tick size of a contract is worked out in different ways, with some examples
as follows:

CME S&P500 Index Future
- The contract size or trading unit is S&P500 Index × $250.
- The price is quoted in index points and the minimum price fluctuation is
  0.10 index points. This gives a tick size of $25 ($250 divided by 10).

NYSE Liffe Short Sterling 3 Month Interest Rate Future

- The tick size is the value of a one-point movement in the contract price. This
  price is arrived at by multiplying the notional contract size by the length of
  time of the notional time deposit underlying the contract in years multiplied
  by the minimum tick size movement of 0.01%.

Tick size = £500,000 × 3/12 × 0.01% = £12.50

Product Range

Liquid exchange traded futures and options markets now exist for all the following asset classes:

Product categories:

Government bonds (2–30 years)
3 month interest rates
Futures on swaps

Stock indices
Individual equities
Currencies (vs USD)
Precious metals
Base metals
Oil (full product range)
Natural gas, coal
Weather
Soft commodities
Agricultural commodities
*Property (residential and commercial)

*Residential property futures were listed by CME in 2006; although the property derivatives market is mainly traded OTC.

Now we will consider two types of futures contract in more detail: equity index futures and commodity futures.

Equity Index Futures

Since the first index based contract was introduced in 1982 on the Kansas City Board of Trade, stock index futures have been among the fastest growing futures contracts. So popular have they become, that in most cases the volume of futures market trading significantly exceeds trading volumes in the associated underlying cash market. The first important equity index contract to be launched, the S&P 500 contract traded on the CME (launched in Jan. 1983), is still the most heavily traded equity index futures contract (by notional value).

An equity index contract allows both investors and speculators to buy or sell the index at a fixed level. The seller, or short, has an obligation to sell (deliver) a fixed amount of the underlying equity market (number of contracts × contract value) at maturity at the price traded. However in practice futures contracts are rarely held to maturity. They are usually closed out prior to settlement by an equal and opposite transaction in the market.

With equity index futures it is very difficult to design a procedure that enables the seller to actually deliver a basket of multiple different shares in the exact proportions (weighting) required to replicate the relevant underlying index. Thus unlike many other futures contracts (eg, Bonds, metals, commodities) equity index contracts are always "*cash settled*." When the contract matures, if the index is above the price at which the futures contract was bought, the seller, instead of having to deliver a basket of shares, simply pays the buyer the cash difference between the index price at maturity and the original traded contract price. If it is lower, then the buyer pays the cash difference. So in practice an equity index futures contract is an agreement to buy or sell the cash value of the index at a future date.

Commodity Futures

Commodity futures contracts differ from financial futures due to the very different nature of the underlying assets. Indeed, historically financial institutions have shied away from commodity futures due to the implications of physical delivery. However when returns on equities and yields on interest rates fall, investors often look for alternative assets to invest in and the commodity markets (including energy and metals) may sometimes offer a potential source of better returns. In practice, the major commodity and energy derivative market participants are the large corporate producers, manufacturers, and consumers of the actual commodity being traded, alongside a number of commodity finance banks and some specialist fund managers.

Physical agricultural and soft commodities have the additional feature of being perishable over time and thus have only a limited lifespan in which they can be consumed. To deal with the complicated issues of physical commodity delivery, the futures exchanges have designed detailed delivery procedures and regulations (eg, regarding warehousing, transportation, and product quality requirements) that must be carefully adhered to by both buyers and sellers involved in any delivery process.

Agricultural and soft commodities are finite in terms of availability and subject to variations in quality due to the forces of nature, such as weather. In order to ensure the product delivered is of the correct quality, as defined in the contract terms, there is a quality checking procedure. Where there is a problem with delivery, arbitration is sought via a trade association or an independent source appointed by the exchange. The delivery months of agricultural and soft commodities are not as standardized as for some other futures contracts. This is because they have to take into account factors such as growing season, harvesting and transportation.

During the delivery period the *"clearing house"* organization that operates the clearing and settlement system and manages the risk on behalf of the exchange, may demand higher margin deposits from holders of open positions in order to encourage traders who do not wish to go to delivery to close out their positions prior to the maturity/delivery date. Less than 0.1% of futures contracts traded actually result in a delivery of the underlying asset.

Example

Purchase of 50 NYSE Liffe July Cocoa futures @ 1750

The buyer has entered into an obligation to take delivery of cocoa from the holder of a short position in Jul. The price is set at £1,750/ton irrespective of the price cocoa might be trading at in Jul.

Basic Trading and Hedging Strategies

Although the fund custodian and administrator are supporting investment funds and their management, it is important to understand the way in which the markets work and the players involved so we will look at trading as well as strategies used in investment management, for example, strategies utilized by hedge funds involve gearing etc.

Trading

The basic rule of trading is the same the world over, regardless of the type of item being traded: "buy low, sell high." Futures contracts are particularly well suited to high risk speculative trading, first because they require only a small percentage of contract value to be put up as a deposit (margin) and second because, unlike most other assets and financial instruments, the trader can readily go short, that is, sell a futures contract and then buy it back later (with a view to making a profit as prices fall). Obviously the skill of any trading activity is to determine how to consistently make profits over a long period of time. Indeed a huge research industry has built up to support traders in their quest for the "perfect" trading system, comprising both fundamental market research and a myriad of various technical analysis and related software; covering such things as pattern, trend, chart and gap analysis, moving averages, momentum indicators, and complex option and derivative pricing models.

Equity index futures are one of the most flexible trading instruments. Traders and speculators can use them to obtain maximum gearing for their strategies on stock market direction, while "*arbitrageurs*" can use them to take advantage of pricing anomalies.

Trading Strategy 1: Market Direction (Using Futures)

An investor, who believes that the market as a whole will rise, can purchase exposure to the relevant stock index in a single transaction by buying the requisite number of futures contracts (rather than a basket of the individual equities). For example, an investor deposits £100,000 with his broker and buys 25 FTSE100 contracts at a price of 5990 (equivalent to a £1,497,500 investment in the index, ie, 25 contracts × £10 × 5990). Against this position, he has to put up a margin deposit of (say) £2,500 per contract (= £62,500). Some weeks later, after several rises and falls in the market the index has risen to 6040. The investor decides to close out his position by selling 25 contracts (now equivalent to an investment of £1,510,000). His margin deposit is returned and he makes a £12,500 profit (25 contracts × 50 points (6040−5990) × £10 per point value).

Trading Strategy 2: Speculating (Using Options)

Options are attractive to speculators because of their limited downside risk. For the buyer of call or put options their maximum potential loss is the amount of option premium paid; while, if the market moves in their favor the potential upside profit is unlimited.

A speculator believes that BP plc shares, which are currently 490 p, will rise in the next few weeks. He has approx. £50,000 to invest. He could purchase 10,200 shares at 490 p or, in the traded option market, he could buy 200 of the 500 p Jun. call option contracts (1000 shares per contract) for 25 p/share or £50,000. These call options give him an exposure to 250,000 shares, so if the BP share price rises high enough before end of Jun., his potential profit far exceeds the amount he would make buying 10,200 shares.

If the underlying share price goes to 550 p, the 500 p call options would be worth at least 50 p so he could sell them for £100,000 for a profit of £50,000. Had he bought the 10,200 shares he could sell them for £56,100 for a profit of £6,100. However, as with most other forms of trading and speculation, higher potential rewards always involve higher risk of loss.

If the BP share price falls to 475 p by the expiry of the options in Jun., the 500 p options will be worth nothing and the option speculator will lose his entire investment (£50,000). While had he used the more conservative strategy and bought the 10,200 BP shares in the cash market, his loss would only be £1,530, and he would still have a holding of shares worth £48,450, the price of which may rise again in the future.

Trading Strategy 3: Gearing

An investor with an existing stock market portfolio and bullish view on market direction can "gear up" by going long (buying) futures contracts. Depending on the particular contract, it is possible to take on additional stock market exposure (and thus additional profits/losses) by putting up margin deposits of just 5–10% of the contract value of the futures position added.

Trading Strategy 4: Arbitrage Trading

When the market price of an equity index futures contract differs significantly from its "*fair value*" (see later section), arbitrage can be used to profit from the perceived mispricing. If the futures contract is trading at a premium to fair value the arbitrage involves buying the shares (which make up the index) and selling an equivalent amount of futures contracts. The cost of holding the shares, net of dividends received, is included in the fair value of the future and consequently an investor holding shares and short an expensive future will be left with a profit after holding costs if he holds the position through to expiry. Conversely, where the future is trading at a discount to fair value (as it does typically), the arbitrageur can sell the shares (which make up the index), to create a short position, and buy the cheap future to lock in the under-valuation. In practice, these arbitrage opportunities are limited by the costs of dealing in multiple shares (which comprise the specific equity index) and futures prices have to differ from fair value by a certain threshold amount before arbitrage trading becomes economically worthwhile.

Hedging

While traders are essential to the healthy liquidity of futures and options markets, the real economic value and importance of these contracts is their potential usage as hedging instruments. As hedging tools, futures and options enable market participants both traders and investment managers to protect themselves from market price risk and better manage their market exposures. This can be best explained with a few examples:

Hedging Example 1: Potato Farmers

Imagine a potato producer. In Mar., at the beginning of the season he must purchase the seeds to plant his potato crop and will tender his crop during the coming months until harvest time. He has no idea at that time how the season will turn out but his livelihood depends on the profits that he can make from growing his potatoes. The farmer has two fields with an estimated yield of 375 tons in each field. He has fixed overheads of £5,000 to produce the potatoes and expects to sell them at around £10 to £12 per ton. He looks to the futures market to "hedge" or protect the value of his expected potato crop.

In order to protect his crop against a fall in prices and to ensure that his overheads are covered, the farmer enters into a futures contract. He sells 25 contracts (20 tons per contract = 500 tons) at £10 per ton for delivery in Oct.

This would cover the £5,000 fixed costs that he has, as he is guaranteed to sell 500 tons at £10 per ton in Oct. He also has his additional 250 tons to sell at the prevailing market price, on which he hopes to make a profit. However, the farmer still has one other problem; what would happen if he were unable to produce the 500 tons that he needs to fulfil his contract?

In this case the farmer enters into a hedging transaction to protect himself. He buys a call option, which gives him the right to buy 500 tons at £10.50 per ton in Oct. To acquire this right costs him £250 in option premium.

This is his insurance in case his harvest fails and in total it costs him £500, because he has paid £250 in option premium and it will cost him an extra £0.50 per ton if he has to exercise his option (500 tons × £0.50 per ton = £250). He would have chosen the £10.50 call option because it was not far from the £10.00 price he wanted and was cheaper to purchase.

At harvest time in Oct. the farmer's crop is poor and potatoes are in short supply. He has only managed to produce 520 tons from his crop. However, the market price of potatoes, given the shortage, is £16 per ton. The farmer must fulfil his futures contract obligation by selling 500 tons at £10 per ton but he sells his additional 20 tons at £16 per ton.

Sell 500 tons @ £10 per ton	= £5,000 cr
Sell 20 tons @ £16 per ton	= £ 320 cr
Net profit before hedge	= £5,320 cr

He also has the option, which he should now exercise because it is "in-the-money" and allows him to buy 500 tons at £10.50 per ton, which he can resell in the market at £16 per ton to make a profit.

Buy 500 tons @ £10.50 per ton	= £5,250 dr.
Sell at market price of £16 per ton	= £8,000 cr
Gross profit	= £2,750 cr

Less option premium paid	= £ 250 dr
Net profit on hedge	= £2,500 cr
Overall profit on the above transactions	= £7,820

Let us look at what would happen if the crop had been successful and the farmer was able to produce 900 tons of potatoes.

Because of the good crop and plentiful supply, the market price of potatoes has fallen to £7 per ton. He fulfils his obligations in the futures market.

The option contracts that he bought as insurance for his crop are "out-of-the-money" and therefore are left to expire worthless.

Sell 500 tons at £10 per ton	= £5,000 cr
Sell remaining 400 tons at £7 per ton	= £2,800 cr
Gross profit	= £7,800 cr
Less option premium paid	= £ 250 dr
Net profit	= £7,550

If the farmer had not entered into any futures or options transactions he would have been able to sell his total crop of 900 tons at the market price of £7 per ton, thus realizing a profit of £6,300. Using the futures and options not only protected his crop but also gave him a better profit than without the protection.

Hedging Example 2: Fixed Rate Mortgages

Other examples of users of futures markets are the banks and building societies that offer customers fixed rate mortgages. Consider the problem that the building society has if it offers you a fixed rate mortgage over five years. It has to pay its savings customers a floating market rate, while it is receiving a fixed rate from you, irrespective of what happens to interest rates over the five year period.

If interest rates were to rise in the first year, the building society would have to raise the rates that they pay to savers but they would not be able to increase the rates that they charge you as the mortgage borrower. In order to balance this mismatch in interest payments, the building society can enter into an interest rate swap transaction with another counterparty, most likely a bank.

The interest swap transaction is an over-the-counter (OTC) derivative (see "Part 2—OTC Derivatives"), which is specifically designed between two counterparties to match their hedging requirements. It involves an agreement to pay the counterparty bank the fixed interest payments that it receives from you as the borrower, and in return the building society receives the floating rate, which is similar to the rate that it pays to its savers. The building society is then back to its matched interest rate status for borrowers and savers.

However, now the counterparty bank has a problem because they are not protected against interest rate changes. Therefore it may choose to hedge this risk using NYSE.Liffe's 3 Month Short Sterling Interest Rate futures contract. This contract allows the bank to fix the interest rate now that will be paid or received in 3 months time. From time to time the bank will roll the contract over, if market conditions are right, so that the interest rate protection is continued.

This involves selling the position that is held in say Jun. futures and buying Dec. futures, thus continuing the protection for another six months. The end result is that everyone has the interest rate protection that they need.

Note: Why would the building society use an interest rate swap transaction? The terms are more flexible and allow them to hedge their requirements in one straightforward transaction. The bank receives a bid/offer spread from the building society, which they would price so that they make a profit on the deal allowing for the hedging costs of their interest rate futures contracts.

Investment Managers

Investment managers can use futures and options in many ways and we will explore these later in this part of the book.

Now let us consider the market infrastructure

Market Structure

Role of an Exchange

The exchange is the place where members, who can be companies or individuals, trade futures and options against each other. The members carry out their business under the rules and regulations of the exchange. Each exchange in turn is subject to regulation by local government agencies. For example; in the UK, the Financial Conduct Authority (FCA) supervises a number of Recognised Investment Exchanges (RIE) and Recognised Overseas Investment Exchanges (ROIE) under the Financial Services and Markets Act 2000; RIEs include ICE, LIFFE and LME; ROIEs include CME, CBOT, NYMEX, and EUREX.

While historically exchanges provided a large physical location for the trading activity to take place, these days most futures and option trading is done electronically through computer "*screen based trading*" systems managed centrally by the exchange organization. The traditional style physical exchanges use "*open outcry*" where the members gather together on an exchange market floor in "*pits*" and shout out their bids and offers. Traders use an exchange authorized method of hand signals to communicate with their colleagues and other market members. The largest futures exchange in the world still using physical open outcry is New York's NYMEX (energy and precious metals) but this activity is undertaken in parallel with screen based trading. However, it is only a question of time before this colorful and visually extraordinary style of trading is finally consigned to history.

Until the late 1990s, the responsibility of the management of most exchanges was vested in a board of directors elected by the membership of the exchange. However, over the years most European and US exchanges have separated exchange membership (ie, trading access) from exchange ownership, allowing exchanges to become stock exchange listed profit-focused commercial organizations (as opposed to "not-for-profit" member owned club style bodies). This change in ownership style also accelerated the consolidation of futures exchanges through a series of corporate acquisitions and mergers. Reporting to the exchange board are the executive staff (employees of the exchange) and various practitioner-based committees who consider specific issues relevant to the day-to-day operation of the exchange. These issues concern price dissemination, trading access and regulations, IT systems, product design, specification and development, marketing and exchange fees from which exchanges derive most of their revenue (and profit).

Exchange members may be divided into a number of different categories, with different trading rights and obligations, in particular with regard to their authority to transact business on behalf of third party customers. The most important sub-division is that between "nonclearing" and "clearing" members. Clearing members are those who have a direct counterparty relationship with the central Clearing House (see later), while nonclearing members need the support of a clearing member in order to trade on the exchange.

Role of the Clearing House

The role of the clearing house is to act as central counterparty to both sides of every trade, thereby replacing any direct counterparty relationship between the two trading counterparties. The clearing house is fundamental to the integrity and credibility of the exchange traded futures or options market for which it operates, as its purpose is to guarantee the performance of each and every transaction; in effect enabling multilateral netting of trading exposures between all clearing members. By assuming the legal responsibility for the trade, the clearing house removes the credit risk that the two original counterparties would otherwise have on each other. It is important to note that the clearing house guarantee only extends to clearing members. All other market participants (end customers and nonclearing exchange members) have a continuing counterparty credit risk with the clearing member through which they have chosen to access the market. Likewise clearing members are exposed to the credit risk of their clients, including any nonclearing members for whom they provide a clearing service.

The process of establishing a futures contract in the name of the clearing house as counterparty, to each clearing member, is called "*novation*." In this process the clearing house becomes buyer to every seller and seller to every buyer, for each transaction. Following novation, the clearing member has no counterparty risk in the market for all their futures trading, other than with the clearing house on one side and their own clients (if any) on the other. The completion of the novation process is called "*registration*." Upon registration the clearing member's open positions in the market are held with the clearing house and it becomes irrelevant regarding which trade counterparties the clearing member actually dealt with originally. Similarly, when closing a position in the market there is no need to seek out the original counterparty of the initial trade. For all registered trades, the clearing house undertakes daily mark-to-market processes and effects automated settlement of the two (buy and sell) transactions the following morning.

There are two categories of clearing house; those that are owned by the same corporate entity as the exchange itself and those that are separately owned and independent of the exchange, with their own financial backing. Today, following extensive exchange consolidation in the United States and Europe, most of the world's clearing houses are combined with their associated exchanges. There are many examples of this integrated exchange/clearing house model, including the CME (including CBOT & NYMEX contracts), ICE (including LIFFE), EUREX (including ECC), KSE, HKSE, and TSE.

Until 2001, LCH.Clearnet (LCH) was the independent clearing house for all London's futures exchanges; LIFFE, IPE, LME, and LCE. However, following the acquisition of these exchanges by various overseas exchanges, this centralized clearing has gradually been superseded. Today LCH provides clearing arrangements for the cash equities for the LSE and interest rate swaps in Swapclear (see later section) plus repurchase agreements (RepoCLear) and other products.

Clearing houses need be financially robust in order to sustain a potential clearing member default in the market(s) in which they operate. The most common structure of financial support for clearing houses is a default fund, into which all clearing members are required to pay significant cash deposits, partly in proportion to the volume of their business. In addition, as a condition of clearing membership, clearing member firms may have to accept some contingent liability (or additional assessment) to "top up" the clearing house default fund in the unlikely event that such cash reserves are insufficient to cover a clearing member failure. Over the last 20 years there have been a number of high profile defaults of clearing member firms, including Barings, Refco, Lehman, and MF Global, but in all cases the default handling procedures of the clearing houses have worked well in practice, without any losses being sustained in their default funds. The financial backing of the clearing house is an important consideration for banks and brokers when they are contemplating becoming clearing members of an exchange. It is also an important issue for companies researching the potential of trading on any particular exchange, as they need to know that their trades will be efficiently settled and that their positions will be secure in the event of another unrelated party defaulting on market. As for exchanges, the clearing houses are themselves subject to regulatory oversight by their local government agencies (eg, FCA in the UK, CFTC/SEC in the United States).

Basics of Futures Fair Pricing Theory

In order that the administrator can value products as well as carry out oversight tasks related to price at which derivatives are traded we need to understand the concept of the fair value or pricing of products.

Equity Index Futures Fair Pricing

The value of a futures contract depends on the level of the index and the basic trading unit of the contract; for the S&P500 futures traded on the CME the unit is $250 for every index point; for the Nikkei225 contract traded in Tokyo the unit is ¥500 for each index point; while for the FTSE100 contract on NYSE. Liffe it is £10 for every index point.

If the FTSE100 index stands at 5,000, the value of one futures contract at that price would equate to £50,000 (£10 × 5,000). In practice the fair market price of the FTSE futures contract will not be the same as the cash market index, as there are important differences between the characteristics of an index futures contract and that of the underlying basket of stocks; as follows:

1. The holder of the basket of shares will receive dividend income. The holder of the future does not and should therefore be compensated for the loss of dividend income by a corresponding discount in the futures price. Higher expected dividend levels will lower the fair value of the futures contract since the holder of the futures does not receive the dividends.

2. Buying the basket of shares involves payment of the full cost of the securities immediately, whereas the purchaser of the futures contract only has to put up a small percentage of the cost of the securities (as his deposit or "margin") initially, and so can earn interest on the remainder. Thus the purchaser of the futures should be willing to pay a premium for the futures, which will be offset by the interest received (on the surplus cash) during the lifetime of the contract. The higher the prevailing interest rate, the higher the fair value of the futures. The longer the maturity of the futures contract, the greater this benefit will be and so the greater the premium. Similarly the higher the index level, the greater the cost of buying the underlying shares, and so the greater the carrying costs reflected in a greater fair value premium.

A simple formula for the calculation of fair value is shown:

$$\text{Fair value} = \text{spot index level} + \text{cost of carry}$$

Where cost of carry = spot index level × $(i/100 - y/100)$ × $d/365$, i = interbank rate, d = the number of days from settlement day for the day of trade to the settlement day for the expiry date of the contract, y = percentage annual yield of FTSE100 Index.

(Source NYSE.LIFFE FTSE Indices booklet)

Assuming an index level of 6000 on 3rd Jan., the first business day of the year, a forecast yield on the index of 4.1% and a three month interbank rate of 5.25%, the above formula can be used to calculate a fair value for the Mar. FTSE future:

$$\begin{aligned}
\text{Fair value} &= 6000 + 6000 \times (5.25/100 - 4.1/100) \times 66/365 \\
&= 6000 + 6000 \times (0.0525 - 0.041) \times 0.18 \\
&= 6000 + 12.42, (\text{or } 6012 \text{ to nearest tick})
\end{aligned}$$

If interest rates are generally higher than dividend yields, the futures generally trade at a premium to the underlying index. This premium is determined by comparing the interest that would be earned by buying futures with the dividends that would be paid on the underlying securities during the remaining life of the contract.

Fair value is a benchmark, not an absolute number, since different investors in the market will use different expectations of unknown future dividends and also different funding assumptions. The above formula is simplistic in the sense that the dividends that are to be paid in the future are not discounted to their present value. Supply and demand factors will also affect the price, making the traded price differ from fair value. The futures contract is described as "expensive" when it is at a premium to fair value and "cheap" when it is at a discount to fair value. The difference between the actual level at which the futures trade and the theoretical fair value is sometimes known as the "*value basis.*"

Settlement and Margining

When a fund has participated in a derivative transaction it will need settling. The custodian may do this or the positions may be held by a derivatives clearing broker and so the fund will settle with the broker.

Futures contracts have a characteristic that is important in terms of their flexibility and usefulness for both hedgers and traders alike. This characteristic is that, unlike cash securities or physical commodity transactions, the full market value of the derivative contract is never actually paid or received, unless delivery of the underlying asset takes place at maturity. In order to trade futures only a small percentage of contract value needs to be paid upfront, albeit that subsequent profits and losses must be settled on a daily basis. This "gearing" feature makes futures contracts efficient and cheap tools for hedgers and traders, but also represents a possible danger if the full underlying market exposure is not properly managed. It was mentioned earlier that the clearing house performs an important credit risk reduction role between clearing members. One way in which the clearing manages its own credit risk exposure to each clearing member is to establish margin (or collateral) requirements on all open positions (both long and short) until the contract obligations have been met.

Initial Margin

The deposit which the clearing house calls from clearing members (and indirectly their clients) to cover their margin requirements is called "*initial margin*" and is returnable to the clearing member once an open position is closed. The amount of initial margin required varies markedly for different futures contracts, being determined by reference to the volatility of each particular underlying market (bond, interest rate, commodity, etc.). The initial margin required (per contract) is set by the clearing house at a sufficient level to cover approx.

95% of likely one day movements in the contract price, but it can be changed at short notice to reflect changing market conditions. This margin deposit is retained by the clearing house throughout the period that the open position is maintained.

The margining of option contracts is more complex than for futures contracts due to the much wider range of contract parameters: puts and calls, strike/exercise prices, and expiry dates. In addition options are normally traded in combination with other options and/or futures such that opposing market risk exposures partly net-off with each other. To calculate the appropriate level of initial margin requirement that is appropriate to the market risk of a given option portfolio, all of the world's main clearing houses now use the SPAN (Standard Portfoilo Analysis of Risk) system, or similar "risk-based" margining software, which is described in more detail later. Option margining requirements also vary depending on whether option premium is payable upfront (eg, equity and index options) or not (eg, options on futures contracts). The OCC use their own process—System for Theoretical Analysis and Numerical Simulations ("STANS") see appendices.

Equity and index option buyers (holders of long option positions) are not charged initial margin because once the option premium has been paid out (to the seller) on T + 1, the buyer has no further downside market risk. The worst that can happen for the buyer is that the option subsequently expires worthless. Equity and index option sellers/writers (holders of short option positions) are required to deposit initial margin as there remains a risk of the writer being unable financially to fulfil their delivery obligations, should the option be exercised on or before expiry.

In contrast, the traded premium on options on futures contracts only flows from buyer to seller gradually over the life of the option. Thus both buyers and sellers have a remaining risk exposure and both are required to deposit initial margin in a similar way as for futures contracts. Their initial margin requirement changes daily in line with the changing market risk exposure in their option portfolio.

Interest

The regulations pertaining to securities held by a third parties mean that to encourage clearing members to pay cash to cover their initial margin requirements, most clearing houses pay interest on the cash deposited. The rate of interest paid by each clearing house varies. The rate is set and published by the clearing house itself, with reference to (and usually slightly below) the local central bank or interbank deposit rate for the relevant currency. For the same reason clearing member firms will use the interest rates set by the clearing house, perhaps minus 0.25% (or plus 1.0%), as the basis of the rates paid to (or charged to) their own clients.

Intraday Margin

In times of high market volatility, with very large daily movements up or down in the price of a specific futures contract, the clearing house may increase the initial margin requirement (per open contract). An additional margin amount may occasionally be called intraday by the clearing house from those clearing members on the wrong side of the price movement, to support their open futures and option positions. If the clearing house believes that the situation is only temporary and that market volatility will quickly decrease to a more stable environment, then they will leave the initial margin requirement at its original level for the next day, only calling the intraday margin as a one-off advance payment. More likely however, the initial margin level will be increased as a result of the volatile conditions.

Intraday margins can be called from the clearing members by the clearing house at any time as determined in their rules. It is important to understand that the clearing members must pay the required amount to the clearing house, regardless of whether they are able to obtain any additional funds from their clients. In this respect, it is necessary that clearing members have the systems capability to recalculate margin requirements during the day so that they can accurately determine how they and their clients are affected. Intraday margin calls also highlight the need for clearing members to be adequately capitalized in that they must draw on their own financial resources to meet the call.

Spot Month Margin

This is an additional initial margin amount which may be charged by the clearing house on futures contracts that are still open after the close of trading on the last trading day, pending delivery of the underlying security or asset on the actual delivery date. (The "spot" month is the earliest delivery month available for futures trading.) This extra margin is designed to cover the potential risk of a party default during the delivery process. It is relevant for deliverable contracts such as government bond futures and equity options and even more important for certain commodity, metal and oil futures contracts, where relatively complicated delivery processes make take several days to for the parties to complete.

SPAN Margin System

The method for calculating initial margin varies from clearing house to clearing house and may be different for futures and traded options. In 1988 the CME devised a methodology known as "SPAN". This risk-based margining system is now used by most exchanges for the calculation of the initial margin on futures and options. On a daily basis SPAN automatically generates a range of 16 possible scenarios rechanging market conditions (the "*risk array*") within the boundaries of the risk parameters (eg, scanning risk, volatility change, spread offsets) set by the clearing house. The potential resulting profit or loss under each of the 16 scenarios is calculated for the combined futures and options position portfolio of each clearing member. By comparing all the different individual arrays, SPAN determines the worst possible loss scenario for each specific clearing member portfolio and sets that as the initial margin amount required.

SPAN is a relatively sophisticated risk-based margining system. For example, SPAN calculates the *"delta"* (see later) value of options to convert them to futures contract "equivalents" when calculating any futures/options and inter-month spread margin amounts.

(Note: The *delta* of an option measures the rate of change in option premium relative, or in proportion, to a given change in the underlying asset price. Roughly speaking, a deep in-the-money option has a maximum delta of 1, a far out-of-the-money option has a minimum delta of 0, while an at-the-money option has a delta of exactly 0.5. As time value decreases toward option expiry, the option delta will also be affected.)

Note: Exchanges may use SPAN or other systems or inhouse developed systems to calculate margin calls.

Margin Offsets

Where market participants employ particular spread trading strategies across related contract types, the clearing house may allow certain reductions in the margin requirements to reflect the reduced overall risk of the combined positions. Spread trading involves the use of two or more options and/or futures to create a position combination, or portfolio, which has limited risk. Movements in the market will have a negative impact on one leg of the spread, but a positive impact on the other leg. The most common strategy of this type is the "calendar spread" (eg, Long Jun., Short Sep.). These spread positions attract a significantly lower initial margin requirement than an outright position, where there is no other balancing leg to offset market risk.

Variation Margin (Settlements)

For futures contracts the clearing house operates a daily overnight mark-to-market and settlement process, whereby it pays out profits and collects in losses generated each day, on all futures trading activity. Mark-to-market is done with reference to the official daily settlement price set and published by the exchange at the close of trading session each day. This process generates daily cash flows (payments and receipts) for all clearing members with either open positions or new trading activity. These profit/loss settlement amounts are known as variation margin (VM). In parallel with this daily clearing house process, clearing members themselves will be processing VM settlements in the accounts of all their clients.

An example calculation of VM is as follows:

A client buys 1 Sep NYSE Liffe Long Gilt Future at 110.13 on Jun, 1st.

The client sells the position at 110.42 on Jun. 8th.

The contract size is £100,000 nominal value with a minimum price fluctuation of £0.01 per £100 nominal. This gives a tick size of £10.

Date	Trade price	Net open	Closing price	Daily price movement	Settlement date	Daily settlement
1/06	110.13	+1	110.09	− 4 ticks	2/06	£40 Loss
2/06		+1	110.28	+ 19 ticks	3/06	£190.Profit
3/06		+1	110.28	No change	4/06	No Movement
4/06		+1	110.35	+ 7 ticks	5/06	£70 Profit
5/06		+1	110.40	+ 5 ticks	8/06	£50 Profit
8/06	110.42	0		+ 2 ticks	9/06	£20 Profit
TOTAL				+ 29 ticks		£290 Profit

The overall profit on the trade was 29 ticks, which is the difference between the buying and selling price; (29 × £10 per tick = £290). The daily variation margin amount is always settled by the clearing members with the clearing house in cash in the currency of the contract on T + 1.

As in the above example, an initial margin of £500 (assuming £500 is the applicable initial margin requirement for LIFFE Long Gilt contract) would also be called by the clearing house on Jun. 2nd and held until Jun. 9th when it would be returned.

Collateral

Initial, but not variation, margin obligations to a clearing house may be covered in various ways, depending on the specific clearing house regulations. As mentioned earlier, cash in the currency of the contract traded is most commonly used form of collateral. However, government treasury bills are also commonly deposited with clearing houses (particularly in the United States). More rarely certificates of deposits, certain equities and approved bank guarantees may also be acceptable by some clearing houses.

The form of collateral that a clearing member will accept from their client is negotiable between the parties. However, there may be restrictions about usage of such collateral and additional transaction costs to be borne by the client. If applicable, the client may have to check with their trustees about whether they have any additional restrictions. By physically transferring the collateral into the name of the clearing member or clearing house, the client loses legal title but not the "beneficial ownership" of the collateral. If this transfer of the asset as collateral is made under hypothecation, the taker of that collateral can only use it if the giver of the collateral fails to meet an obligation (defaults). However, if the agreement between the giver and taker of the collateral allows rehypothecation, the taker can use this collateral. This gives rise to a credit risk with the clearing member, as the collateral provided could be used to cover (say) a loan between the clearing member and a counterparty and may be seized in the event of a default by that organization, even though the client is not involved in the default situation. All noncash collateral lodged with any clearing house will be subject to a "haircut" or discount when being valued. A typical haircut for equity collateral may be 30–50%; (eg, a stock priced at 100 would have a collateral value of between only 50 and 70).

Margining Customers

It is relatively easy to understand the concept and calculation of variation margin. Nearly all corporate customers and other market end users will calculate the daily profit and loss amounts generated by their trading activities, using their own inhouse trading and accounting systems. These figures can be readily reconciled with those of their clearing broker, as reflected on the daily (online) statements they receive.

However the initial margin calculations of the clearing house and clearing member firms are much harder for customers to replicate, unless their positions are very simple without options and intermonth or intercontract spreads to include in their portfolio margin calculations. Therefore, although risk based margining systems (such as SPAN) are very efficient and result in the client depositing a lower overall initial margin, clients generally have to accept that the clearing broker's calculated amount is correct. In order for the client to accurately verify the initial margin required, they would need to receive the daily risk arrays from all the relevant clearing houses and have their inhouse system capability to compute the figures; which for many clients is not cost effective. For much larger volume clients, a solution is for them to buy an established commercial futures back-office software package for their own processing and accounting. This software is expensive but has all the margining capability required.

Single Currency Margining and Settlement

For fund clients trading in various different markets around the world and working with a high number of settlement currencies, the settlement process can be quite cumbersome. Therefore, many clearing brokers offer a service known as "single currency margining."

This facility involves the deposit of only one currency by the client, which is equal to or more than the total equivalent amount of all the currency settlements due to the broker. In order to calculate this, each currency is notionally converted to the base currency chosen by the client as the preferred settlement currency. Interest would normally be received on the currency deposited and would be charged on the other currencies which are in debit/overdraft. Both the clearing broker and the client take on an intraday FX risk, as the amount due in the settlement currency is only calculated once overnight, using the end of day FX rates. Where this service is offered to many clients, it needs careful control by the clearing broker's operations team to ensure that the FX exposures are properly managed. Cash held in any other currency than the selected base currency may be subject to a valuation haircut.

Although no specific fee may be levied for this service, clearing brokers will recoup their expenses through the interest rates that are paid and received. While such rates need to be relatively competitive, in order to make the service viable, they are designed to cover at least any financing costs that the broker incurs on behalf of the client. From the client's point of view it may make the settlement process more efficient; in particular reducing bank charges and administration for foreign currency transactions.

Treasury Management

As discussed above, initial margin requirements, and the collateral used to cover them, are vital to controlling risk. The margin and treasury management implications regarding funding costs, cash utilization, foreign exchange risk, etc. will become more important as the use of derivatives by an investment fund grows. From a regulatory point of view, the efficient management of margin calls enforces discipline on the operations teams of the clearing brokers, who must cover the nonreceipt of margin from a (defaulting) client using its own funds.

With a variety of acceptable collateral available, market participants need to carefully assess the most efficient alternatives of meeting the margin calls from their clearing broker. It is important to note that most clearing houses margin their clearing members on a net basis, that is, the initial margin requirement for a clearing broker will be based on the broker's overall net position after offsetting any equal and opposite, long and short positions held for all the broker's clients. The broker holds positions on a gross basis and collects margin from every client, thus creating a pool of client cash (and collateral) held by the clearing broker, which is not passed on to the central clearing house. With efficient treasury management this excess client cash, the interest rate spread earned provides important additional revenue. An effective treasury management function within the fund is about the administrator and custodian producing accurate and timely information about all aspects of the margining process, in addition to all the other cash flow and FX issues affecting the cash flow of the fund on a day-to-day basis.

Interest Rate Calculations

For all futures and options market participants including investment funds, the disciplines associated with treasury management include the regular monitoring of interest rates applicable to both the accounts they maintain with their clearing broker(s) and/or central clearing house and, if applicable, the accounts they maintain for their fund customers—in each case potentially across multiple currencies. In most cases interest rates are not symmetrical between credit and debit balances; with market participants charged for maintaining overdraft account balances in any currency. Errors regarding interest rate setting and interest rate changes are not uncommon; these mistakes can lead to unexpected funding costs and financial loss as well as disputes between brokers and clients, if regular monitoring and checking procedures are not put in place.

We can now look more specifically at the use of derivatives by investment funds.

Usage of Futures and Options in Investment Management

There are many ways in which derivative products may be used in investment management. For each fund entity, the specific investment strategy and objectives, mandate guidelines, and restrictions, as well as actual market conditions, will determine trading activity and product selection. In this section, we look at some basic examples of different ways that fund managers can use futures and options.

Stock index futures are particularly flexible tools for equity investment management. Fund managers can use them to protect the value of a portfolio in a falling stock market; to provide a leveraged investment at a time of bullish sentiment; to enhance yields; to allocate assets easily, cheaply, and quickly; and to track the performance of indices. A fund manager who has an underlying portfolio of shares whose performance is correlated with the index and whose value he wishes to protect against falls in the market, can sell futures contracts. In this way the fund manager removes the market risk from all or part of his total position, such that the fund will profit or lose to the extent that the portfolio out-performs or under-performs the underlying market.

Pension Funds

Pension funds own significant holdings in many of the UK's largest quoted companies. In order to manage the risks of these holdings against the value of share prices falling, the pension fund manager can look to using the NYSE. Liffe FTSE100 index futures contract. If a pension fund manager's analysis of the UK stock market concluded that it was likely to fall in the next six months, they can take one of two actions;

1. Select some of the shares and sell them in the market before the value goes down, with a view to buying them back at a later date at a cheaper price; or
2. Sell FTSE100 futures with a six month delivery date immediately with a view to buying them back at a later date at a cheaper price.

On the surface there does not appear to be a lot of difference in these two strategies. However, there are some important differences, which make the selling of the futures contracts a much more viable choice.

- The FTSE100 futures contract represents the value of the whole FTSE100 companies whereas if the pension fund manager wanted to sell shares he would have to choose which specific stocks to sell and how many of each.
- Selling the shares may take time and will involve some dealing costs. Share dealing costs may be up to 1% against possibly 0.1% for futures.
- FTSE100 index futures can be bought or sold very quickly in one transaction.
- FTSE100 futures do not disturb the underlying shareholdings—an attractive feature for pension funds where investments are held for the longer term.

- Futures also help the manager to smooth out fluctuations in the value of the fund. Investors find this reassuring.

If the pension fund manager is correct and the value of the UK stock market falls over the six months then he can buy back the futures contracts at the lower value. The profit from this transaction would be used to offset the fall in value of the underlying shares, thus protecting the value of the portfolio.

If the pension fund manager gets it wrong and the value of the stock market rises, he can buy back the futures contracts. The loss made on this transaction would be offset against the rise in value of the underlying portfolio. Of course he will not make as much profit in this case as he would have done without the futures contracts hedge in place, but he has the advantage of the temporary protection (or insurance) against the possible fall in value, without disturbing the portfolio. Indeed, the pension fund manager can close out his futures position at any time during the six months if he feels that it is right to do so, thus limiting his losses. He is not locked in for the full six months.

Basic Illustration of Derivatives Use in Asset Allocation

Investment opportunities often arise quickly and unpredictably. Fund managers wishing to take advantage of such events would traditionally have had to liquidate part of their existing holdings in order to reinvest the proceeds elsewhere; this is costly and time consuming exercise. Index futures contracts offer a cheap, quick, and efficient method of shifting exposure from one market to another.

Example: A fund manager has a portfolio made up of US, UK, and Japanese equity shares, plus UK Gilt stocks and cash. The fund's portfolio is currently made up of 40% US equities, 20% UK equities, 20% UK Gilt stock, 10% Japanese equities and 10% cash.

The fund manager believes that the US equity market is due a fall and that Japan will rise. He expects this to occur in the next six to eight weeks. The fund manager can adjust the balance of the portfolio by selling US shares and purchasing stocks in Japanese companies. He will need to research both markets to determine which shares to buy and sell and then execute the transactions needed, which all takes time to implement. Dealing costs will be incurred on each transaction.

Alternatively the fund manager can use derivatives, in this case index futures, to gain and reduce exposure to the respective markets. He needs to sell S&P Index futures contracts and purchase Nikkei Index futures. If he is correct in his assumptions, the sale of the S&P futures will offset the fall in value of the US equities he holds while the Nikkei futures will rise enabling the fund to participate in the increase.

There are several advantages for the fund manager.

- The futures transactions are very quick to effect with low dealing costs.
- Exposure adjustment is immediate, thus reducing the risk of loss should the market move before the relevant shares can be sold and bought.
- The futures transactions can be quickly reversed if the assumptions are wrong.

- The fund manager can still affect the actual sale/purchase of the underlying shares when he is ready (unwinding the futures trades at the same time).

Note:

Before a manager uses this strategy he should first ensure that his portfolio closely matches the index. Each index consists of a number of individual stocks, which are "weighted" according to their capitalization. If the manager's portfolio differs from the index portfolio he may be exposed to "basis" risk when the two portfolios react differently to changes in market; (see also "Part 2—OTC Derivatives").

Income Enhancement

A fund manager buys or holds significant amounts of equity shares. He is happy to sell some of these holdings at certain levels and would like to increase income over and above the dividend if possible. He looks to the traded options market.

Example: He has purchased 500,000 BP shares at 600 p and will be happy to sell half of the holding if the stock rises more than 10%. He notes that the 650 call options expiring in two months can be sold for 25 p. He sells 250 contracts (1000 shares per contract) at 25 p. The fund manager has given the right to the option buyer to call/buy the 250,000 shares at 650 p anytime in the next two months in return for £62,500 (250 × 1000 × 25 p) of premium paid to him immediately.

If the stock rises above 650 p he may have to deliver the stock at 650 p. If it does not rise above 650 p he will not have to deliver the stock.

In the first scenario, he has effectively sold the stock for 675 p (650 + 25) which meets his criteria of selling on a 10%+ share rise. But note that his profit is restricted to the difference between 600 p and 675 p, no matter to what price the stock rises. In the second scenario, he still has the stock but has received income of £62,500 or looked at another way he has reduced the purchase price to 575 p. This means he is protected against a fall to this level on half of his holding.

Hedging

The fund manager is reviewing his portfolio and is concerned that the UK stock market may fall in the short term. However he does not wish to change the weighting in the portfolio nor any form of asset allocation or to sell his shares. He looks at two possibilities. First he can sell FTSE futures contracts, which will provide him with a profit as the market falls thereby offsetting the fall in value of the stocks (as seen earlier). Second he could buy a three-month FTSE Put option.

With the futures contracts, the fund manager risks incurring a loss if the market should rise until he decides to close the position. With the put option he can determine how much the "insurance" against a fall in the market will cost and has the comfort that if the market should rise he will never pay more than the original cost of the option.

Index stands at 5960 on January 3rd

The March Futures contract is trading at 5975

The FTSE Feb 5950 Put is quoted at 50 p

Scenario One: Fund manager sells 2 FTSE futures contracts @ 5975.
Market *rises* to 6010 by mid Feb. and fund manager decides the market will
not fall and buys 2 contracts at 6050 to close the position.
Outcome—The hedge has cost the fund manager 2×75 points or 150 ticks
$(6050-5975) \times £10 = £1500$

Scenario Two: Fund manager buys 2 Feb 5950 Puts @ 50 p
Market rises to 6010 by mid Feb.
The 5950 Puts are priced at 10 p
Outcome—The hedge has cost the fund manager £1000 in option premium
paid to open the position. If he closes the position by selling the put option
he receives £200, a net cost of £800 excluding dealing fees.

Both strategies gave protection against a *Fall* in the market. The put option
restricted the cost of the hedge against a *Rise* in the market. However bear in mind
that while there is a loss occurring on the futures position as the index rises, the value of the stock has increased to compensate. With the option, the rise in the stock
prices accrues to the portfolio once the £1000 outlay has been compensated for.

These are very simplistic examples and the decision on whether to use futures or options to hedge a portfolio or stock will be made taking into account
many factors. In both cases the position could be quickly closed out if desired.
In the above examples, we have seen how the fund manager can disperse or
minimize the impact of risk on his portfolio.

Index Tracking

Index Tracker funds perform to their benchmark equity market indices and a
such a fund can match the performance of a given index by simply buying and
rolling over the relevant equity index futures positions to provide the exposure
required in combination with the interest earned on the fund's cash, without the
cost and difficulty of buying the underlying basket of shares.

If the fund has set a target investment objective of index performance plus
x%, then sophisticated fund investment strategies have been designed in which
futures and options are used in combination with other instruments to both enhance yields and reduce risk.

OTC DERIVATIVES

Introduction

The over-the-counter derivatives market is extremely large; the notional value
of outstanding OTC derivative contracts is enormous with nearly $20 bn at 31st
Dec. 2015 in credit default swaps alone. (see Appendices for statistics related
to various products).

There is no useful means of comparing the size of the OTC derivative market with that of the exchange traded derivative market, but suffice to say both are vast and also closely related to one another. In terms of notional value, by far the largest segment of the OTC derivative market comprises interest rate swaps, followed by currency swaps and options, currency forwards and interest rate options. Although credit derivatives attracted all the negative headlines during the financial market meltdown in 2008, they represent as noted above a fair chunk of outstanding OTC derivative notional value. OTC equity swaps and options and OTC commodity swaps and options are the other main product categories, albeit much smaller than the other categories mentioned earlier.

The OTC derivative markets are constantly evolving with new product innovations being introduced on a frequent basis. Indeed over the last 10–15 years credit derivatives (see later) have grown to become a very important derivative market, having previously been almost unknown.

ISDA is at the heart of the OTC derivatives market. ISDA was founded in 1985 by a group of 25 banks, which were already active in the fledgling interest rate swap market. Since then ISDA has worked very successfully to make the global OTC derivative markets more efficient and safer and the association provides continuous guidance and commentary regarding the latest OTC derivative market developments (see www.isda.org). ISDA now has over 800 member institutions from 62 countries including a broad range of derivative market participants.

To quote from the ISDA website:

> *"ISDA's pioneering work in developing the ISDA Master Agreement and a wide range of related documentation materials, and in ensuring the enforceability of their netting and collateral provisions, has helped to significantly reduce credit and legal risk."*

However, the 2008 market crash highlighted some serious transparency issues and systemic risks within the OTC derivatives markets and led to a major review and overhaul of the OTC space by government regulators, particularly in the United States and Europe; initiatives which have received strong support from ISDA members as well. In the United States, the Federal Reserve toughened up its regulatory supervision of the US banking sector with a range of initiatives specifically targeted at reducing credit and operational risks in the OTC derivative markets. A range of new directives have emerged since 2008, including the Dodd-Frank Act in the United States and the Markets in Financial Instruments Directive (MiFID) and Alternative Investment Fund Managers Directive (AIFMD) in Europe. In Europe the new European Market Infrastructure Directive (EMIR) is having an even more far reaching impact as the regulators seek to make OTC transactions more standardized and transacted on centralized trading systems wherever possible. An additional new requirement is that OTC transactions should be recorded with some form of central trade repository and reported to the local regulator.

On both sides of the Atlantic the regulators are pushing for OTC transactions, at least those between banks (to start with), to be voluntarily cleared (and margined) by a central counterparty (CCP), or clearing house, in a similar way to how exchange traded futures and options have always been cleared in the past. In the three years (2011–13) significant progress was made toward this goal with major growth in the clearing of interest rate swaps through Swapclear (run by LCH.Clearnet) and EurexOTC Clear and also of credit default swaps (CDS) through CME and, to a lesser extent, ICE Clear.

The main different types of OTC derivative product are described in more detail later.

1. *Differences from exchange-traded products*

We have seen earlier how exchange traded products are standardized in the form of futures and options contracts and how they are actively traded on screen based trading systems in the secondary market (ie, you buy can a futures contract from one party and then sell it in the market to someone else, to close out your position).

However the standardization of exchange traded futures and options contracts (in terms of contract size, maturity, and underlying asset specification) is often a disadvantage to their use as hedging instruments, as the standardized terms may not accurately match the existing market exposure that needs to be hedged by the end user. In addition, depending on the market conditions and liquidity, a better buy/sell price may be achievable in the OTC market than on-exchange (or vice versa).

Example: A fund manager has a portfolio of UK equity shares in combination of FTSE100 stocks and smaller companies and wants to hedge his portfolio for 12 months. The value of the portfolio is £2,425,000 and the FTSE100 index future is currently trading at 5823.5.

If the fund manager decides to use the FTSE100 index future there are some problems.

1. The most liquid futures contract will be the nearest maturity, a maximum of only 3 months away. Therefore the futures position will need to be "rolled" over through different several quarterly maturities in the course of the twelve month hedge period.
2. The FTSE100 index future will not reflect any change in value of those smaller companies in his portfolio that are not in the index. Thus the price correlation between the index futures contract and the fund portfolio may not be good enough for a hedging transaction.
3. The number of contracts required to hedge the portfolio would be:

$$\frac{\text{Portfolio}}{(£10 \times \text{index point})} = \frac{2,425,000}{(£10 \times 5823.5)}$$

$$\frac{2,425,000}{58235} = 41.64 \text{ contracts}$$

You cannot trade part contracts, so the fund manager must trade either 41 or 42 contracts. In either case the portfolio is not precisely hedged.

It is because of these types of issue (and others) that hedgers often look to arrange an OTC deal with another counterparty, usually a dealer bank that is tailored to meet their precise hedging requirements. On the other hand the fund manager recognizes that an OTC transaction may involve additional credit risk (on the OTC dealer counterparty) and liquidity risk, in that the position cannot easily be closed out if the fund manager later changes his mind.

In general, unlike exchange traded futures and options, once transacted between two counterparties, most OTC derivative contracts will be held to maturity (in the case of forwards or swaps) or expiry (in the case of OTC options). However it may be possible to negotiate the terms and price for an "early termination" of the swap or option with the original counterparty. Alternatively an early termination may be achieved through the negotiation of a novation of the existing swap or option to a third party. In practice many participants will simply reduce their net market exposure by entering into another equivalent but opposite bargain with the same or different counterparty, albeit that this may increase both the associated operations work required and the number of counterparties (and credit risks) involved.

Both OTC and exchange traded derivatives (ETD) are often used by the same organizations and the choice of product will depend on the trade price, trade size, strategy, risk appetite, liquidity, dealing costs, and market conditions at the time.

	Derivative product	
Characteristics	OTC	ETD
Contract terms	Tailored, negotiated, very flexible and confidential.	Standardized quantity, grade and maturity. Some product types not available on exchange.
Contract documentation	Trade confirmation supported by ISDA Master Agreement, definitions and schedules.	Standard contract specification published by futures/options exchange.
Maturity/ Delivery	Negotiable dates. Most trades held to maturity.	Defined delivery dates. Most contracts are closed out before maturity.
Price transparency	Can be limited, often depend on quote comparisons from different OTC dealers.	Full, last trade price and bid/offer spread displayed on screen.
Cost transparency	None. Dealer spread/costs built into price quoted.	Full. Negotiated commissions agreed in advance, plus published exchange fees.
Liquidity	Variable. May be better than exchanges for very large trades and long term maturities. But can take time to negotiate and be limited by available counterparties.	Variable. Price and time priority regardless of order size. Instant execution for all major contracts with near term maturities. But many listed products with less liquidity.

	Derivative product	
Characteristics	OTC	ETD
Credit risk	Risk is with selected counterparty to OTC transaction. But collateral can be used to mitigate the risk. *Since 2008 crash more OTC products are being centrally cleared.*	Clearing broker (or central clearing house) becomes counterparty to all trades and manages risk through daily revaluations and margin calls. Original trade counterparty irrelevant.

With the terms of OTC derivatives being customized and negotiated between counterparties, the operations function is much less automated and routine than that required to process and settle exchange traded products. Instead of standardized daily margin and settlement processes and procedures, there is periodic settlement (usually monthly or quarterly) and more event driven procedures. We will illustrate these differences as we look at some of the derivative products traded OTC in more detail later.

Products

Forwards

As defined in Part I above, forwards are very similar to futures contracts. Although a few forward contract types are traded on exchange (eg, London Metal Exchange), the bulk of all forwards trading occurs OTC, in particular with respect to foreign exchange and bulk commodities. OTC forwards are settled only on the delivery date (payment against delivery of the underlying currency or physical commodity), or on a predetermined date during the life of the forward contract. The largest forward market in the world by far is that for global foreign exchange, which is traded by phone (and online) on a bilateral OTC basis, through myriad banks and brokers.

While open forward positions can be revalued on a daily basis, for accounting, valuation, and risk management purposes, any profits or losses accrued are not paid out until the settlement date of the forward contract. This applies even if the position is effectively "closed out" by a new equal and opposite trade (at a different price) prior to the settlement day.

Note: The LME is in effect an exchange regulated and cleared forward market, where most of the trading is done on an OT style phone basis, but all the resulting contracts and open positions are then registered with a clearing house, by which initial margin requirements are calculated and profits and losses are settled.

Forward Rate Agreements

A forward rate agreement (FRA) is an agreement to pay or receive, on an agreed future date, the difference between a fixed interest rate at the outset and a reference interest rate prevailing at a given date for an agreed period. FRA's are transacted between buyers who agree to the fixed rate and sellers who agree to the floating rate or benchmark.

Example: Suppose a manufacturer needs to borrow £5m in one month's time and needs the loan for a period of three months. Concerned about interest rates rising, the manufacturer decides to buy a FRA that will fix the effective borrowing rate today, even though they have no wish to borrow the money now when it is not needed.

The terms of the FRA are that the fixed rate is 5.25% and the benchmark is LIBOR. It will start in one months time and finish three months later and would be known as a "one versus four" FRA. In one month's time the calculation of the settlement of the FRA can take place. The prevailing 11.00 am LIBOR is 5.5%.

The formula used to calculate settlement is:

Notional Principal Amount $\times$ (Fixed Rate $-$ LIBOR) $\times$ days in FRA period/days in year divided by $(1 + ($LIBOR $\times$ days in FRA period/days in year$))$

Calculation

$$£5,000,000 \times (0.0525 - 0.055) \times 91 / 365 \text{ over} (1 + (0.055 \times 91 / 365)) = £3,074.28$$

The LIBOR rate was higher than the fixed rate so the buyer (the manufacturer) receives this amount from the seller. There is no exchange of the £5 m, the manufacturer will borrow the money from a lending source and the money received from the FRA will offset the higher borrowing costs of around 5.5%. Had LIBOR been lower than the fixed rate, the manufacturer would have paid the difference to the seller but of course would borrow the money at a lower rate. The manufacturer "locked" in a rate of 5.25% for their planned future borrowing.

As far as settlement is concerned, the amount due is known on the settlement date, the date at which the FRA period starts (ie, 1 month time) and the calculation period is known (3 months). Unlike most transactions that settle on maturity a FRA can be settled at the beginning of the calculation period. The amount may be discounted to reflect the interest that would accrue if the amount paid was deposited to the end of the FRA period.

SWAPS

As mentioned previously, swaps are the most widely used OTC derivative product. As defined in Part I, swaps involve the exchanging of one future cash flow for a different future cash flow, where both flows are calculated by reference to an agreed notional amount of an agreed asset, entity, or benchmark. The most common examples of swaps are: interest rate swaps, currency swaps, commodity swaps, and equity swaps.

Interest Rate Swaps ("IRS")

An IRS is an agreement to swap, over an agreed period, two payment streams each calculated using a different interest rates (typically fixed versus floating) but based on the same notional principal amount. By using an IRS, a company can change their future interest rate exposure (eg, from floating to fixed) in advance for a specific period, typically 1–10 years.

Fixed rate

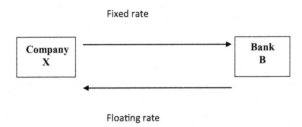

Floating rate

During the life ("*term*") of the above swap there will be periodic settlements of the netted payment flows on "*payment date,*" calculated at what is known as "*reset dates*" (eg, quarterly semiannually, or annually) and valued against the benchmark rate(s). The payments cannot be netted at each reset date if the payment dates are different, for example, where the fixed rate is paid annually but the floating rate is paid semiannually.

An IRS is transacted to start immediately, or at a forward date, and will run for the agreed period. The start date is known as the "*effective date*" and the end date is known as the "*termination date.*" The floating rate is reset at the effective date for the next period, and then at reset dates for the following period throughout the term of the swap.

Suppose a company XYZ currently pays a floating rate of interest, say LIBOR + 0.4% for a loan of $10m over 5 years. Concerned that rates will rise, the treasurer wants to change the payment flow to a fixed rate but is unable to alter the terms of the loan. Company XYZ approaches Bank ABC and agrees a five year IRS, the terms of which are that:

Company XYZ will pay 6.3% fixed, paid annually on an ACT/360 basis and receive LIBOR, semiannually on an ACT/360 basis. If at the beginning of the swap LIBOR is 6%, than at the end of the first six months the floating-rate payment is:

$10,000,000 × 6.00% × 181/360 = $301,667, which is paid by Bank ABC to Company XYZ [Note: there is no netted payment against the fixed rate cash flow for the period, as the terms state that the fixed rate leg only settles annually.]

At the beginning of the next six months LIBOR is 6.25% and after that second six month period the swap payments are:

Floating: $10,000,000 × 6.25% × 184/360 = $319,444 (due by Bank ABC to Company XYZ).

Fixed: $10,000,000 × 6.30% × 365/360 = $638,750 (due from company XYZ to Bank ABC).

This time the settlement can be netted so that Company XYZ pays $319,306 to Bank ABC.

In this IRS Company XYZ has a risk as their view on interest rates over the next five years may be wrong and rates might actually fall, not rise. By agreeing to pay a fixed rate, in this case 6.3%, their cost of borrowing may end up higher than it would have been, if they had not entered into the swap. *Note: In a CCP cleared swap the settlement flows pass through the CCP.*

Currency Swap

A currency swap is simply a specific type of IRS. A currency swap involves the exchange of a series of cash flows in one currency for a series of cash flows in another currency, at agreed intervals over an agreed period, with both cash flows calculated by reference to specific interest rates.

It is possible to have a combination of fixed and floating rates in two currencies in a currency swap; for example,

- Fixed interest in one currency against floating rate in another currency.
- Fixed interest in one currency against fixed interest in another.
- Floating rate in one currency against floating interest in another.

Unlike an IRS where there is no exchange of the principal amount, with a currency swap there may (or may not) be a negotiated exchange of the principal amounts at both the beginning and end of the swap term, at an FX rate agreed at the beginning.

Example: A UK company plans to expand its business in the United States and needs to borrow USD to do so. The company believes it can borrow money (albeit GBP) much cheaper in the UK (where it is well known to its bankers). To facilitate its currency requirements the company can negotiate a currency swap.

The UK company borrows British Pounds (GBP) on a floating rate basis from its own bank and then swaps this GBP principal amount for USD with the swap bank counterparty. It might agree to pay a fixed rate of interest on the USD and receive a floating rate of interest on the GBP, which it uses to pay the floating rate interest on the original GBP loan from its bank.

It agrees to exchange the principal amounts at the beginning of the term at an agreed FX rate and decide to fund the future repayment of the GBP loan, (which is a totally separate transaction from the swap) from its own resources.

The USD amount is invested in its US business and the subsequent income stream is used to pay the swap counterparty the fixed rate interest on the USD leg of the swap. During the swap term, which will correspond to the loan duration, the payment streams will be settled on reset dates. They are not netted because they are in different currencies.

This currency swap has provided the company with protection against foreign exchange movements during the period of the swap and protection against interest rate movements in the UK market rate during the period of its borrowing.

OTC Options

As specific terms can be freely customized and negotiated between counterparties, OTC options vary significantly in their terms and complexity. At one end of the spectrum there are simple "vanilla" OTC options that look very similar to the standardized exchange traded options described in Part I. At the other end of the spectrum are complex "exotic" options, or option combinations, that build in additional characteristics and variables that can change the relatively simple call and put profit and loss outcomes. Although some common OTC option types and related jargon are briefly described ahead, there is no substitute for reviewing the specific option terms on a case-by-case basis.

Common OTC Option Types

- *Calls and Puts* with specific customized amounts and durations negotiated between the two parties, for example, a £1.1 m, two year call option on the FTSE100 index at a strike of 5905.2.
- *Interest Rate Guarantee (IRG)* is an option on a FRA.
- *Swaption* is an option to enter into a swap. Like all options it gives the buyer the right, but not the obligation, to enter into the swap at or before the expiry date of the swaption.
- *European, American, and Bermudan* style options, which have a variety of different exercise characteristics; (ie, exercise at expiry only, at any time prior to expiry, or only at specific times prior to expiry).
- *Asian, average rate, or average price options*, which use different benchmarks rather than the price of the underlying asset on expiry to determine if they are in- or out-of-the-money (eg, the average price of the underlying asset over the last month).
- *Barrier options* refer to a family of different options, which are either cancelled or activated if the underlying price reaches a predetermined level. They are also known as *knock-out, knock-in* or *trigger* options.
- *Caps and floors* refer to a related series of call or put options with sequential expiry dates over a predetermined period. Commonly used to manage interest rate exposures; for example, "capping" the interest rate payable, or fixing a "floor" to the interest rate receivable. May be linked to a series of "rollover" rates agreed, whereby the difference in rates is paid, if applicable at the time of the rollover.
- *Collars* refer to a combination of buying a cap and selling a floor (or vice versa) in order to maintain a price or interest rate between two limit levels while minimizing the net premium cost payable/receivable.

We also have *Puttable* and *Callable* swaps, which allow the fixed rate receiver and fixed rate payer respectively to terminate the swap early. They are traded with European, American, and Bermudan styles of exercise right.

Another popular product used by some investment managers is a total return swap.

Total Return Swap

As the name implies, a total return swap is a swap of the total return out of a credit asset against an agreed fixed return. The total return out of a credit asset can be affected by various factors, some of which may be quite unconnected to the asset in question, such as interest rate movements, exchange rate fluctuations etc. Nevertheless, the protection seller guarantees a fixed return to the originator, who in turn, agrees to pass on the entire collections (both income and capital gain/loss) from the credit asset to the protection seller. That is to say, the protection buyer swaps the total return from a credit asset for a negotiated predetermined fixed return.

Also popular in hedging issuer risk is a credit default swap.

Credit Default Swap

A credit default swap (CDS) is not a swap at all, but much more akin to a re-fined form of a traditional financial guarantee or insurance. As with insurance the protection buyer is required to pay premium (either upfront or on regular preset quarterly dates) to the protection seller. If within the agreed period of protection, a predefined "credit event" occurs the protection seller is obliged to pay the protection buyer a compensation amount as defined in the terms of the CDS. The terms of a CDS need not be limited to compensation only upon an actual default (of a reference security or entity), but may also cover other types of credit event such as the downgrading of the issuer of specific security. Credit default swaps cover only the credit risk inherent in the specified security or asset (as defined in the CDS terms), while price risks due to other factors such as market sentiment or interest rate movements remain with the originator.

Contracts for Differences (Equities)

Contracts for differences (CFD's) have become popular over the last 10 years, especially among professional traders and sophisticated retail investors. There are a number of specialist CFD broker-dealers (normally equity market-makers) with whom CFD "customers" can trade. A CFD is a contract to receive (or pay) the difference in value on an agreed quantity of shares, in a specific listed company, between the agreed share price on the day when the CFD deal is opened and the subsequent share price on the day when the CFD deal is closed out. The market risk on the CFD transaction exactly matches that of the underlying company shares to which it is referenced, including equivalent dividend payments (by CFD seller) and receipts (by CFD buyer).

CFD transactions have no fixed maturity date (ie, no time limit) and are not closed until the customer wishes to do so (or in the rare event of a customer default). At no point does the customer ever take or make delivery of the underlying shares.

The CFD broker-dealer requires a margin deposit, typically 10% of the underlying, to protect themselves from the risk of the customer defaulting on the

CFD. The position is marked-to-market daily and the broker may call for additional margin. Charges include a commission and a cost-of-carry charge based in the underlying amount.

The main advantages and disadvantages in using CFD's are:

- No stamp duty
- The ability to go short
- Leverage through trading on margin
- The opportunity to trade shares which are not listed on a futures or option exchange
- Daily mark-to-market and settlement of losses
- Commission and financing costs payable to the CFD dealer
- No voting rights

Settlement of OTC Products

The settlement procedures for OTC derivatives are determined by the terms of the transaction negotiated agreed between the two counterparties, as set out in the trade confirmation and any associated supporting documentation and or the CCP. In practice, thanks in large part to the work of ISDA, most OTC derivative dealers now use very standardized terms, language, and definitions in their trade documentation, which has simplified the settlement process and reduced the number of exceptions. Indeed complete standardization of derivative trade and settlement terms is achieved for those IRS and CDS transactions where the two trade counterparties agree to register and clear it through a CCP (eg, Swapclear, ICE Clear, etc.). As a result the market now has evolved to a point where there are relatively standard settlement characteristics for the main OTC products types.

Operational or settlement events are triggered by such things as the:

- Effective date, reset date, and payment date for IRS.
- Settlement dates and calculation periods for FRAs, equity and commodity swaps.
- Premium payment dates for options and CDS.
- Exercise notifications and trigger events for options.
- Maturity/expiry of all products.

In general most products settle at the end of a period or on maturity, with the exception of FRAs and IRGs where the settlement takes place using a discounted present value of the future cash flows.

Key to the settlement of OTC products is the terms of the transaction. Unlike exchange traded futures and options where the terms are stipulated, each OTC trade is effectively a new set of terms, even though the product may be the same each time. All OTC derivative trades should be supported by documentation that ensures that the terms of the derivative transaction are fully disclosed and understood.

In the past, documentation was a major obstacle to the use of OTC derivatives, as each trade had a separate agreement. These agreements had to be vetted by the legal department by both parties and consequent delays and disputes caused considerable problems. ISDA have greatly helped to resolve the problems by developing standard documents for use by counterparties for many types of OTC derivative product. The British Bankers Association has also developed standard documentation for FRAs.

The standard ISDA document negotiated between the two parties (before their first trade) is known as a "Master Agreement." This key agreement can later be supplemented with schedules, annexes, and appendices to cover any additional issues and trades that are agreed between the parties.

The ISDA master documents cover all the legal terms and conditions that are relevant for both parties, in particular with respect to their rights and obligations in respect to the netting of any OTC transactions executed between them. These provisions include:

- Legal entities and multibranch facilities
- Payment netting provisions
- Default procedures and rights of set-off
- Termination events
- Warranties, covenants, and representations
- Tax indemnities
- Assignment
- Legal jurisdiction
- Waiver of immunities
- Notices

Confirmations

For every OTC transaction executed outside of a trading system, a confirmation document (either electronic or paper) is generated by one or both of the counterparties as evidence of all the specific commercial terms of the trade. The confirmation excludes all the general terms under which business is being transacted between the two counterparties, as these matters will already have been preagreed in the ISDA Master Agreement.

The confirmation sets out the key trade details to be reconciled (see example). Confirmations should be issued by one counterparty (the bank dealer issuing the OTC product), as quickly as possible so that the trade details can be checked and "affirmed" by the other party. Affirmation can be evidenced either by the return of a signed copy of the initial confirmation, or the receipt of a separate confirmation from the other party. Where no affirmation is quickly forthcoming, the counterparty should be chased up, as the confirmation is not legally enforceable until both parties have acknowledged that the details of the trade have been agreed. [Note: Typically two banks participating in a trade will send each other confirmations while a bank and a client trade will result in a confirmation from the bank to the client which the client will then sign and return.] Over the last 10 years the use of online confirmation and affirmation systems has greatly improved efficiency and reduced delays and costs. Ensuring the efficient settlement of OTC products requires a high degree of skill in managing the flow of trade information both at, and immediately after, the time of trade execution. Accurate trade confirmation details are essential to the subsequent position maintenance and periodic settlement of the resultant OTC derivative position, through to the date of maturity or expiry.

Example: FRA confirmation (which will typically be sent via SWIFT) and would contain information such as:

Confirmation from Mega Bank	To: InterBank Inc
Buyer: *Mega Bank*	
Transaction Date	19/06/2012
Effective Date	21/06/2012
Terms	ISDA
Currency/Amount	GBP 3,000,000
Fixing	19/09/2012
Settlement	21/09/2012
Maturity Date	21/12/2012
Contract Period	91 days
Contract Rate	2.79% pa on a actual/360 basis

Example: IRS confirmation for a fixed/floating swap transaction would contain information such as:

Confirmation from Mega Bank	To: Interbank Inc
Interest Rate swaps	
Transaction Date	19/06/2012
Effective Date	21/06/2012
Maturity Date	21/12/2012
Terms	ISDA
Currency/Amount	UDS 5,000,000
We pay	2.76%
Frequency	Annual
Calculation Basis	Actual/365
We receive	6-Month LIBOR
Frequency	Semiannual
Calculation Basis	Actual/360

There are other pieces of information that may be added to this, such as frequency being modified following convention.

The global OTC derivative market is rapidly automating to improve the way the industry operates. There is significant pressure on OTC dealers to increase efficiency and decrease operational and compliance costs, in part driven by new regulatory requirements. One of the main communication platforms is MarkitSERV. MarkitSERV was originally created from systems collaboration between

Markit and DTC. This system provides posttrade confirmation, allocation, clearing, and regulatory reporting solutions to over 2,000 market participants and 12 OTC clearing houses. MarkitSERV supports all the main OTC derivative product types including CDS, IRS, FRA, FX (forwards and options), equity options, and equity swaps. Increased usage of this type of online system service for trade confirmation/affirmation has significantly reduced the manual processing involved.

Post Trade Environment

There are many processes in the post trade environment that are common to all transactions. These include:

- Trade capture and verification
- Confirmation and affirmation
- Reconciliation
- Position maintenance
- Daily mark-to-market and profit/loss calculation
- Periodic settlement
- Presettlement advice and postsettlement check
- Notification of relevant trigger events
- Closing of transaction at maturity/expiry
- Risk and collateral management

Trade capture and verification requires all the trade details to be input (whether automated or manual) to the back-office systems. From a risk and control point of view, the system must be capable of handling certain key information about a trade such as:

- Title of instrument traded
- Buy or sell (FRAs, options), pay or receive (swaps)
- Currency
- Size of contract (option), notional amounts (FRAs, swaps)
- FX rate, price, rate of premium (two rates in the case of a fixed/fixed rate currency swap)
- Floating rate references
- FX rate agreed for conversions of principal (currency swap)
- Strike price or rate (options)
- Trigger level (barrier option)
- Trade date and time
- Underlying asset (notional amount, security, equity, bond, and commodity)
- Effective date
- Settlement date(s)
- Term and maturity date
- Expiry date (option)
- Exercise styles and dates
- Credit event notification (CDS)
- Day/year calculation basis (swaps)

- Physical/cash settled (options)
- Special conditions, for example, for Asians options
- Trader
- Counterparty
- Deal method, for example, screen, telephone

This list is not exhaustive and certain types of products will need additional information. In cases where the full details cannot be recorded in the main system, additional manual records, processes, and checks must be employed. Details of the settlement instructions, including netting if agreed, will also be input to the system together with information such as the reference sources for fixings and possibly the documentation type (ISDA, BBA) and governing law.

It is important that all this data is captured in the back-office systems so that key reports and information can be supplied to operations, dealers (positions and profits/losses), risk managers, general ledgers, reconciliation systems, etc. There will always be queries related to transactions, settlement, and events and it is important that the respective operations staff at the two parties to the trade work closely together to resolve any problems quickly. This has been highlighted in recent years by the strong guidance issued by the Federal Reserve Board of the United States, and the UK FCA, concerning the length of time taken to match bargains in the OTC credit derivatives market. They were concerned with the number of bargains remaining unmatched for a number of weeks thus exposing both parties to operational and counterparty risk. OTC equity derivatives have come under a similar regulatory spotlight.

Event Calendar

This trade and settlement information also helps to provide a calendar of future OTC events in order for the relevant operations, treasury, and dealing staff to track the settlement events that will be occurring, for example, resets, expiry, settlement dates.

Some events are mandatory obligations of the trades done (and/or automatic), such as those involved with swaps, barrier options, caps, collars and floors, FRAs. Other event types may require an instruction and/or decision by the dealer or client, for example, option exercise, credit default events, early terminations of OTC contracts.

Other Settlement Issues

It is important to regularly (ideally daily) revalue OTC positions for profit/loss reporting purposes and to reconcile all open positions against both the dealers' records and the counterparty's records for overall exposure, limit, and risk control management. A fund with a daily NAV will have to value OTC positions on a daily basis.

The use of collateral in conjunction with OTC trades is also a key risk control, especially where one party has a much lower credit rating than the other. Where collateral has been lodged as part of the risk management process it is important to ensure that the collateral value remains sufficient to cover the exposure risk. Aside from market risk, counterparty default is the second most important concern of OTC derivative market participants. Where a trader has the fixed side of a swap "matched" between two counterparties (eg, he is receiving a fixed rate from one counterparty and paying a lower fixed rate to the other) and the first counterparty defaults, the second counterparty must still be paid. The trader is likely to incur financial loss in replacing the defaulted swap with another at current market prices.

Derivatives Valuation and Accounting

The use of both exchange traded and OTC derivatives for both hedging and speculation is now very widespread. Participants include all banks, large corporates (including energy and commodity producers and consumers), insurance companies, investment managers (pension funds, hedge funds, retail funds), professional traders, and a variety of government agencies. In practice nearly all investment fund participants access the derivative markets through a bank or Prime Broker; either as their clearing broker (exchange traded futures and options) or their OTC derivative dealer.

Some of the control issues in using derivatives revolve around the ability to price and value open derivative positions for the purpose of profit/loss calculations for regular accounting and fund net asset value requirements. Being able to value the derivative, recognize potential market exposure and to understand the way in which different derivatives are treated for accounting purposes (in line with the relevant accounting standards) are all essential requirements for any organization using these products.

Exchange traded futures and options are relatively easily valued using the independently sourced prices published at the end of each day by the relevant exchange. These same prices drive the resultant variation margin settlements on the following day.

OTC derivative valuation can be much more complex. For simple commonly traded products where there is high market liquidity (eg, many FX, IRS, FRA, and CDS transactions), then there is normally a ready supply of third party generated bid/offer prices (sourced from brokers or quote vendor screens) from which to determine a "fair" market price. It is still better for those OTC derivatives that are cleared through a CCP, the CCP generates and publishes daily mark-to-market prices for its own margin and collateral purposes. However for less liquid, longer dated or more exotic OTC derivatives, there may be no easily available source of current market value. In these instances it is important for the investment funds and the administrator to predetermine their own internal pricing policy along the guidelines of "best industry practice."

OTC Derivatives Clearing

It has long been recognized that the establishment of a CCP (or clearing house) facility for OTC derivative trading could bring many of the same benefits that have always been taken for granted in the exchange traded (and cleared) derivative markets; namely multilateral netting of trade exposures between all the CCP members and significant reduction of bilateral credit risks between these firms. However for many years this type of initiative was blocked by some of world's largest banks; they doubted that a major bank default was a realistic scenario and were reluctant to see a "leveling of the OTC playing field." Times have changed, helped in part by much more onerous regulatory capital adequacy requirements on banks in respect of their credit risk exposures.

The pioneer for OTC derivatives clearing was LCH.Clearnet. LCH launched SwapClear in Sep. 1999 to provide a group of the largest interest rate swap dealing banks in London (who could meet the high financial criteria required for SwapClear membership), the ability to clear some of their interest rate swap portfolio (ie, all swap trades between one another within certain contract type, currency and date parameters agreed by SwapClear) under similar procedures as used for exchange traded derivatives (ie, multilateral netting with daily mark-to-market, variation and initial margin requirements). The 2008 default of Lehman (then an active clearing member of SwapClear) clearly highlighted the value and robustness of the OTC CCP structure and finally ushered OTC derivative clearing into the mainstream of strategic thinking for regulators (particularly the SEC and CFTC in the United States) and market participants alike.

Since 2008, several other organizations have set up their own OTC derivative clearing facilities and there has been a sharp increase in the cleared volumes year on year ever since. The leading clearing houses for IRS are currently SwapClear and the CME, but EUREX has also geared itself up to compete for a share of the IRS market. Both CME and ICE Clear provide competing clearing services for CDS transactions. Activity also increasing at LCH's ForexClear, which provides clearing for OTC nondeliverable FX forwards in more than 10 currencies. Meanwhile in Asia, SGX and HKEC have launched their own CCP OTC derivative clearing services and similar initiatives have commenced in India and elsewhere.

Summary

The use of derivatives by investment funds is extensive although some funds may not use them at all either out of choice or because of the regulation applicable to the fund.

For the administrator and custodian derivatives should not present a major problem although some of the more bespoke negotiated products may be more difficult to value.

Key issues are the concept of margin calls and collateral management, potential delivery, and ensuring that unwanted and or unauthorized exposures are not created.

All funds should have a policy for the use of derivatives and reference must be disclosed in the offering documents.

While not inherently dangerous, a failure to identify, record, reconcile, and value positions and to account for them correctly can cause a fund potentially serious and unwanted problems.

APPENDIX A—USEFUL REFERENCE WEBSITES

Derivative markets are already a very important component of the world's financial markets and continue to grow in variety, complexity, and usage, with new products constantly being researched and designed. The infrastructure in the industry evolves and changes constantly to meet these challenges. The following websites may be particularly useful:

Futures and option exchanges:

www.cmegroup.com

www.theice.com

www.eurexchange.com

www.CBOE.com

www.asx.com.au

www.LME.com

www.NYSELiffe.com

www.ccilindia.com

www.markit.com

www.sgx.com

www.Hkex.com.hk

Clearing houses/CCPs/Repositories:

www.theocc.com

www.LCHClearnet.com

https://www.theice.com/clear-europe

www.euroclear.com

Industry general and Regulators:

www.futuresindustry.org

www.isda.org

www.fca.gov

www.sec.gov

www.cftc.gov

www.esma.europa.eu

www.cisi.org (Exchange Traded and OTC Derivatives Administration Qualification)

www.cltinternational.com/funds (Advanced Certificate and Diploma in Fund Administration)

Derivative definitions and jargon:
www.thefreedictionary.com
www.investopedia.com

APPENDIX B—OCC STANS

Methodology

Introduction

This page offers an overview of OCC's margin methodology. Section 2 describes the general features of the methodology. Section 3 adds an explanation of the basis upon which CMs can make intraday withdrawals of excess margin or substitute one collateral asset for another.

General Features

OCC applies margin requirements on a daily basis to each account maintained at OCC by its CMs. Intraday calls for additional margin may be made on accounts incurring significant losses.

Under the STANS methodology, which went into effect in Aug. 2006, the daily margin calculation for each account is based on full portfolio Monte Carlo simulations and—as set out in more detail below—is constructed conservatively to ensure a very high level of assurance that the overall value of cleared products in the account, plus collateral posted to meet margin requirements, will not be appreciably negative at a two-day horizon. Long option positions held in customer accounts of CMs, and not part of various designated spread positions, are excluded altogether from OCC margin calculations for investor protection reasons. The effect of the exclusion is that the value of such options does not get used to collateralize other customers' short positions.

Until Feb. 2010, securities posted as collateral were not included in the Monte Carlo simulations, but were subjected to traditional "haircuts." Since then, the "collateral in margins" scheme has taken effect, whereby some collateral securities—specifically equity securities and, more recently, US Treasury securities (excluding TIPS)—have instead been included in the Monte Carlo simulations. Thus, the margin calculations now reflect the scope for price movements in these forms of collateral to exacerbate or mitigate losses on the cleared products on the account.

The Monte Carlo simulations are based on econometric models of the joint behavior of the risk factors affecting values of CM accounts at OCC. There are currently in the region of 7,000 such risk factors, of which the majority pertain to individual equity securities. The modeling of each risk factor allows for volatility clustering and fat-tailed innovations. The joint behavior is addressed by combining the marginal behaviors of individual risk factors by means of a copula function that takes account of correlations and allows for tail-dependence.

The Monte Carlo simulations use, for the volatility of each risk factor, the greater of the short-term level predicted by the model and an estimate of its longer-run level. In between the monthly reestimations of all the models, volatilities are automatically rescaled upward if a model of the behavior of the S&P 500® Index, reestimated daily, indicates heightened turbulence in the financial markets.

The base component of the margin requirement for each account is obtained from the risk measure known as 99% Expected Shortfall (ES). That is to say, the account has a base margin excess (deficit) if its positions in cleared products, plus all existing collateral—whether of types included in the Monte Carlo simulation or of types subjected to traditional "haircuts"—would have a positive (negative) net worth after incurring a loss equal to the average of all losses beyond the 99% VaR point.

The base component is adjusted by the addition of a stress test component. The stress test component is obtained from consideration of the increase in ES that would arise from market movements that are especially large and/or in which various kinds of risk factor exhibit perfect or zero correlations in place of their correlations estimated from historical data, or from extreme adverse idiosyncratic movements in individual risk factors to which the account is particularly exposed.

Brief technical details concerning the base and stress components are provided in the Appendix. Several other components of the overall margin requirement exist, but are typically considerably smaller than the base and stress test components, and many of them affect only a minority of accounts. CMs on elevated Watch Levels as specified in OCC rules may be subject to additional margin requirements.

3. Intraday Withdrawal and Deposits of Collateral

A CM may make intraday withdrawals of excess collateral on an account, and/or deposit fresh collateral assets in place of others.

For collateral types that are subject to a traditional "haircut," the impact of a withdrawal or deposit upon the margin excess incorporates the "haircut."

For collateral types that are subject to "collateral in margins" treatment, the impact of a withdrawal or deposit is based upon a "portfolio specific haircut" (PSH) that is communicated to the applicable CM concerned on a daily basis. The PSH represents the sensitivity of the risk profile of that particular account to its position in the relevant security. In other words, the PSH applicable to any given movement of collateral is designed to provide an estimate of the resulting change in margin requirements if the entire margin calculation was recalculated following the movement.

APPENDIX C—DEPENDENCE AND CONCENTRATION

The base component corresponds to the ES of the portfolio computed at a 99% confidence level using historical estimates of correlations between risk factors:

$$Base = ES_{0.99}^{H}$$

The stress test component is whichever is the greater of two subcomponents called Dependence and Concentration.

The Dependence subcomponent can be thought of as a proportion of the extra risk that would arise if we go further out into the tail of the PandL distribution and consider the effects of replacing historical estimates of dependence between single-stock returns with either perfect correlation or zero correlation. ES is computed at a 99.5% confidence levels for each of the historic, perfect, and independent correlation assumptions. The Dependence subcomponent equals a proportion of the difference between the maximum of the three computations and the base risk requirement:

$$Dependence = 0.25 * \left[\max\left(ES_{0.995}^{H}, ES_{0.995}^{P}, ES_{0.995}^{Z}\right) - ES_{0.99}^{H} \right]$$

where the H, P, and Z superscripts refer to the correlation structure used.

The Concentration subcomponent can be thought of as a proportion of the extra risk that would arise from extreme adverse idiosyncratic moves in two risk-factors to which the portfolio is especially exposed, coupled with marginally less severe experience in the remainder of the portfolio. The single-factor sub-portfolios consist of all positions (options, stock loans, futures etc.) corresponding to one single risk factor. Not all risk factors are considered when selecting these risk factors: for instance positions pertaining to indices are excluded. This reflects the capture only of idiosyncratic risks in this test. If a portfolio contains exposure to less than two sources of idiosyncratic risk, then the formula is adapted in the obvious way. Source: http://www.optionsclearing.com/risk-management/margins/. ES is computed at a 99.5% confidence level for each of the two single-factor sub-portfolios having the greatest exposure at that level, and those two results are added to the ES of the residual portfolio computed at a 99% confidence level. The Concentration component is a proportion of the amount by which this sum exceeds the base component:

$$Concentration = 0.25 * \left({}_{c}^{2}CES_{0.995}^{H} + {}^{2}RES_{0.99}^{H} - ES_{0.99}^{H} \right)$$

where: ${}_{c}^{2}CES_{0.995}^{H}$ is the sum of the ES of the two single-factor sub-portfolios reporting the greatest exposure at a 99.5% confidence level; and ${}^{2}RES_{0.99}^{H}$ is the ES of the residual portfolio at a 99% confidence interval.

In order to maintain a conservative approach, all calculations of ES are computed using techniques from Extreme Value Theory, and the results are increased to take account of an estimate of the sampling error that arises in the Monte Carlo sample.

APPENDIX D—SUGGESTED FURTHER READING

In addition the following reading and information sources are suggested:
Clearing and Settlement of Derivatives www.books.elsevier.com/finance

Part 6

Summary—Fund Administration Notes

The following is a summary of the subject matter of this book

1. Investment industry—Still recovering from market crash and liquidity problems with investors, both private and institutional, wary of issues like security and reconciliation over the assets of a fund (Madoff), large and sudden drop in Net Asset Value of some funds (suggesting unrealistic valuation of assets), and a general negative view of participants in the financial markets (short selling, high performance fees, bank rip offs, lack of control etc.). Alternative investments are popular, for example, buying gold, art etc.

    There has been significant regulation and legislation introduced including the Alternative Investment Fund Managers Directive (AIFMD), The European Markets Infrastructure Regulation (EMIR), UCITS V, Markets in Financial Instruments Directive II (MiFID) Dodd-Frank (United States) with more emphasis on transparency and reporting.

    Also legislation aimed at tax avoidance like Foreign Account Tax Compliance Act (FATCA).

2. Types of fund entity—Three main structures found with the oversight responsibility for each:

    a. Investment company—board of directors—established under company law in the jurisdiction.

    b. Unit trust—trustee—established under trust law of a jurisdiction.

    c. Partnership—general partner—established under partnership law of a jurisdiction.

    d. There can also be funds with no legal personality often called Common funds operated by a management company.

    e. Retail fund—Can be sold to anyone, high level of regulatory protection for investors, usually has to have transferability (can enter/exit fund on demand), diversity in the portfolio and does not have liabilities like cash borrowing.

    f. Qualifying Investor, Expert, Market Professional funds, some Fund of Funds, Exempt funds—restricted investor base (market professionals, institutions, high net worth individuals (c. $1 or 2 m), need and have less regulatory protection.

3. Investment—Revolves around key concepts as follows:
   a. Risk and return are related.
   b. Time to realize the return is important—long, medium, and short.
   c. Risk appetite—
      - Low-conservative—Diversified across many assets, no use of derivatives (except for currency risk management and hedging risk) and other "risky" assets, no borrowing (gearing/leverage created liabilities), no risky strategies, for example, short selling, foreign exchange risk removed through forward contracts, often benchmarked or tracker type funds (passive).
      - Medium—Diversified portfolio of assets, some use of derivatives mainly to hedge risk, limited gearing and exposures, major part of the portfolio in low risk assets like G7 government bonds, blue chip equities, rest in more volatile assets, for example, high yield bonds, speculative equities—example split 80–20% or 70–30%, often actively managed.
      - High-low diversification, wide use of derivatives and structured products, use illiquid assets like private equity and property (real estate) gearing/leverage common, unlikely to distribute income, use high risk strategies like short selling, skewed exposures, mainly absolute return funds.

4. Types of product used in investment—
   a. Assets and asset allocation used to create the portfolio.
   b. Asset classes.
      - Equities—shares
      - Debt—bonds (long term), Notes (medium term), Bills and money markets (short term).
      - Cash—deposits and currencies.
      - Property—housing and commercial (offices, shopping malls, warehouses).
      - Commodities—agricultural, softs (coffee, cocoa, butter etc.), metals, energy.
      - Alternatives—antiques, art, wine, forestry.
      - Capital growth—for example, equities, currencies, property, and private equity.
      - Income—for example, debt (interest), equities (dividend), and property (rental income).
      - Ethical and specific funds—environmental/green funds, and Islamic funds.
      - Master/feeder funds and fund of funds—investment in another fund or funds rather than assets.

5. Operating structure of funds—
   a. Type of entity—company, trust, partnership, or common fund.

b. Owner/sponsor—investment company operating sub funds, for example, the SICAV in Europe, hedge fund run by fund companies or individuals—track record/reputation major importance.

c. Investment manager(s) and advisers—make investment decisions or provide suggested investments (decision made by investment committee/board/general partner based around the mandate/offering documents plus regulatory constraints, risk appetite/profile of the fund. Operate under an Investment Management/Advisory Agreement (IMA).

d. Fund administrator—often an external, "independent" party covering potentially three main areas:
  - Operations—transaction inputs, reconciliation, recordkeeping.
  - Accounting and valuation—pricing, NAV calculation, accounting records of the fund.
  - Transfer agency—dealing with subscriptions, redemptions, fund register, investor due diligence, AML checks, investor communication etc.
  - Other areas—fund set up, secretarial services.

e. Custodian—holds the assets of the fund in either physical or electronic format depending on the asset and offers other support services.

6. Services and issues in setting up a fund.

a. Jurisdiction/location—onshore/offshore.

b. Regulator—who is the regulatory authority (some investors wary of funds that are not regulated/authorized but lower cost can be attractive).

c. Regulation—what is applicable to different types of funds.

d. Tax related to the the fund business as well as investors. Tax on income and capital gain, with holding tax (WHT) and tax treaties plus tax exempt status where applicable.

e. Legal—agreements, constitutive documents, offering documents.

f. Fund set up—applications, licenses, registrations, listing etc.

g. Offering documents—prospectus (investment company—retail and alternative), offering memorandum (hedge fund/PE/Property), scheme particulars (trust).

h. Investment management—inhouse, outsourced, combination.

i. Secretarial.

j. Banking.

k. Sales and marketing—outlets—fund management company, prime broker, financial advisers, banks, brokers, online selling, coupons in journals etc.

l. Administration services—records, valuations, dealing with investors (inhouse/outsourced).

m. Prime broker/broker relationships including possible custody service.

7. Prospectus/offering memorandum/scheme particulars—contain all the relevant information and disclosures about the fund including:

a. Investment objectives, risk profile, functionaries (including investment manager, management company, trustee, directors, general partner, administrator, custodian, auditors), subscription and redemption details, investor constraints, taxation, etc.

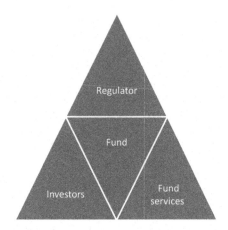

DIAGRAM 6.1   Investment funds relationships.

    b. Legal details, regulator.
    c. Fees and charges applicable to the fund including any performance fee payable to the investment managers if targets are met.
    d. Rights of the share or unit holders or the limited partners in a partnership.

The regulator oversees the whole process authorizing funds under the terms of the relevant legislation in the jurisdiction (Diagram 6.1).

Funds can be authorized for general sale, for example, European UCITS funds or for sale to qualifying investors only (nonretail funds).

There can also be unauthorized funds with restricted investor base and Exempt funds, given exemption from the local regulation as they are regulated elsewhere to a satisfactory standard (these funds usually cannot be sold to domestic investors even qualifying investors).

The general structure of a fund is shown in Diagram 6.2.

The management company deals with the day to day process of the fund operation.

Investment management is done by managers and or advisers in conjunction with investment management agreement, investment committee etc. and

DIAGRAM 6.2   General structure.

through brokers, the prime broker for securities, commodities and derivatives, agents for property, advisers/agents/directors of private equity firms for opportunities for PE funds etc.

The administrator manages the day to day processing of the activity of the fund and the custodian holds the assets and deals with settlement of the asset transaction.

1. Fund administration—A service based product that has developed from the independent provision of pricing and valuations of assets and portfolios into a broad based product covering:

    a. Fund operations—Asset trade capture and inputs to records, validation and verification of positions (exposure limits/mandate), assets (settlement status and location, eg, custodian), and reconciliations.

    b. Fund accounting and valuations—Statutory accounts, general ledger, pricing of assets, posting of actual and accrued income (from assets, eg, dividends, interest from debt instruments and cash deposits), and expenses (from transactions, eg, broker commissions, services, eg, custody fees, audit fees, licenses and registrations, bank charges etc.).

    c. Transfer agency—Managing subscriptions and redemptions, client due diligence, AML checks, the fund register, and communication with clients.

    d. Secretarial services, risk and compliance management, fund set ups.

2. Change to the service requirement—Driven by the need for funds to show higher degree of control and management over the day to day operation of the fund including risk management and compliance—Key issue is quality and professionalism.

3. Product characteristics—Essential that the administrator understands the structure and characteristics of different products the fund may have in the portfolio, for example, the process of accrued interest on bonds, margin, and collateral associated with derivatives, for example, and the possibility of corporate action events. Also the valuation issues surrounding "easy to value" assets like listed equities and "difficult to value" like property and illiquid assets.

4. Workflow—The ability for the administrator to manage the workflow associated with the process of subscription and redemption, through cash forecast update, asset trades, postings, reconciliation, and finally the pricing and valuation process.

5. Identifying problems—Data quality crucial as is the timings and cut offs associated with key processes, for example, asset trade capture from investment manager, receipt of subscription/redemption requests etc. Managing situations in a practical way.

6. NAV calculations—Pricing policy, tolerances and parameters, exception management, initial reasonableness checks, for example, portfolio change versus a benchmark, and correct accruals.

7. Private Equity—Drawdown capital, growth, and then distribution periods, fund has a projected life (5–10 years). Distribution pays off in order:
   a. The initial capital of the investors.
   b. The preference return to the investors.
   c. The carried interest of the general partner.
   d. Remaining return distributed across investors/general partner.

   Fund is charged fees throughout the life of the fund so initially investors have a negative situation.

8. Futures contracts have:
   a. Variation margin based on the contract size/tick size and value—the end of day price and any closing trades.
   b. Creates a daily settled process of unrealized profits/losses, realized profit/losses, and commission payments.
   c. Initial margin is collateral held by the broker until obligations are closed.
   d. Cash covering initial margin still part of the NAV but not available for investment by the manager.
   e. Futures have a contract specification, for example, tick size and value, maturity size (FTSE index future on Euronext is £10 × index).

9. Property fund—Often based around the following:
   a. Physical property.
   b. Shares in property companies, land etc.
   c. Rental income from properties.

   Property is often managed by a property management company with assets like title deeds held at a legal firm and assets like shares at a custodian.

10. Sources of data are important—Subscriptions/redemptions from 3rd parties, asset trades for investment manager/prime broker, valuations from PE accountants and property management company, price feeds and data from Bloomberg, accruals from ledgers/invoices etc.

11. Cash flow—forecasts and cash management oversight.

EXERCISE ANSWER

Day one:

Variation margin—purchases 10 contracts × £10 × 5900 = £590,000
End of day (EOD) price 5907 = £590,700 creating a profit of £700 less commission of £15 = net £685 receivable (this amount is called variation margin or VM).

Cash balance now £60,685—initial margin = 10 × £2500 = £25,000 so cash balance for NAV purposes is £60,685 but for the cash forecast, that is, available cash is £35,685.

Day two:
  BFwd 10 contracts @5907
  Sell 5 contracts @ 5912 VM = 5 contracts $\times$ 10 ticks $\times$ £5 = £250
  CFwd 5 contracts
  EOD price 5915 VM = 5 $\times$ 16 $\times$ £5 = £400
  Total VM = £650 profit less £7.50 commission = £642.50 to receive
  New cash balance = £60685 + £642.50 = £61327.50—initial margin = 5 $\times$
  £2500 = £12,500
Day three:
  Bfwd 5 contracts @ 5915
  Buy 5 contracts @ 5920 and Sell 10 contracts @ 5906
  VM = 5 $\times$ 18 $\times$ £5 = £450 and 5 $\times$ 28 $\times$ £5 = £700
  Both are losses so total VM = (£1150) plus commission £15 $\times$ 1.5 = £22.50
  Final cash balance = £61327.50 minus £1172.50 = £60,155
  Note: Each day the initial margin is covered by cash so the amount available
for investment is the balance minus the initial margin.

1. Fund accounting (Part 2)—Important for an administration team to understand the characteristics of products used in the assets allocation process.
   Some of the key points are:
   a. Realized and unrealized profits and losses.
   b. Accruals for income and expenses.
   c. Ability to value products issued at a discount—The accreting amount
      per day.
   d. Using correlations to measure the value movement, that is, a relevant
      index versus the portfolio change.
   e. Illiquid (hard to value) products—Use the pricing policy, balance sheet,
      use similar products, last price traded if not "old," write up write downs
      based on economic research etc.
   f. Private equity—Often Board representation which can be source of
      value.
   g. Day count convention important—days for accrued interest, that is, 360
      (US), 365 (UK).
   h. Equalization—High watermark, hurdle rate, calculated excluding any
      capital inflow/outflow, resets, method of equalization (refer to handout
      document).
2. Transfer agency—Managing subscriptions and redemptions, client due diligence, AML checks, the fund register, communication with clients to the
   service requirement.
   a. AML checks vital—Individuals, financial institutions (other funds), and
      corporate companies must have due diligence carried out.
   b. Policy for investors introduced by third party, for example, financial ad-
      visers, banks etc. Some form of confirmation needed or due diligence
      must be done by the T/A.
   c. Power of attorney over deceased investors.

    d. Segregation of distributions into segregated bank account prior to the payment.

    e. Update of share register with accumulation shares resulting from distribution.

    f. Update cash flow forecast with result of subscription/redemptions amounts.

    g. Know the constraints on redemptions—gates, embargoes, shut outs etc.—early exit fees may apply—dealing periods and cut offs.

    h. Know constraints on subscription—size, cut off times.

    i. Distribution of investor communications—financial statements, periodic statements, notices (pre or post event—"material information" prior to event).

3. Fund compliance—Increasing in importance and the tasks are often outsourced to the administrator (but not the responsibility which remains with the fund directors, trustee, or general partner)—two elements apply—regulatory compliance and internal controls compliance.

    a. Fund compliance and Fund Administrators Compliance

    b. Regulatory compliance
- Authorization/License terms
- Rules and Regulations pertaining to Collective Investment Schemes, for example, FCA UK "COLL"
- Directives like UCITS, ESD, MiFID, AIFM
  – Best execution
  – Marketing
  – Investment constraints—strategies, borrowing, gearing, investor type
- Responsibilities of functionaries
- Fiduciary responsibility
- Offering documents and disclosures
- Reporting

    c. Internal controls
- Mandates and agreements
- Procedures
- Checklists, for examples, for a corporate action
- Management information
- Audit trails
- Logs—administrators should always log any incident, request to waiver any control or procedure etc.
- Compliance checklist

4. Risk management—Also increasing in importance for both fund promoters and investors. Three key risk areas:

    a. Market risk—largely the investment managers area based around investment decisions, assets allocation and selection, liquidity, risk etc. Issuer risk—default on a bond for instance.

  b. Credit/Counterparty risk—mainly around default possibilities, very important for private equity and other draw down funds as investor default has major risks. Also risk of failure of counterparty holding positions, collateral, assets belonging to the fund, for example, prime broker failure (Lehmans), breach of Custody Agreement or Administration Agreement—failure of investment manager to adhere to Investment Management Agreement (case study–Peter Young Morgan Grenfell Asset Management).

  c. Operational risk—mainly day to day operation of fund but also includes personnel/HR risk, technology risk (performance, scope, maintenance, and security), settlement risk, access risk (premises, travel etc.).

  d. Other risks include—legal—unenforceable contracts/agreements and regulatory—breaches of rules, mandates, offering documents (prohibited product, unsuitable investor etc.), failure to carry out duties (Fiduciary risk).

5. Killer and key risks—Killer risk is an actual event that would destroy the fund, management company, administrator—key risk would be so serious it would damage the fund or custodian, administrator and may leave it so weak (loss of capital/assets, investors) that they/it eventually closes.

6. Fund and administrator should have Procedure Manuals and Policies for dealing with key processes and controls, including identifying key risk indicators (KRIs) and key performance indicators (KPIs).

7. Must be consistent in the way in which the fund operates key tasks and functions, that is, pricing and valuation, accounts etc.

8. Secretarial services can include risk and compliance management (documenting minutes of meetings, filing returns etc.

9. Fund set ups—key risk for promoter so may use an administrator in the jurisdiction to set up the fund including providing directors etc.

10. Administrator risks—mainly about viability of the business (fees revenue—percentage fee plus some usage basis fees versus costs—premises, salaries, systems etc.) and compliance with Administration Agreement and Service Level Agreement between fund and administrator.

11. Operational risk is often assessed by carrying out a process of "self-assessment" to measure the level of risk.

Part 7

The Future of Fund Custody and Administration

We have commented in this book on the fact that not only the regulatory environment changes have created the need to change to the custody and administration product and how this creates challenges for the teams providing the services. We have also seen changes in the market infrastructure such as the T2S project which is creating a single platform for securities and cash settlement (https://www.ecb.europa.eu/paym/t2s/about/about/html/index.en.html) with a significant challenge for custodians as well as the growth of CLS Bank in the FX settlement space (https://www.cls-group.com)

Another potential key change will be in the area of technology and particularly the block chain or distributed ledger technology (DLT) space.

While it is early days, the potential to radically change and improve the efficiency of the post trade environment is gaining support and interest for example look at the following press release.

7th April 2016

Bank of America Merrill Lynch, Citi, Credit Suisse, J.P. Morgan, and the Depository Trust & Clearing Corporation (DTCC) successfully traded credit default swaps on the blockchain, according to an announcement today.

SWIFT has published a most interesting paper on the whole question for DLTs, what the current status is, and what R&D is needed to bring the concept to fruition.

Appendix 11 contains the paper. There is much change happening and in the pipeline and administrators and custodians will need to meet the challenges and provide the solutions. Watch this space!

Appendix 1

The Investment Association Categorization of Funds

Funds principally targeting capital protection
  SHORT TERM MONEY MARKET
  MONEY MARKET
  PROTECTED FUNDS

Funds principally targeting income (by asset category) fixed income sectors
  UK GILTS
  UK INDEX LINKED GILTS
  £ CORPORATE BOND
  £ STRATEGIC BOND
  £ HIGH YIELD
  GLOBAL BONDS
  GLOBAL EMERGING MARKETS BOND

Equity sectors
  UK EQUITY INCOME
  GLOBAL EQUITY INCOME

Mixed asset sectors
  UK EQUITY & BOND INCOME

Funds principally targeting growth (by asset category)
Equity sectors
UK equities
  UK ALL COMPANIES
  UK SMALLER COMPANIES

Overseas equities
JAPAN
ASIA PACIFIC INCLUDING JAPAN
ASIA PACIFIC EXCLUDING JAPAN
CHINA/GREATER CHINA SECTOR
NORTH AMERICA
JAPANESE SMALLER COMPANIES
NORTH AMERICAN SMALLER COMPANIES
EUROPE INCLUDING UK
EUROPE EXCLUDING UK
EUROPEAN SMALLER COMPANIES
GLOBAL
GLOBAL EMERGING MARKETS

Mixed asset sectors
MIXED INVESTMENT 0–35% SHARES
MIXED INVESTMENT 20–60% SHARES
MIXED INVESTMENT 40–85% SHARES
FLEXIBLE INVESTMENT

Specialist funds
PERSONAL PENSIONS
PROPERTY
SPECIALIST
TARGETED ABSOLUTE RETURN
TECHNOLOGY & TELECOMMUNICATIONS

Unclassified
UNCLASSIFIED

This document is sourced from The Investment Association website and the full details including definitions of the individual sectors can be found at http://www.theinvestmentassociation.org/investment-industry-information/ fund-sectors/sector-definitions.html. Readers are encouraged to study the definitions.

Appendix 2

Source-Investment Association

http://www.theinvestmentassociation.org/investment-industry-information/
research-and-publications/asset-management-survey/the-industry-in-figures.
html#undefined

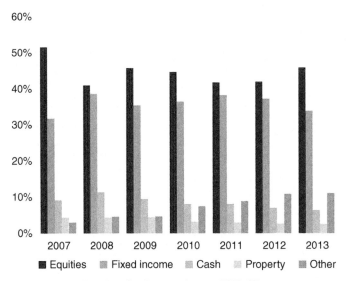

CHART 9   Overall asset allocation of UK-managed assets (2007–13)

Appendix 3

Glossary of Risk Terminology

Risk	Description	Associated Risk Type
Accounting Risk	This will occur when a business engages in accounting practices for products or services that are either not suitable, are deliberately misinterpreted or are implemented incorrectly or do not comply with accepted market principles. The risk can also occur if there is doubt about the acceptable accounting standards or where there is conflict between different standards by the setting organizations.	Audit, Regulatory, Reporting
Actioning Risk	The risk of an action being implemented erroneously, accidentally, in unsuitable situations or being authorized or under taken by unqualified personnel. The risks that arise could create losses (costs, fines etc.), reputation damage (outcome and impact) and regulatory problems.	Management, Settlement, Payment
Audit Risk	This is the risk that the audit process and people are unable or do not have the ability to, or do not understand sufficiently the processes and procedures being audited.	
Basel Directives	Inability to demonstrate compliance with the requirement as set out by the Committee of the Bank for International Settlement.	Regulatory
Business Risk	A risk that is derived from the specific services and products and are particular to the industry of the firm concerned. These risks are often sub sets of strategic risk and occur or originate from business units.	Operations Risk, Technology Risk, People risk.

(Continued)

Fund Custody and Administration

Risk	Description	Associated Risk Type
Business Continuity Risk	The impact of internal or external events that in some way interrupt or curtail the operation of the business for a significant period of time or in some catastrophic financial or logistical way as to make normal or viable operation of business difficult.	Operations Risk Client Risk Counterparty/ Supplier Risk.
Client Risk	The risk of being unable to manage the processes associated with the services provided to clients. Money Laundering Fraud Noncompliance with client regulation (Regulatory Conduct of Business Rules etc.)—key areas being suitability (Funds) risk warning distribution, client money/asset segregation.	Operations Risk People Risk Regulatory (including fines) Reputation - Loss of clients/revenue
Competition Risk	A complex risk that can arise in a number of ways and is quite different from business risk, which is about internal decisions and actions. Competition risk could arise from the entrance of a new competitor or product into a market with potential loss of market share and or increase in investment/costs to compete. This is particularly the case where new competitors cherry pick profitable market segments, where they have or adapt to new technology and practices quicker, or can respond to changing customer requirements more rapidly. Examples here could be found in e-banking, socially responsible investment products etc. Competition risk can also apply to prolonged declining market share created by inability to change as well as by poorly managed mergers and takeovers resulting in massive loss of customers that in turn renders the strategic aims unobtainable and likely to entail severe losses for some period of time.	
Compliance Risk	The inability to adequately comply with external regulations or internal rules and controls. This may be caused by lack of knowledge of certain markets, products and regulatory requirements and or oversight of business units involved.	Regulatory Financial
Counterparty Risk	This is the risk associated with dealing with or taking services or products from another party. Includes: ongoing support and enhancement of services, insourcing/outsourcing.	Operations Risk

Risk	Description	Associated Risk Type
Country Risk	Risk of clearing, settlement, and client money regulation not being as strong as in the UK/US Law Infrastructure Information distribution may be less transparent and or obtainable Instability Tax environment/changes	Operation Risk Legal Risk
Credit Risk	Risk associated with the default of a counterparty on an obligation.	Financial – replacement loss
Creeping Risk	A risk that starts in one part of a business and then moves across and within the business potentially having a greater impact in other areas (Similar to a computer virus).	
Custody/ Depositary Risk	The failure to protect assets and any resulting benefits on those assets that are entrusted to the care and safekeeping of the firm.	Reputation, Financial, Regulatory
Data Risk	Occurs when data is incorrectly generated, updated, stored or used. Corrupted or incorrect data in critical systems (including risk systems) can have a devastating impact. Unauthorized access, use or publication of confidential client or business data can have such an impact as to put at risk the very existence of the organization.	Technology, Control, Fraud
Demand Risk (liquidity)	A risk where there is uncertainty about future demand for a product caused by uncontrollable or unforeseen changes in the market, for instance regulatory changes. It also manifests itself in situations where there is greater demand than can be satisfied effectively and efficiently causing delays and penalties to be incurred. Demand risk is relevant in terms of the passing of risk from one business unit to another, that is, the aggressive marketing of a product creating risk for the production team (meeting alterations "sold" by the sales team) or client support teams (delays in delivery, quality etc.)	Strategic, Operational, Operations
Documentation Risk	As well as errors within and the ineffectiveness of legal documentation, there is the risk inherent in the publication of documents to clients including correctness of information, suitability of the document (KYC and restricted product documents), confidentiality, and frequency requirements (regulatory, agreements etc.)	

(Continued)

Risk	Description	Associated Risk Type
Fiduciary Risk	Breaching either of the following: 1. A person legally appointed and authorized to hold assets in trust for another person. The fiduciary manages the assets for the benefit of the other person rather than for his or her own profit. 2. A loan made on trust rather than against some security or asset.	
Fraud Risk	This is the risk that because of weak controls in respect of payments, asset movements, authorizations, access to systems, and static data in an organization, it is vulnerable to an act of fraud by an individual, group of individuals or from external sources e-banking presents potential for fraud if security over access and data is poor.	
H R Risk	See Personnel Risk	
Insource Risk	A risk associated with the taking on of additional operational workload with inadequate resource, knowledge, and systems.	Operations Risk, Financial—compensation for performance, Reputation
Key Performance Indicators (KPI)	Indicators showing a change in performance that may be evidence of increasing or decreasing efficiency and effectiveness of processes and procedures Often linked into KRIs	
Key Risk	Identified as risks that could significantly impact on the achievement of the objectives of a business unit. Likely to be proactively managed by Head of Function/Department on a frequent (ie, monthly basis). Typically 15–20% of total risks. Firms develop key risk indicators to measure profile changes of the key risks.	
Key Risk Indicators (KRI)	The identification of risks and their indicators used in the risk management process. Important that KRIs are monitored for evidence of increasing or decreasing risk levels and also for their continued relevance.	
Killer Risk	Identified as risks that could significantly impact on the achievement of firm, divisional, and or strategic business unit objectives including a risk that's impact is so severe that it would render the firm incapable of continuing in business or would make the firm so vulnerable that it would subject to takeover or wipe out by competitors. Typically, 2–5% of total risks. Managed and tracked through key risk indicators.	

Risk	Description	Associated Risk Type
Know Your Client (KYC)	A risk control measure that demands the organization has adequate and up to date knowledge of the client, its activities, restrictions that apply to the client's actual or potential business and the suitability of products and services marketed and sold to the client.	
Legal Risk	The risk associated with the business of a firm in a jurisdiction. From an operations point of view it would be related to areas such as netting, agreements, claims etc.	Settlement Risk
Limit Risk	A risk that a control measure is accidentally or deliberately circumvented or is incorrectly set or is not reviewed and amended according to changed circumstances.	
Loss Database	A database that records incidents where a risk event has created a loss at or above a set threshold.	
Management Risk	A risk associated with the failure of management to be structured or operate effectively in relation to the business. Poorly trained, under resourced/overworked or ineffective managers, and supervisors are a massive operations risk.	Operations Risk, Reputation, Regulatory
Market Risk	Risk associated with the transactions undertaken by a firm in a market/product. Mainly about price and liquidity but can also be related to other risk like legal and competition.	
Money Laundering Risk	A major risk for many organizations that can result in heavy penalties for individuals and loss of authorization to do business for firms for breaches of the regulations. Any organization covered by the Regulations must ensure effective controls over possible money laundering including making sure employees are adequately trained.	
New Market Risk	This is the risk of operating in a new market environment where knowledge and experience may initially be low. It is also about the risk that procedures and controls are not immediately at the acceptable standard level of existing market usage. Can also apply to activity that is undertaken in emerging markets where the market infrastructure, practices and operation is itself untried and tested.	Operations Risk, Systems Risk, Settlement Risk
New Product Risk	This risk will manifest itself if the launch of or the commencement of trading in a new product or when the launch or use of a new service is undertaken without sufficient infrastructure in place, including controls, systems, knowledge skills etc. and prior training of personnel.	Operations Risk, Systems Risk, Settlement Risk

(Continued)

Risk	Description	Associated Risk Type
Operational Risk	There are various definitions of operational risk. The Basle Committee define it as "the risk of loss resulting from inadequate or failed internal processes, people and systems, or from external events." Most organizations would add in "loss of reputation."	
Operations Risk	Part of operational risk it applies to the functions that deal with areas like clearing, settlement, payments, delivery of client services, custody, systems etc. Operations risk is the failure to provide the required process, procedures and controls for the above.	
Operational Risk Management (ORM)	The process of actively managing operational risks in a structure that adds value as well as reduces potential unnecessary losses. Often run by a Risk Group and usually has one or more operational risk managers in the structure. Likely to include audit and compliance in some capacity.	
Operational Risk Officers (OROs)	Name given to a person who is part of the group managing risk and is usually closely related to the business so that they can liase with both the business and the risk managers on risk issues. Can also be called ORCs—operational risk coordinators.	
Outsource Risk	A risk associated with the outsourcing of operational functions and processes. Risk is that you can outsource the function but not the responsibility.	Operations Risk, Reputation
Payment Risk	A risk associated with the erroneous payment of monies. Often but not always associated with fraud it can be nevertheless a risk that is created by poor training, supervision and procedures for making and or receiving payments.	Fraud, Reputation—errors on client accounts
People Risk	This is the risk associated with individuals or teams of people and is often about their potential as a source of risk and also their potential to be a significant contributor to managing some risks like operational risk. One obvious people risk is the level of human error in the processes, the knowledge levels both procedural and business and the ability to work in environments particular to business units, products, services etc.	Operations, Financial, and Reputation Risk

Risk	Description	Associated Risk Type
Personnel Risk	Different from people risk in so much as this may occur because of poor recruitment environments, uncompetitive remuneration, lack of or ineffective training and development etc. Loss of key personal is a major personnel risk. Employment Law is also part of this risk and includes areas such as Diversity in the Workplace Directives and training, unfair dismissal etc.	Operations, Financial, and Reputation Risk
Regulatory Risk	The risk of non-compliance with the regulatory environment where the business is operating. Particularly areas such as Authorization, Marketing and Sales, Conduct of Business, Client relationships etc.	
Risk Event	The occurrence of a possible risk situation becoming an actual risk situation with resultant actual impact.	
Standard Risk	A risk that is identified and managed as part of the day-to-day business process by the boys and girls doing their jobs effectively and efficiently. Controls devised and implemented by managers and supervisors in the business. Monitored by risk managers from management information provided by the business but essentially not, what the risk managers or OROs should be focusing on.	
Strategic Risk	A risk that is associated with decisions and leadership, that is, the adoption of a working practice that is old, untried, or ill thought out that result in unnecessary pressure, workloads, costs and falling performance of people, systems, and the business.	
Technology Risk	The risk associated with the use of technology in a firm. Most obvious risks are: 1. lack of knowledge of systems 2. inability to manage projects 3. lack of support for systems 4. lack of awareness of systems capability and scope 5. inappropriate systems for the business 6. old and outdated technology 7. access—hackers and viruses, malicious attack.	
Value At Risk (VAR)	A technique used to estimate the probability of portfolio losses based on the statistical analysis of historical price trends and volatilities.	

(Continued)

Risk	Description	Associated Risk Type
Workflow Risk	Risk associated with workflow and processes covering: 1. variable flow 2. under resourcing 3. pressure points 4. disruption 5. lack of knowledge 6. unnecessary complex procedures 7. poor technology 8. lack of STP 9. cross border processes 10. data sources	

This Glossary of Terms is compiled from various sources and is believed to be correct although no responsibility can be taken for any errors or omissions.

Appendix 4

Organization of the SESC

The SESC is within the Financial Services Agency (FSA), which is based on Article 54 of the Act for Establishment of the Cabinet Office and Article 6 of the Act for Establishment of the Financial Services Agency. The SESC consists of a chairman and two commissioners. They are appointed by the Prime Minister with the consent of both Houses and may use their authority independently. To ensure their independence, basically, both the chairman and the commissioners may not be dismissed during their tenure of 3 years. In Dec. 2013, Chairman Kenichi Sado and Commissioners Masayuki Yoshida and Mari Sono were appointed and started their new 3-year term (8th term).

The Executive Bureau, under the control of the SESC is composed of the following six divisions: the Coordination Division, the Market Surveillance Division, the Inspection Division, the Administrative Monetary Penalty Division, the Disclosure Statements Inspection Division, and the Investigation Division. In addition, the SESC has staff members at the Local Finance Bureaus mainly in charge of inspections of financial instruments business operators located in the regional area. In total, there are 739 staff members (of which 400 work for the head office) as of fiscal year 2013.

For the purpose of appropriate market surveillance, the SESC has been strengthening its framework of market surveillance by recruiting lawyers, certified public accountants, real-estate appraisers, etc.

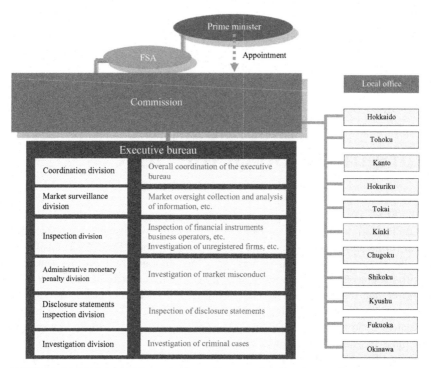

NOTE: In Jul. 2006, the SESC was transformed from two divisions (the Coordination and Inspection Division and the Investigation Division) and three offices (the Compliance Inspection Office, the Market Surveillance Office and the Office of Penalties Investigation and Disclosure Documents Examination under the Coordination and Inspection Division) into five divisions (the Coordination Division, the Market Surveillance Division, the Inspection Division, the Civil Penalties Investigation and Disclosure Documents Inspection Division, and the Investigation Division). Furthermore, in Jul. 2011, the Civil Penalties Investigation and Disclosure Documents Inspection Division was divided into two divisions (the Administrative Monetary Penalty Division and the Disclosure Statements Inspection Division), meaning that the SESC was transformed into six divisions. In Aug. 2011, the Office of Investigation for International Transactions and Related Issues was established within the Administrative Monetary Penalty Division, to investigate transactions, etc. conducted by persons in foreign countries.

Appendix 5

Financial Conduct Authority

Reporting Annex IV Transparency Information Under the Alternative Investment Fund Managers Directive

FOR FULL-SCOPE UK AIFMs, SMALL AUTHORIZED UK AIFMs AND SMALL REGISTERED UK AIFMs

As a full-scope UK AIFM (Alternative Investment Fund Manager), small authorized UK AIFM or small registered UK AIFM, you are required under the Alternative Investment Fund Managers Directive (AIFMD) to report information (referred to as transparency information) to the FCA.

This transparency information is about yourself as the AIFM and the Alternative Investment Fund(s) (AIFs) that you are managing and where relevant, marketing.

The requirement for you to report transparency information has now begun: it began on the date when you were authorized or registered by the FCA.

It is important that you understand our requirements for the reporting of transparency information that apply to you.

You must comply with the FCA's transparency reporting requirements.

Regulatory reporting is an integral part of the FCA's supervision strategy and transparency information is one element of this. Receiving accurate information from firms on time enables us to focus its supervisory resources appropriately. This helps us to meet our operational objectives of protecting and enhancing the integrity of the UK financial system, including financial stability, and securing an appropriate degree of protection for consumers.

This communication provides you with a summary of the transparency reporting obligations applying to you as a full-scope UK AIFM, small authorized

UK AIFM or small registered UK AIFM. It does not constitute FCA rules or guidance but provides important information about:

- The transparency reporting requirements of the FCA.
- Procedures for reporting transparency information to the FCA.
- The FCA's approach for reporting transparency information for the quarterly reporting period ending Sep. 30, 2014.
- Where to go for more information on transparency reporting.
- The FCA's approach to missed or late transparency reporting.

It is your responsibility to know:

- *How the FCA's transparency reporting requirements apply to you.*
- *What transparency information you have to report.*
- *When you have to report transparency information and the reporting deadlines.*
- *The procedures for reporting transparency information to the FCA.*

TRANSPARENCY REPORTING REQUIREMENTS

Reporting to the FCA

1. The requirement for all types of AIFMs to report transparency information to competent authorities is established by Articles 3 (Exemptions) and 24 (Transparency Requirements) of the AIFMD. These require AIFMs to report transparency information to competent authorities about the AIFM, as manager, and the AIFs they are managing and, where relevant, marketing.
2. The FCA has incorporated the AIFMD transparency reporting requirements which apply to all types of AIFMs into the FCA Handbook, the "*Handbook*," which is available online at: http://fshandbook.info/FS/html/FCA.
3. The Handbook is divided into blocks and each block is subdivided into modules, which include Sourcebooks (containing regulatory obligations, which are binding on firms). Transparency reporting requirements are set out in the Supervision sourcebook (*SUP*) and Investment Funds sourcebook (*FUND*).
4. All authorized or registered AIFMs should refer to *SUP* and the transparency reporting requirements set out at *SUP* 16.18 (AIFMD reporting) which defines three authorized and registered AIFM types for the purposes of reporting:
   a. A full-scope UK AIFM.
   b. A small authorized UK AIFM.
   c. A small registered UK AIFM.
5. If you are a full-scope UK AIFM, you should also refer to FUND and the reporting requirements set out at FUND 3.4 (Reporting obligations to the FCA).
6. You may also find it helpful to refer to Annex I of ESMA's "Guidelines on reporting obligations under Articles 3(3)(d) and 24(1), (2) and (4) of the

AIFMD" which sets out "Reporting obligation diagrams" including a diagram for "Authorized AIFMs." ESMA's final version of guidelines was published on Aug. 8, 2014 and took effect from Oct. 8, 2014. The guidelines can be found at: http://www.esma.europa.eu/content/Guidelines-reporting-obligations-under-Articles-33d-and-241-2-and-4-AIFMD-0.

7. For more information about reporting, AIFMD transparency information you should refer to section "More Information on Transparency Reporting" at the end of this communication, which provides links to the AIFMD, AIFMD Level 2 Regulations, and ESMA guidelines on reporting.

Transparency Information to be Reported

8. SUP 16.18 and FUND 3.4 identifies the transparency information to be reported to the FCA as follows:
   d. Full-scope UK AIFMs, small authorized UK AIFMs and small registered UK AIFMs must report the information required by the Reporting to competent authorities table set out at SUP 16.18.4EU paragraphs 1 and 2.
   e. Full-scope UK AIFMs must also report the information required by FUND 3.4.2R, FUND 3.4.3R, FUND 3.4.5R and FUND 3.4.6AR (1).
   f. Full-scope UK AIFMs must also, under FUND 3.4.6AR (2), report the information required by FUND 3.4.3R for each non-EEA AIF that it manages that is not marketed in the EEA, if that AIF is the master AIF of a feeder AIF that it also manages, and that feeder AIF is (a) an EEA AIF; or (b) a non-EEA AIF that is marketed in the EEA.

Form of Transparency Information Reports

9. You must provide the required transparency information in accordance with the proforma reporting templates set out in Annex IV of the AIFMD Level 2 Regulation. The FCA will use two reports to collect transparency information which must be used by all AIFMs:
   a. AIF001—Manager Report: This is the report you must use to provide AIFM-specific information.
   b. AIF002—Fund Transparency Report: This is the report you must use to provide AIF-specific information.

Identifying the AIFM and the AIFs

10. The AIF001 and AIF002 reports require you to identify the AIFM and AIF(s) and when doing so you must only use:
   a. Your Firm Reference Number (FRN) issued by the FCA, which uniquely identifies you as the AIFM.
   b. Your Product Reference Number(s) (PRN(s)) issued by the FCA, which uniquely identify the AIF(s) that you are managing and, where relevant, marketing.

11. We have not yet generated and issued:
    a. FRNs to small registered UK AIFMs (who are not FSMA authorized firms).
    b. PRNs to full-scope UK AIFMs, small authorized UK AIFMs or to small registered UK AIFMs (with the exception of AIFMs that manage QIS or NURS AIFs who will have already been issued PRNs for an Umbrella AIF (but not the sub-funds) and/or standalone AIFs).
12. We will generate and issue FRNs and PRNs in conjunction with providing access to transparency reporting in GABRIEL. More information about how and when we will issue these reference numbers provide access to GABRIEL transparency reporting and the actions you must take, is set out below.
13. However, the AIF001 and AIF002 reports also request that you provide alternative identification code(s) elsewhere in the reports. You are encouraged to obtain as many as possible and, in particular obtain, and provide a Legal Entity Identification code (LEI code—the identifier referred to in the Financial Stability Board's recommendations on (A Global Legal Entity Identifier for Financial Markets). More information about LEI codes can be found on the website of the Legal Entity Identifier Regulatory Oversight Committee (ROC) at http://www.leiroc.org/. The issuance of LEI codes in line with the agreed principles for pre-Local Operating Unit solutions (LOUs) is currently underway. A list of globally endorsed pre-LOUs can be found on the ROC website and includes the London Stock Exchange under the sponsorship of the FCA.

Transparency Reporting in Relation to Different Fund Structures

14. If you are managing and, where relevant, marketing an AIF that is a fund-of-funds, feeder AIF and/or umbrella AIF, the information that you should report in respect of those AIFs has been addressed in guidance published by ESMA in "Guidelines on reporting obligations under Articles 3(3)(d) and 24(1), (2) and (4) of the AIFMD." ESMA's final version of guidelines was published on Aug. 8, 2014 and took effect from 8 Oct. 8, 2014. The guidelines can be found at: http://www.esma.europa.eu/content/Guidelines-reporting-obligations-under-Articles-33d-and-241-2-and-4-AIFMD-0.

Feeder AIFs

15. AIFMs should treat feeder AIFs of the same master fund individually. They should not aggregate all the information on feeder AIFs of the same master(s) in a single report. AIFMs should not aggregate master-feeder structures in a single report (ie, one report gathering all the information on feeder AIFs and their master AIFs).
16. When reporting information on feeder AIFs, AIFMs should identify the master AIF in which each feeder invests but should not look through to the holdings of the master AIFs. If applicable, AIFMs should also report

detailed information on investments that are made at feeder AIF level, such as investments in financial derivative instruments.

17. In addition to reporting on feeder AIFs, full-scope UK AIFMs must also, under FUND 3.4.6AR (2), report the information required by FUND 3.4.3R for each non-EEA AIF that it manages that is not marketed in the EEA, if that AIF is the master AIF of a feeder AIF that it also manages, and that feeder AIF is (a) an EEA AIF; or (b) a non-EEA AIF that is marketed in the EEA.

Funds of Funds

18. When reporting information on an AIF that is a fund of funds, AIFMs should not look through to the holdings of the underlying funds in which the AIF invests.

Umbrella and Subfund Structures

19. When reporting information on an AIF that takes the form of an umbrella AIF with several compartments or subfunds, AIF-specific information should be reported at the level of the compartments or subfunds.

20. In considering how to report in respect of umbrella and subfund structures you should have regard to The Perimeter Guidance Manual (PERG) Chapter 16 (Scope of the Alternative Investment Fund Managers Directive) and PERG 16.2G (What types of funds and businesses are caught?). Questions 2.61 to 2.65 are concerned with investment compartments and provide guidance on the identification and treatment of investment compartments.

Frequency of Transparency Reporting

21. SUP 16.18 sets out reporting frequencies and reporting periods for full-scope UK AIFMs, small authorized UK AIFMs and small registered UK AIFMs as set out below.

Small Authorized UK AIFM

22. Under SUP 16.18.6R a small authorized UK AIFM must report annually and its reporting period must end on 31 Dec. in each calendar year.

Small Registered UK AIFM

23. Under SUP 16.18.7D a small registered UK AIFM must report annually and its reporting period must end on 31 Dec. in each calendar year.

Full-Scope UK AIFM

24. Under SUP 16.18.4EU paragraph 3 a full-scope UK AIFM can be required to report on quarterly, half-yearly or annual basis. A full-scope UK AIFM determines its reporting frequency with reference to the AUM thresholds and other criteria set out in SUP 16.18.4EU paragraph 3 (a) to (d) inclusive.

25. Under SUP 16.18.5R the reporting periods of a full-scope UK AIFM must end on the following dates:
   a. AIFMs that are required to report annually, on 31 Dec. each calendar year.
   b. AIFMs that are required to report half-yearly, on 30 Jun. and 31 Dec. in each calendar year.
   c. AIFMs that are required to report quarterly, on 31 March, 30 June, 30 Sep. and 31 Dec. in each calendar year.

Transparency Reporting Submission Dates

26. Under SUP 16.18.4EU paragraph 1 you must provide your completed AIF001 and AIF002 reports to the FCA as soon as possible but not later than one month after the end of the annual (31 Dec.), half yearly (30 Jun. and 31 Dec.) and quarterly (31 Mar., 30 Jun., 30 Sep., and 31 Dec.) reporting periods.
27. If you are reporting in respect of an AIF that is a fund-of-funds you may extend the period available for reporting of the AIF001 and AIF002 reports by 15 days. This extended submission date applies only to AIFs that are fund-of-funds.
28. If you manage both (1) AIFs that are not fund-of-funds and also (2) AIFs that are fund-of-funds (for which you have extended the reporting date), you must submit reports to the FCA as follows:
   a. As soon as possible but not later than one month after the end of a reporting period—you must submit AIF001 and AIF002 reports in respect of all AIFs that are not fund-of-funds.
   b. Before the end of an extended 15 day reporting date—you must submit an AIF002 report in respect of all AIFs that are fund-of-funds and you must also submit an amended AIF001 report updated to accurately take account of the fund-of-funds transparency information being reported on the fund-of-funds AIF002 report.

First Transparency Reports

29. You are subject to the FCA transparency reporting requirements from the date of your authorization or registration.
30. In determining when you should begin reporting you should follow guidance issued by ESMA set out in Section VII (Procedure for first reporting) of "Guidelines on reporting obligations under Articles 3(3)(d) and 24(1), (2) and (4) of the AIFMD," ESMA/2014/869EN. ESMA's final version of guidelines were published on Aug. 8, 2014 and took effect from Oct. 8, 2014, they can be found at: http://www.esma.europa.eu/content/Guidelines-reporting-obligations-under-Articles-33d-and-241-2-and-4-AIFMD-0.

31. Your obligation to begin reporting starts from the first day of the following quarter after you have information to report until the end of the first reporting period. Your first report will due after the end of your first reporting period as determined in accordance with your reporting frequency.

32. Following authorization or registration there may be cases in which you do not have any information to report on AIFs, such as where there is a delay between the authorization or registration being granted and the actual start of activity or between the creation of an AIF and the first investments. In such a scenario, we expect to receive from you AIF001 and AIF002 reports for the (earlier) reporting periods for which you have no information to report (which starts from the first day of the following quarter after authorization or registration) indicating that you have no information to report by using the specific field to indicate a Nil return.

Example

33. An AIFM is authorized on 31 Jan. and has information to report as from 24 Apr. The AIFM determines that it is required to report on a quarterly basis with reporting period end dates 31 Mar., 30 Jun., 30 Sep. and 31 Dec. In this case the AIFM must:

   a. Submit a Nil return for its AIF001 and AIF002 reports for the quarterly reporting period ending 30 June. The report will cover the quarterly period from 1 Apr. to 30 Jun. (the quarter following the date of authorization). The report must be received by the FCA as soon as possible but not later than one month after the end of the reporting period which may be extended by 15 days for an AIF that is a fund-of-funds.

   b. Submit full report information in AIF001 and AIF002 reports for the quarterly reporting period ending 30 Sep. The report will cover the period from 1 Jul. to 30 Sep. (the first quarter following the first point from which information to report arose). The first AIF001 and AIF002 reports must be submitted to the FCA as soon as possible and not later than one month after the end of the 30 Sep. reporting period end date, which may be extended by 15 days for an AIF that is a fund of funds.

REPORTING TRANSPARENCY INFORMATION TO THE FCA

GABRIEL reporting

Access to GABRIEL

34. GABRIEL is the FCA's online regulatory reporting system for the collection, validation, and storage of regulatory data. We will use GABRIEL for the purposes of transparency reporting.

35. GABRIEL and supporting systems have been developed to enable submission and reporting of AIF001 and AIF002 reports by all AIFMs.
36. Transparency reporting in GABRIEL is live and we provided access to the reporting functions in phases in conjunction with the generation and issuance of PRNs and FRNs as required.
37. Once you have been given access to GABRIEL transparency reporting, as set out below, we will only accept AIF001 and AIF002 reports submitted via GABRIEL.

Full-Scope UK AIFMs with Quarterly Sep. 30, 2014 Reporting Obligations

38. We are prioritizing access to GABRIEL transparency reporting for full-scope UK AIFMs with quarterly transparency reporting obligations that are required to report to the FCA for the quarterly period ending Sep. 30, 2014. We have provided more information about prioritized access in the section titled "Transparency Reporting Requirement—Quarterly Reporting Period Ending Sep. 30, 2014" below.

Full-Scope UK AIFMs and Small Authorized UK AIFMs

39. Once we have completed the prioritized access we will begin the roll out of GABRIEL transparency reporting for the remainder of full-scope UK AIFMs and small authorized UK AIFMs, when we will also generate and issue PRNs. To determine when you have access to GABRIEL transparency reporting and to obtain details of your PRNs you must continue to access and check your GABRIEL user account after Oct. 20, 2014. We do not intend to communicate directly with individual full-scope UK AIFMs or small authorized UK AIFMs to provide notification of GABRIEL access or details of PRNs.

Small Registered UK AIFMs

40. Small registered UK AIFMs will be will be given access to GABRIEL transparency reporting during Nov. 2014.
    a. To register, access, and use GABRIEL you will need to have received certain information from the FCA. We intend to send this information to you by email to the address of the contact person identified during the FCA's registration procedure.
    b. The FCA email (the notification email) will contain all of the information you will need to register in GABRIEL as follows:
       - Your FRN that identifies you as the AIFM.
       - The PRN(s) of your AIF(s).
       - A unique GABRIEL registration key—a unique access code that you must use when registering with GABRIEL and activating your user account which we will have established for you.

All AIFM Types — Initial Action Required in GABRIEL

41. You are responsible for verifying that AIF001 and AIF002 transparency reporting functionality has been correctly established in your GABRIEL user account which will include completing the following actions as applicable:

  a. Register with GABRIEL—you must first register with GABRIEL (this step will not apply to existing users of GABRIEL). Information about registering to use GABRIEL and submitting reports to the FCA is available on the FCA website at the following address: http://www.fca.org.uk/firms/systems-reporting/gabriel/firm-registration.

  b. Access your GABRIEL user account.

  c. Review your schedule of regulatory reporting shown on the "Firm Schedule—Reporting Period" page (the reporting schedule) that will be displayed when accessing your GABRIEL account. The reporting schedule displays the returns you are required to submit on a rolling 12 months basis, which you should ensure includes AIF001 and AIF002 reporting obligations.

  d. Verify that the AIF001 and AIF002 reports in your reporting schedule are correctly identified with your unique FRN and PRN(s) that identify you as the AIFM and your AIF(s).

  e. Verify that your reporting schedule accurately records your actual reporting obligation for AIF001 and AIF002 reports.

  - The initial schedule of reporting obligations that will be displayed in GABRIEL will be established by the FCA based on your authorization and registration status and without reference to information that will be contained in up-to-date AIF001 and AIF002 reports.

  - The obligations that will be initially established will be: *half-yearly reporting for full-scope UK AIFMs and annual reporting for small authorized UK AIFMs and small registered UK AIFMs.*

  - This is an initial scheduling only and it *should NOT be relied upon as being correct.* You are responsible for assessing your own reporting obligations and determining the date by which your first AIF001 and AIF002 reports must be received by the FCA, and the subsequent frequency of reporting, so that you submit these reports within the required timeframe.

  - It is your responsibility to ensure that the reporting obligation displayed in your reporting schedule is correct. If the reporting frequency is incorrect you must submit AIF001 reports and AIF002 in which you have recorded the actual reporting obligation using the appropriate change in reporting frequency codes to communicate a change in frequency. These reports would be submitted at your next scheduled reporting period or the next reporting period, which you have determined to be your actual reporting period.

Example—If the frequency is too low

- In this case your GABRIEL reporting schedule displays half-yearly reporting when you determine it should be quarterly. Regardless of the reporting obligation displayed on your reporting schedule, you would submit AIF001 and AIF002 reports for the next quarterly reporting period once the relevant period end date has passed and within the reporting deadline. You would complete both reports using the appropriate change in frequency code to communicate the future change in reporting frequency to quarterly reporting. The code provided in the reports will be used by GABRIEL to reschedule and display your transparency-reporting obligation according the submitted frequency code (in this example quarterly reporting).

Example - If the frequency is too high

- In this case GABRIEL reporting schedule displays half-yearly reporting when you determine it should be annual. Regardless of the reporting obligation displayed on your reporting schedule, you would submit AIF001 and AIF002 reports for the next half-yearly reporting period once the relevant period end date has passed and within the reporting deadline. You would complete both reports using the appropriate change in frequency code to communicate the future change in reporting frequency to annual reporting. The code provided in the reports will be used by GABRIEL to reschedule and display your transparency-reporting obligation according the submitted frequency code (in this example annual reporting).

- Frequency and content change code information is set out in the Data Reference Guides for the AIF001 and AIF002 reports which are published on the FCA website at: http://www.fca.org.uk/firms/systems-reporting/gabriel/system-information/data-reference-guides/aifmd.

- If you have any other difficulties with the set-up of transparency reporting please contact our Customer Contact Centre at the telephone number and/or email address set out in the section titled "GABRIEL support" below.

Ongoing Responsibility

42. Reporting transparency information according to your actual reporting obligation and maintaining the accuracy of your reporting schedule in GABRIEL is an ongoing responsibility. You must use the change in reporting frequency and change in reporting content codes to indicate a future change in your reporting obligations. As set out in the section above 'All AIFM types—Initial action required in GABRIEL', regardless of the reporting obligation displayed in your reporting schedule, you can submit AIF001 and AIF002 reports to remain in compliance with your assessment of actual reporting obligations and to indicate changes in your reporting obligations. We will continue to monitor compliance with transparency reporting requirements including the submission of AIF001 and AIF002 reports within timescales as scheduled in GABRIEL and also whether AIFMs, regardless of the GABRIEL reporting schedule, are reporting according to the actual reporting requirement.

Submitting Transparency Reports Using GABRIEL

43. GABRIEL provides the following methods for you to load AIF001 and AIF002 reports for submission to the FCA (the loading and submitting of data are two independent actions found in different parts of the GABRIEL system). You are able to select the most suitable method to your business for loading data from the following methods:
   a. Online Forms (manually keying data into GABRIEL forms).
   b. File upload via webpage (manually controlled, XML only).
   c. Direct communication (system-to-system data service for XML).

44. You must use only v1.1 of the ESMA reporting documents when reporting to the FCA. We recognize that this approach differs from the ESMA guidance regarding completion of v1.2 and may also differ from the requirement of other competent authorities. We have provided technical information regarding the use of v1.1 in our Questions and Answers published on the "Reporting" page in the AIFMD section of the FCA website—the link can be found in the section titled "More Information on Transparency Reporting" set out below.

45. GABRIEL provides functionality that will allow you to: load and/or enter information during multiple system sessions, report multiple AIFs on a single AIF002 report, and to make amendments to information during and after formal submission.

46. Importantly, when you are required to submit AIF001 and AIF002 reports for a particular reporting period you must, in all cases, after the end date of the quarterly, half-yearly or annual reporting period, and before the end of the period in which your transparency reporting must be submitted, complete the following actions:
   a. For the AIFM and each AIF (for which there is a reporting obligation), enter and/or load the required AIF001 report and AIF002 reports into GABRIEL with all required and relevant data fields completed (reports are loaded via the "AIFMD section" of GABRIEL)—GABRIEL monitors reporting compliance at an AIF level.
   b. After AIF001 and AIF002 reports have been entered and/or loaded they must be submitted which is a separate action and takes place in a different part of GABRIEL. To complete the reporting process you must use the "Firm Schedule—Reporting Period" page to select a "Return Due Date" item which leads to the "Data Items in Reporting Period" page. This page displays the "completion status" of data items due on the reporting date. To submit a report you must click the "submit" button for

each required AIF001 and AIF002 report which changes the GABRIEL status of the report to "submitted." Only when the GABRIEL status of the report changes to submitted will you have satisfied the reporting obligation for that particular report.

47. Although GABRIEL permits the amendment of AIF001 and AIF002 submitted reports, we expect this function to be used sparingly in exceptional circumstances only. At the expiry of the relevant reporting deadline, we expect AIFMs to have submitted all applicable AIF001 and AIF002 reports that have been completed using the most accurate data and up-to-date information available to the AIFM at that point in time. In any event, the FCA must receive amended data by resubmission, which is complete, accurate and final no later than one month after the reporting deadline (ie, no later than two months after the end of the relevant reporting period). Although amendment of data may be necessary, for example to add important precision, we do not expect that AIFMs will need to use this function to make wholesale or fundamental changes to data already submitted.

48. An overview of the available submission methods is provided on the FCA website at the following address: http://www.fca.org.uk/firms/systems-reporting/gabriel/system-information/overview-of-submission-methods.

49. AIFMs should also refer to the GABRIEL Data Reference Guides (DRGs) which sets out the specifications for GABRIEL data items and other related material to help firms submit data using system-to-system (direct communication) and XML upload submission methods.

   a. GABRIEL DRGs can be found on the FCA website at the following address: http://www.fca.org.uk/firms/systems-reporting/gabriel/system-information/data-reference-guides.

   b. Specific GABRIEL DRGs for transparency reporting using the AIF001 and AIF002 reports can be found on the FCA website at the following address: http://www.fca.org.uk/firms/systems-reporting/gabriel/system-information/data-reference-guides/aifmd.

MISSED OR LATE TRANSPARENCY REPORTING

50. FCA will use GABRIEL and supporting systems to monitor the compliance of all AIFMs with our transparency reporting requirements.

51. If you fail to submit an AIF001 and/or AIF002 report(s) by the due date following the end of an annual, half-yearly or quarterly reporting period as scheduled, FCA may require you to pay an administrative fee of £250.

52. FCA may, from time to time, send reminders when AIF001 and/or AIF002 reports are overdue. You should not, however, assume that the FCA have received a report merely because you have not received a reminder.

53. If an AIFM still does not complete and submit its AIF001 and/or AIF002 reports after receiving a reminder of non-compliance, the FCA are able to take enforcement action. Ultimately, this could result in a full-scope UK

AIFM or a small authorized UK AIFM having its authorization cancelled or a small registered UK AIFM having its registration revoked including, where applicable, its registration as a EuSEF manager or EuVECA manager.

54. You are permitted to delegate the function of transparency reporting to an external vendor. At all times, however, you will be responsible for ensuring that reports are submitted in full compliance with the transparency requirements set out in the FCA's rules.

TRANSPARENCY REPORTING REQUIREMENT—QUARTERLY REPORTING PERIOD ENDING SEP. 30, 2014

55. Certain full-scope UK AIFMs with quarterly reporting obligations will be required to complete and submit the required AIF001 and AIF002 reports to the FCA for the quarterly reporting period ending Sep. 30, 2014.

56. To ensure that the FCA can prioritize the establishment of GABRIEL transparency reporting for the whole population of full-scope UK AIFMs with a Sep. 30, 2014 reporting obligation the FCA request that AIFMs in this category contact the FCA using the following email address: firm.queries@fca.org.uk. AIFMs should include in the subject line "Quarterly Reporting Sep. 30, 2014." This will complement the actions we are also taking to identify this population of full-scope UK AIFMs.

57. The FCA will prioritize access to GABRIEL transparency reporting for full-scope UK AIFMs that are required to submit AIF001 and AIF002 for the quarterly reporting period ending Sep. 30, 2014 starting from 8:00 am Monday Oct.20, 2014 when GABRIEL first becomes available. GABRIEL can then be used by these AIFMs to meet their Sep. 30, 2014 quarterly reporting obligation.

MORE INFORMATION ON TRANSPARENCY REPORTING

58. More information about transparency reporting requirements can be found in the publications set out below with links. All documents should be considered in the context of ESMA's IT technical guidance regarding the use of XML v1.2 and the FCA's current position that it will only accept reports submitted using XML v1.1.

   a. Article 3 (Exemptions) and 24 (Reporting obligations to competent authorities) of the AIFMD - Directive 2011/61/EU of The European Parliament and of The Council of Jun. 8, 2011. The Directive can be found at: http://eur-lex.europa.eu/legal-content/EN/TXT/PDF/?uri=CELEX:32011L0061&from=EN.

   b. Article 110 (Reporting to competent authorities) and Annex IV Reporting Templates - Commission Delegated Regulation (EU) No 231/2013 of Dec. 19, 2012. The Regulation can be found at: http://eur-lex.europa.eu/legal-content/EN/TXT/PDF/?uri=CELEX:32013R0231&from=EN.

    c. Final report, Guidelines on reporting obligations under Articles 3(3)(d) and 24(1), (2) and (4) of the AIFMD, dated Nov. 15, 2013, ESMA/2013/1339. The guidelines can be found at: http://www.esma.europa.eu/content/Guidelines-reporting-obligations-under-Articles-33d-and-241-2-and-4-AIFMD-revised.

    d. Questions and Answers, Application of the AIFMD, dated Jul. 21, 2014, ESMA/2014/868. The questions and answers can be found at: http://www.esma.europa.eu/content/Update-Questions-and-Answers-QA-application-AIFMD.

    e. ESMA's final version of its guidelines, Guidelines on reporting obligations under Articles 3(3)(d) and 24(1), (2) and (4) of the AIFMD, ESMA/2014/869EN, referred to in the above document (c), were published on Aug. 8, 2014 and will take effect from Oct. 8, 2014. The guidelines can be found at: http://www.esma.europa.eu/content/Guidelines-reporting-obligations-under-Articles-33d-and-241-2-and-4-AIFMD-0.

59. The FCA have also published a set of Questions and Answers on transparency reporting (Reporting Transparency Information to the FCA) our website at the address below which are relevant to all types of AIFM: http://www.fca.org.uk/firms/markets/international-markets/aifmd/reporting.

Appendix 6

European Securities and Markets Authority

Questions and Answers

Application of the AIFMD

17.02.2014 | ESMA/2014/163

 European Securities and
Markets Authority

Date: 17 February 2014
2014/ESMA/163

Contents

I. Background

1. The Alternative Investment Fund Managers Directive (AIFMD) puts in place a comprehensive frame- work for the regulation of alternative investment fund managers within Europe. The extensive requirements with which AIFMs must comply are designed to ensure that these managers can manage AIFs on a cross-border basis and the AIFs that they manage can be sold on a cross-border basis.

2. The AIFMD framework is made up of the following EU legislation:

   a. Directive 2011/61/EU[1], which was adopted in 2011. It is a "framework" Level 1 Directive which has been supplemented by technical delegated and implementing measures.

   b. Commission Regulation (EU) No 231/2013[2], Commission Regulation (EU) No 447/2013[3] and Commission Regulation (EU) No 448/2013[4].

3. ESMA is required to play an active role in building a common supervisory culture by promoting common supervisory approaches and practices.

---

1. DIRECTIVE 2011/61/EU of the European Parliament and of the Council of 8 June 2011 on Alternative Investment Fund Managers and amending Directives 2003/41/EC and 2009/65/EC and Regulations (EC) No 1060/2009 and (EU) No 1095/2010

2. COMMISSION DELEGATED REGULATION (EU) No 231/2013 of 19 December 2012 supplementing Directive 2011/61/EU of the European Parliament and of the Council with regard to exemptions, general operating conditions, depositaries, leverage, transparency and supervision

3. COMMISSION DELEGATED REGULATION (EU) No 447/2013 of 15 May 2013 establishing the procedure for AIFMs which choose to opt in under Directive 2011/61/EU of the European Parliament and of the Council

4. COMMISSION DELEGATED REGULATION (EU) No 448/2013 of 15 May 2013 establishing a procedure for determining the Member State of reference of a non-EU AIFM pursuant to Directive 2011/61/EU of the European Parliament and of the Council

In this regard, the Authority develops Q&As as and when appropriate to elaborate on the provisions of certain EU legislation or ESMA guidelines.

4. The European Commission has already published its own Q&A on AIFMD[5].

II. Purpose

5. The purpose of this document is to promote common supervisory approaches and practices in the application of the AIFMD and its implementing measures. It does this by providing responses to questions posed by the general public and competent authorities in relation to the practical application of the AIFMD.

6. The content of this document is aimed at competent authorities under AIFMD to ensure that in their supervisory activities their actions are converging along the lines of the responses adopted by ESMA. However, the answers are also intended to help AIFMs by providing clarity as to the content of the AIFMD rules, rather than creating an extra layer of requirements.

III. Status

7. The Q&A mechanism is a practical convergence tool used to promote common supervisory approaches and practices under Article 29(2) of the ESMA Regulation.[6]

8. Therefore, due to the nature of Q&As, formal consultation on the draft answers is considered unnecessary. However, even if they are not formally consulted on, ESMA may check them with representatives of ESMA's Securities and Markets Stakeholder Group, the relevant Standing Committees' Consultative Working Group or, where specific expertise is needed, with other external parties.

9. ESMA will review these questions and answers on a regular basis to identify if, in a certain area, there is a need to convert some of the material into ESMA guidelines. In such cases, the procedures foreseen under Article 16 of the ESMA Regulation will be followed.

IV. Questions and answers

10. This document is intended to be continually edited and updated as and when new questions are received. The date each question was last amended is included after each question for ease of reference.

11. General questions on the practical application of the AIFMD may be sent to the following email address: AIFMD-questions@esma.europa.eu. However, questions that relate specifically to technical IT issues regarding the AIFMD reporting requirements (such as on the XSD documents or the IT technical guidance) should be sent to: info.it.aifmd@esma.europa.eu.

---

5. http://ec.europa.eu/yqol/index.cfm?fuseaction=legislation.show&lid=9

6. Regulation (EU) No 1095/2010 of the European Parliament and of the Council of 24 November 2010 establishing a European Supervisory Authority (European Securities and Markets Authority), amending Decision No 716/2009/EC and repealing Commis- sion Decision 2009/77/EC Regulation, 15.12.2010, L331/84.

QUESTION 1: FIRST APPLICATION OF THE REMUNERATION RULES

Date Last Updated: 17 February 2014

Question 1a: To which accounting period should AIFMs performing activities under the AIFMD before 22 July 2013 and submitting an application for authorisation under the AIFMD between 22 July 2013 and 22 July 2014 apply the AIFMD remuneration rules for the first time?

Answer 1a: Paragraph 4 of the Guidelines on sound remuneration policies under the AIFMD (ES- MA/2013/232) (the Remuneration Guidelines) states that *"These Guidelines apply from 22 July 2013, subject to the transitional provisions of the AIFMD"*. The Commission Q&A on the AIFMD provided specific guidance on the interpretation of the transitional provisions under Article 61(1) of the AIFMD.[7]

According to Article 61(1) of the AIFMD, AIFMs performing activities under the AIFMD before 22 July 2013 have one year from that date to submit an application for authorisation. Once a firm becomes authorised under the AIFMD, it becomes subject to the AIFMD remuneration rules and the Remuneration Guidelines. Therefore, the relevant rules should start applying as of the date of authorisation.

However, as for the rules on variable remuneration (ie, the ones for which guidance is provided under Sections XI. (Guidelines on the general requirements on risk alignment) and XII. (Guidelines on the specific requirements on risk alignment) of the Remuneration Guidelines), AIFMs should apply them for the calculation of payments relating to new awards of variable remuneration to their *identified staff* (as defined in the Remuneration Guidelines) for performance periods following that in which they become authorised. So the AIFMD regime on variable remuneration should apply only to full performance periods and should first apply to the first full performance period after the AIFM becomes authorised. For example:

- An existing AIFM whose accounting period ends on 31 December and which obtained an authorisation between 22 July 2013 and 31 December 2013: the AIFMD rules on variable remuneration should apply to the calculation of payments relating to the 2014 accounting period.
- An existing AIFM whose accounting period ends on 31 December obtains an authorisation between 1 January 2014 and 22 July 2014: the AIFMD rules on variable remuneration should apply to the calculation of payments relating to the 2015 accounting period.

---

7. ID 1180. Transitional provisions, available at: http://ec.europa.eu/yqol/index.cfm?fuseaction=question.show&questionId=1180.

However, for an existing AIFM whose accounting period ends on 31 December which submits an application for authorisation by 22 July 2014 and obtains an authorisation after that date (including when the authorisation is obtained after 31 December 2014), the AIFMD rules on variable remuneration should apply to the calculation of payments relating to the 2015 accounting period.

Question 1b: To which accounting period should AIFMs not performing activities under the AIFMD before Jul. 22, 2013 and obtaining an authorization under the AIFMD after 22 July 2013 apply the remuneration rules for the first time?

Answer 1b: Once a firm becomes authorised under the AIFMD, it becomes subject to the AIFMD remuneration rules and the Remuneration Guidelines and the relevant rules should start to apply as of the date of authorisation.

However, as for the rules on variable remuneration (ie, the ones for which guidance is provided under Sections XI. (Guidelines on the general requirements on risk alignment) and XII. (Guidelines on the specific requirements on risk alignment) of the Remuneration Guidelines), AIFMs should apply them for the calculation of payments relating to new awards of variable remuneration to their *identified staff* (as defined in the Remuneration Guidelines) for performance periods following that in which they submit an application for authorisation. An AIFM submitting an application for authorisation in the year N (after 22 July 2013), should apply the AIFMD remuneration regime on variable remuneration only to the calculation of payments relating to the accounting period for year N + 1.

QUESTION 2: REMUNERATION RULES IN CASE OF DELEGATION OF PORTFOLIO MANAGEMENT OR RISK MANAGEMENT ACTIVITIES

Date Last Updated: 17 February 2014

Question 2a: Which staff of the delegate should be covered by the "appropriate contractual arrangements" that ensure there is no circumvention of the remuneration rules as set out in paragraph 18(b) of the Remuneration Guidelines?

Answer 2a: Such contractual arrangements must only be in place in respect of the delegate's *identified staff* who have a material impact on the risk profiles of the AIFs it manages as a result of the delegation, and only in respect of the remuneration for such delegated activities.

Question 2b: In a delegation arrangement where the delegate is subject to the CRD rules, can the delegate be considered to be subject to regulatory requirements on remuneration that are equally as effective as those applicable under the Remuneration Guidelines?

Answer 2b: Provided that the staff of these entities who are *identified staff* for the purpose of the Remuneration Guidelines are subject to the CRD rules, these entities are subject to regulatory requirements on remuneration that are equally as effective as those applicable under the Guidelines.

QUESTION 3: ANNEX IV OF THE AIFMD

Date Last Updated: 17 February 2014

Question 3: What additional information should be provided under letter (f) of Annex IV of the AIFMD?

Answer 3: Letter (f) of Annex IV of the AIFMD should be understood as requesting all information set out in Article 23(1) of the AIFMD that is not already contained in Annex IV of the AIFMD.

QUESTION 4: NOTIFICATIONS OF AIFs

Date Last Updated: 17 February 2014

Question 4: Should AIFMs that wish to market new investment compartments of AIFs in a Member State where these AIFs have been already notified undertake a new notification procedure via their competent authority?

Answer 4: Yes.

QUESTION 5: REPORTING UNDER ARTICLE 42 OF THE AIFMD

Date Last Updated: 17 February 2014

Question 5: When a non-EU AIFM reports information to the national competent authorities of a Member State under Article 42 of the AIFMD, which AIFs have to be included in the reports?

Answer 5: When a non-EU AIFM reports information to the national competent authorities of a Member State under Article 42, only the AIFs marketed in that Member State have to be taken into account for the purpose of the reporting.

Appendix 7

China Securities Regulatory Commission (CSRC)

China Securities Regulatory Commission (CSRC), a ministerial-level public institution directly under the State Council, performs a unified regulatory function, according to the relevant laws and regulations, and with the authority by the State Council, over the securities and futures market of China, maintains an orderly securities and futures market order, and ensure a legal operation of the capital market.

China Securities Regulatory Commission is located in Beijing, with appointed one chairman, four vice chairmen, one secretary of the Disciplinary Inspection Commission (on the vice-ministerial level) and three assistants to the chairman. CSRC has 18 functional departments, one inspection division and three centers. In accordance with Article 14 of the "Securities Law of the People's Republic of China," CSRC has set up a public offering review committee, which is formed of professionals of CSRC and invited experts from without the committee. China Securities Regulatory Commission has established 36 securities regulatory bureaus in provinces, autonomous regions, municipalities directly under the Central Government and cities specifically designated in the state plan, and, in addition, Shanghai Commissioner Office and Shenzhen Commissioner Office.

Pursuant to the relevant laws and regulations, China Securities Regulatory Commission performs the following duties in the supervision and administration of the securities market:

1. Study and formulate policies and development plans for the securities and futures markets; draft the relevant laws and regulations on the securities and futures markets as well as put forward suggestions for formulation or modification of the said laws and regulations; and work out the relevant rules, regulations, and measures for the securities and futures markets;
2. Exercise a vertical administration over the domestic securities and futures regulatory institutions and conduct a unified supervision over the securities and futures markets; and perform a regulatory supervision over the managements and the managerial officials of the relevant securities companies;

Fund Custody and Administration

219

3. Supervise the issuance, listing, trading, custody and settlement of stocks, convertible bonds, bonds of securities companies, and bonds and other securities under the charge of CSRC as assigned by the State Council; supervise the securities investment bonds; approve the listing of corporate bonds; and supervise the trading of the listed treasury bonds and corporate bonds;

4. Supervise the securities market behaviors of the listed companies and their shareholders who shall fulfill the relevant obligations according to the relevant laws and regulations;

5. Supervise the listing, trading, and settlement of domestic contract-based futures; and monitor the overseas futures businesses of the domestic institutions in accordance with the relevant regulations;

6. Supervise the securities and futures exchanges as well as their senior managerial personnel in accordance with the relevant regulations; and supervise the securities and futures associations in the capacity of a competent authority;

7. Supervise the securities and futures business institutions, securities investment fund management companies, securities depository and clearing corporations, futures clearing institutions, securities and futures investment consulting institutions, and securities credit rating institutions; examine and approve the qualifications of fund custodian institutions, and supervise their fund custody businesses; formulate and implement measures on the qualifications of senior management for the relevant institutions; and guide the Securities Association of China and the Futures Associations of China in the administration of the qualifications of the personnel engaged in securities and futures businesses;

8. Supervise the direct or indirect issuance and listing of shares overseas by domestic enterprises as well as the listing of convertible bonds by the companies listed overseas; supervise the establishment of securities and futures institutions overseas by domestic securities and futures business institutions; and supervise the establishment of securities and futures institutions in China by overseas institutions for securities and futures businesses;

9. Supervise the communication of the securities and futures information; and take charge of the management of the statistics and information resources for the securities and futures markets;

10. Work with the relevant authorities in the examination and approval of the qualifications of the accounting firms, the asset evaluation institutions and their personnel for securities and futures intermediary businesses; and supervise the law firms, the lawyers and the eligible accounting firms, the asset appraisal institutions and their personnel in their securities and futures business activities;

11. Investigate and penalize the activities in violation of the relevant securities and futures laws and regulations;

12. Administer the foreign exchanges and international cooperation affairs of the securities and futures sector in the capacity of a competent authority; and
13. Perform other duties as assigned by the State Council.

Source: CSRC

SUGGESTED FURTHER READING

http://www.brookings.edu/~/media/research/files/papers/2013/07/01-chinese-financial-system-elliott-yan/chinese-financial-system-elliott-yan.pdf

Appendix 8

October 2015—Top 10 Performing Funds

Fund	October return
Invesco Perpetual US Equity Acc	10.14%
Legal & General Global Technology Index R Acc	9.67%
CF Ruffer Japanese O Acc	9.29%
Invesco Global Technology A Annual Dist USD	9.23%
Henderson Global Technology A Net Acc	9.16%
Neuberger Berman China Equity USD A Acc	9.1%
Neptune China A Acc GBP	9%
UBS US Growth Acc A	8.96%
NFU Mutual Global Growth A	8.94%
Invesco Perpetual Hong Kong & China Acc	8

Source: City AM/Hargreaves Lansdown Nov. 4, 2015 http://www.cityam.com/227976/worried-about-your-pension-investments-chinas-staged-a-glorious-return-to-the-10-best-performing-funds?utm_medium=Email&utm_source=Email&utm_campaign=151104_CMU

Appendix 9

Global OTC Derivatives Market-Source BIS

In billions of US dollars   Table D5

	Notional amounts outstanding				Gross market value			
	H2 2013	H1 2014	H2 2014	H1 2015	H2 2013	H1 2014	H2 2014	H1 2015
All contracts	*710,633*	*691,640*	*629,142*	*552,909*	*18,825*	*17,438*	*20,878*	*15,521*
Foreign exchange contracts	*70,553*	*74,782*	*75,879*	*74,519*	*2,284*	*1,724*	*2,944*	*2,547*
By instrument								
Outright forwards and fx swaps	33,218	35,190	37,076	37,238	824	572	1,205	936
Currency swaps	25,448	26,141	24,204	23,724	1,186	939	1,351	1,286
Options	11,886	13,451	14,600	13,558	273	213	389	326
By counterparty								
Reporting dealers	31,206	31,971	31,933	30,741	1,011	709	1,315	1,025
Other financial institutions	30,552	33,700	34,334	33,323	887	693	1,163	1,001
Nonfinancial customers	8,794	9,111	9,612	10,456	386	321	466	522
By maturity								
Up to one year	51,198	55,115	56,831	56,843	...	...	...	...
Between one and five years	13,658	13,912	13,664	12,405	...	...	...	...
Over five years	5,696	5,756	5,384	5,271	...	...	...	...
By currency								
USD	61,019	65,135	67,235	64,096	1,917	1,399	2,653	2,193
EUR	25,177	26,450	25,515	27,340	707	602	972	988
JPY	14,122	13,179	14,244	13,495	721	352	785	493
GBP	8,789	9,184	8,420	9,034	256	243	241	311
CHF	4,070	3,945	4,178	3,927	133	110	139	143
CAD	3,263	3,252	3,143	3,583	74	85	103	126
SEK	1,407	1,334	1,117	1,227	28	24	41	29
Other currencies	23,258	27,087	27,905	26,336	731	632	954	810
Interest rate contracts	*584,799*	*563,290*	*505,454*	*434,740*	*14,200*	*13,461*	*15,608*	*11,081*
By instrument								
FRAs	78,810	92,575	80,836	74,641	108	126	145	143

(Continued)

Fund Custody and Administration

225

	Notional amounts outstanding				Gross market value			
	H2 2013	H1 2014	H2 2014	H1 2015	H2 2013	H1 2014	H2 2014	H1 2015
Swaps	456,725	421,273	381,028	319,954	12,919	12,042	13,946	9,814
Options	49,264	49,442	43,591	40,145	1,174	1,292	1,517	1,124
By counterparty								
Reporting dealers	95,762	84,520	69,806	61,031	3,741	3,719	3,981	3,104
Other financial institutions	471,870	463,021	421,397	359,808	9,673	8,871	10,682	7,180
Nonfinancial customers	17,168	15,749	14,251	13,901	786	871	946	797
By maturity								
Up to one year	198,655	228,898	200,800	180,500	...	...	...	...
Between one and five years	234,352	208,309	184,661	151,870	...	...	...	...
Over five years	151,793	126,083	119,992	102,369	...	...	...	...
By currency								
USD	173,382	160,805	172,546	159,811	4,314	3,246	3,601	2,751
EUR	241,668	221,855	167,267	126,106	6,989	7,362	8,185	5,273
JPY	52,551	51,706	46,127	44,041	696	759	798	585
GBP	52,626	60,823	57,008	46,563	1,294	1,079	1,828	1,391
CHF	5,750	5,343	4,776	3,994	121	113	128	131
CAD	10,385	10,471	10,086	10,532	139	126	163	213
SEK	6,662	6,229	4,830	4,158	81	114	115	92
Other currencies	41,777	46,059	42,814	39,535	566	661	790	645
Equity-linked contracts	*6,560*	*7,084*	*6,968*	*7,545*	*700*	*678*	*612*	*606*
By instrument								
Forwards and swaps	2,277	2,505	2,495	2,801	202	199	177	168
Options	4,284	4,579	4,473	4,744	498	479	435	438
By counterparty								
Reporting dealers	2,097	2,444	2,364	2,529	244	228	200	212
Other financial institutions	3,874	3,939	3,909	4,279	348	346	288	268
Nonfinancial customers	589	702	696	737	108	105	124	126
By maturity								
Up to one year	3,688	4,116	4,491	4,958	...	...	...	...
Between one and five years	2,265	2,366	2,038	2,149	...	...	...	...
Over five years	607	602	440	438	...	...	...	...
By market								
US equities	2,187	2,522	2,904	3,239	301	302	289	258
European equities	2,752	2,900	2,428	2,692	243	229	179	192
Japanese equities	565	501	510	416	66	56	49	51
Other Asian equities	297	341	351	444	21	23	20	20
Latin American equities	163	178	178	178	10	11	11	11
Other equities	596	643	597	576	60	57	66	74

Appendix 10

Global OTC Derivatives Market-Source BIS

In billions of US dollars   Table D5

	Notional amounts outstanding				Gross market value			
	H2 2013	H1 2014	H2 2014	H1 2015	H2 2013	H1 2014	H2 2014	H1 2015
Commodity contracts	*2,204*	*2,206*	*1,869*	*1,671*	*264*	*269*	*318*	*237*
By commodity								
Gold	341	319	323	247	47	32	34	26
Other precious metal	63	94	66	61	7	7	7	7
Other commodities	1,800	1,792	1,481	1,363	210	230	277	205
By instrument and commodity								
Forwards and swaps	1,462	1,474	1,215	1,101	...	...	...	...
Gold	202	191	177	156	...	...	...	...
Other precious metal	31	50	35	37	...	...	...	...
Other commodities	1,228	1,233	1,003	908	...	...	...	...
Total options	742	732	654	570	...	...	...	...
Gold	139	128	145	92	...	...	...	...
Other precious metal	31	44	31	24	...	...	...	...
Other commodities	572	559	478	454	...	...	...	...
Options sold (gross basis)	436	432	396	350	...	...	...	...
Gold	86	76	88	56	...	...	...	...
Other precious metal	21	28	19	15	...	...	...	...
Other commodities	329	328	289	278	...	...	...	...

(Continued)

	Notional amounts outstanding				Gross market value			
	H2 2013	H1 2014	H2 2014	H1 2015	H2 2013	H1 2014	H2 2014	H1 2015
Options bought (gross basis)	472	463	404	348	...	...	...	...
Gold	84	81	90	56	...	...	...	...
Other precious metal	18	26	19	14	...	...	...	...
Other commodities	370	356	295	278	...	...	...	...
Credit default swaps	*21,020*	*19,462*	*16,399*	*14,596*	*653*	*635*	*593*	*453*
By instrument								
Single-name instruments	11,324	10,845	9,041	8,205	369	368	366	278
Multiname instruments	9,696	8,617	7,358	6,391	284	266	227	175
Index products	8,746	7,939	6,747	5,909	...	...	...	...
By counterparty								
Reporting dealers	11,053	9,540	7,717	6,505	369	313	289	211
Other financial institutions	9,779	9,719	8,485	7,885	276	313	296	235
Central counterparties	5,518	5,196	4,790	4,505	123	143	144	117
Banks and securities firms	1,724	2,042	1,348	1,229	53	70	46	36
Insurance firms	209	197	216	179	7	6	7	5
SPVs, SPCs, and SPEs	363	270	219	186	16	15	12	10
Hedge funds	1,034	1,112	814	787	44	45	42	31
Other financial customers	931	901	1,098	999	33	33	44	35
Nonfinancial customers	188	203	197	206	9	9	8	7
By rating category								
Investment grade	13,205	12,606	9,741	9,321	...	...	...	...
Non-investment grade	4,867	4,223	3,599	3,253	...	...	...	...
Non-rated	2,948	2,634	3,059	2,023	...	...	...	...
By maturity								
Up to one year	3,655	3,718	3,010	2,426	...	...	...	...
Between one and five years	16,162	14,491	12,367	10,944	...	...	...	...
Over five years	1,203	1,252	1,022	1,226	...	...	...	...
By sector								
Sovereigns	2,633	2,686	2,467	2,284	...	...	...	...
Financial firms	5,709	5,000	3,962	3,259	...	...	...	...
Non-financial firms	7,230	6,539	5,624	5,275	...	...	...	...
Securitized products	566	480	227	215	...	...	...	...
Multiple sectors	4,879	4,756	4,117	3,564	...	...	...	...

	Notional amounts outstanding				Gross market value			
	H2 2013	H1 2014	H2 2014	H1 2015	H2 2013	H1 2014	H2 2014	H1 2015
By location of counterparty								
Home country	4,091	3,734	3,423	3,510	...	...	...	...
Abroad	16,929	15,728	12,976	11,087	...	...	...	...
United States	4,486	4,014	3,412	3,162	...	...	...	...
European developed	10,871	10,173	8,205	6,782	...	...	...	...
Japan	162	151	117	116	...	...	...	...
Other Asian countries	170	148	127	100	...	...	...	...
Latin America	780	785	686	607	...	...	...	...
All other countries	461	458	430	320	...	...	...	...
Unallocated	*25,496*	*24,815*	*22,573*	*19,837*	*724*	*671*	*803*	*597*
Gross credit exposure	...	...	...	...	*3,033*	*2,826*	*3,356*	*2,870*

Appendix 11

 accenture

Position paper

**SWIFT on distributed
ledger technologies**

Delivering an industry-
standard platform through
community collaboration

Fund Custody and Administration
231

Contents

ecutive Summary

ce the emergence of
ckchain and distributed
ger technologies (DLTs), the
estion of how this technology
be deployed in a business
ironment has captivated
industry. The search for
lementations and use
ses is now a key focus of
D and innovation teams in
or financial institutions, and
p of mind for executives
king to determine future
ategies for their transaction
inesses and other data-
en operations.

a financial industry
perative, SWIFT's focus
n building technical,
rational and business
abilities with a view to
lving our platform such
DLT-based services could
offered to our 11,000+
mbers, when the technology
ures and firm business use
es emerge. Such DLT-based
ices could be provided by
IFT, our community or third
ies. In this context, we
continue to work with the
ncial industry to guarantee
-to-end automation and
kward compatibility with
cy processes.

It is clear that industry-standard DLTs should be developed collaboratively with the industry in order to ensure the technology can be universally adopted. Drawing upon its long history of fostering industry collaboration, SWIFT will leverage its unique set of capabilities – unrivalled standards expertise and track record in security as well as our strong governance, operational efficiency, reliability and reach – to deliver a distinctive DLT platform offer for the benefit of its community.

This paper is the result of an in-depth assessment of the capabilities of existing DLTs carried out by SWIFT with the support of Accenture. Our analysis has confirmed that DLTs have the potential to bring new opportunities and efficiencies to the financial industry with their key strengths including the ability to create:

- Trust in a disseminated system;
- Efficiency in broadcasting information;
- Complete traceability of transactions;
- Simplified reconciliation; and
- High resiliency.

However, SWIFT's assessment has also demonstrated that, while some solutions have been successfully deployed in proofs of concept, existing DLTs are currently not mature enough to fulfil the requirements of the financial community. The following key requirements that DLTs need to attain in order to be widely adopted by the financial industry have been identified:

- Strong governance;
- Data controls;
- Compliance with regulatory requirements;
- Standardisation;
- Identity framework;
- Security and cyber defence;
- Reliability; and
- Scalability.

Our assessment concludes that significant further R&D work is required in each of these domains before DLTs can be applied at the scale required for the financial industry.

It is apparent that business standards will be key to the success of DLTs – it is always necessary to gain clarity and consensus about the meaning of shared data in a multi-party business environment, whatever the technology used. Existing standards, principally ISO 20022, will have an important role to play, both as sources of industry definitions and as enablers of interoperability between DLTs and existing automation technology, including financial messaging.

Equally, our assessment has highlighted that DLTs should not be viewed as a silver bullet to resolve all business issues; potential use cases should always be assessed to determine whether or not the key strengths of the technology could combine to resolve the business issue in question.

As part of its R&D programme, SWIFT is actively experimenting with DLTs and engaging with its community to identify areas in which they could bring concrete business benefits. We are developing proofs of concept in our SWIFT Innovation Labs spanning various ecosystems of available underlying technologies. As a Board Member of the Linux Foundation's Hyperledger Project, SWIFT is collaborating in an industry-wide effort to evolve open source Blockchain technology and build the foundation of a production grade distributed ledger implementation. In addition, through Innotribe, SWIFT's innovation initiative, we are forging collaboration between our members and FinTech companies. We will continue to engage with our community throughout our R&D process.

To find out more about SWIFT's work on distributed ledger technologies, please contact DLT@swift.com

Technology assessment
of existing DLTs

SWIFT and Accenture have conducted an extensive assessment of existing DLTs in order to contrast the current technologies with the requirements that apply to any new solution to be adopted by the financial industry. Our multi-disciplinary team has examined the governance and compliance implications of the technology as well as technical aspects such as security, reliability, resilience, legacy integration and standardisation. The investigation has centred on operational matters and, as such, has not covered the legal implications of embracing DLTs. Moreover, our assessment is focused on inter-institution use cases, where SWIFT is providing services to the financial industry. It does not cover any potential DLT application within a financial institution, where SWIFT is not present.

Key strengths of DLTs

Our analysis has demonstrated that DLTs have the potential to bring new opportunities and efficiencies to the financial industry. The strengths of the technology include:

- **Information propagation** – Efficient means of keeping a full network up to date with latest information; distributed up-to-date ledgers allow the latest data to be updated and replicated in close to real time, ensuring all nodes are working from the same source of the truth.
- **Full traceability** – Participants or warranted trusted third-parties such as regulators are able to trace information flows back through the entire chain. Entries can be added to, but not deleted from, the distributed ledger, making ledger information immutable. This information potentially includes, but is not limited to, ownership, transaction history, and data lineage of information stored on the shared ledger.
- **Simplified reconciliation** – Local access to complete and verified data could ease reconciliation processes; since information is mutualised and all participants are working from the same data set in real time or near-real time. Current reconciliation processes, which suffer from latency and require significant human intervention, could be optimised and perhaps eliminated altogether.

- **Trusted disseminated system** – Participants are able to trust the authenticity of the data on the ledger without recourse to a central body. Transactions are digitally signed; the maintenance and validation of the distributed ledger is performed by a network of communicating nodes run dedicated software which replicate th ledger amongst the participants in a peer-to-peer network, guaranteeing t ledger's integrity.
- **High resiliency** – Operates seamles and removes dependency on a centr infrastructure for service availability. Distributed processing allows particip to seamlessly operate in case of failu of any participants. Data on the ledge is pervasive and persistent, creating a reliable distributed storage so that transaction data can be recovered fr the distributed ledger in case of local system failure, allowing the system to have very strong built-in data resilienc

chnology assessment
existing DLTs

lying DLTs in the financial services
istry

rly, DLTs have the capacity to open up
iderable opportunities for the financial
stry. However, DLTs emerged from the
sumer-to-consumer (C2C) market with the
ange of cryptocurrencies as a decentralised
iod of value transfer without third-party
nediaries. Evidently, the wider financial
stry has an altogether different set of
irements than the application of individual
umers seeking alternative methods of value
fer. As part of our technology assessment,
ave identified the following key requirements
DLTs need to attain in order to be widely
ted in the financial industry:

Strong governance – Governance
models to clearly define the roles and
responsibilities of the various parties
as well as the business and technical
operating rules;
Data Controls – Controlled data
access and availability to preserve data
confidentiality;
**Compliance with regulatory
requirements** – The ability to comply
with regulatory requirements (e.g.
Sanctions, KYC, etc.);
Standardisation – Standardisation at
all levels to guarantee straight-through
processing (STP), interoperability and
backward compatibility;
Identity framework – The ability
to identify parties involved to ensure
accountability and non-repudiation of
financial transactions;
Security and cyber defence – The
ability to detect, prevent and resist cyber-
attacks which are growing in number and
sophistication;
Reliability – Readiness to support
mission-critical financial services;
Scalability – Readiness to scale to
support services which process hundreds
or thousands of transactions per second.

following sections we detail these
ements, set out the current maturity of
n each of these domains, and identify
ture research & development needed
dge the gap between the capabilities of
g DLTs and the industry's requirements.
equently, we present the conclusions of
chnology assessment.

Scalability

Strong governance

Data controls

Reliability 99,999%

**Key industry
requirements**

Compliance
with regulatory
requirements

Security and
cyber defence

Standardisation

Identity
framework

Industry requirement
Strong governance

Delivering an indus standard platform

Industry requirement

The services used by the financial industry need to rely on strong governance models, clearly defining the roles and responsibilities of the various parties involved as well as the business and technical operating rules supporting a particular business service. Strong governance is key to ensuring the delivery of effective, predictable and sustainable financial services.

Current maturity of DLTs

DLTs emerged through cryptocurrencies and use a community self-governing model, and, while it may be seen as fairly effective in that context, we believe that it does not provide the level of trust, transparency and accountability required by the financial industry. We have identified several governance issues. It is a fully open model under which anybody can join to submit and view transactions (i.e. a 'permissionless ledger'). While this may be a desirable characteristic in a consumer-to-consumer context, we are in favour of models in which only duly authorised participants can access the service and assess whether or not the interactions between participants are done in line with business pre-agreements and technical enforcement by the ledger. While 'permissioned ledgers' are a step in that direction, there is still work needed in order to provide the level of granularity – in terms of role profile definitions – required for the access control and participant interaction. Existing implementations of permissioned ledgers remain basic, only providing support for generic read/write profiles, the 'tokenisation of assets', and limited validation methods.

Future R&D

For applications in financial services, there much debate over the role of a 'centralised authority, creating and administering distributed ledgers with defined business rules versus open-source, or consortium-based models. While the former offers a stronger governance structure to reassure participants, it can also be perceived as limiting functionality and negating some of benefits of DLTs versus the consortium mo The role of centralised governance versus open-source models needs to be investiga further, especially in the context of regulato requirements and reporting, in order to ascertain the appropriate level of governar required.

ustry requirement

a exchange in financial
nsactions is, in most
ses, confidential. This is
her because transactions
ntain personal data such
beneficiary details (and
therefore subject to
cific laws governing the
nagement of personal
a) or because they contain
rmation which could be
d to derive competitively
nsitive information regarding
activities of the parties
olved. Data confidentiality is
refore a key requirement for
solution supported by the
ncial industry, and strong
trols must be put in place to
ure that only duly authorised
ties have exclusive access
he data relevant to them.

Current maturity of DLTs

Data on the ledger is held by all DLT
participants with data broadcast between all
parties. Although the identity of the parties
involved in a transaction is theoretically
hidden, thanks to the usage of an anonymous
address instead of individuals or company
names, this anonymity faces potential
challenges in a business-to-business context.
Here all participants will need to know the
"anonymous" address of their business
counterparties allowing addresses to be
rapidly linked to the individuals or company
concerned, giving full transparency and
visibility on the ledger content.

Solutions to this problem are being
investigated from a number of angles, but
work is required to have a solution in line
with the core confidentiality requirement.
Encryption of the data is the typical solution
used to address this problem, but one must
be aware of the following considerations:

- It can be an operational challenge to
  manage encryption/decryption keys
  when there are multiple parties required
  to have access to the data as keys are
  required for each combination of parties
  involved. When more than two parties
  are involved, it can quickly become
  impractical.
- Data encryption may prevent verification
  of transactions as the transaction content
  may be hidden to the point where the
  network is unable to validate transactions
  or broadcast information to the ledger.

Future R&D

Work is required to better define what kind of
data must reside in the ledger and should be
distributed between participants. Alternative
models should be investigated which are
capable of distributing data sets only between
the participants of a given transaction, either
through peer-to-peer communication or
another solution capable of truly guaranteeing
privacy.

An interesting solution to the data privacy
issue currently being explored is Zero-
Knowledge-Proof (ZKP) algorithms which aim
to allow the verification of content without
having any knowledge of transaction content.

Industry requirement

The financial industry is heavily regulated and regulatory pressure is only increasing. Any solution must ensure that financial institutions are able to comply with their regulatory requirements and enable operations such as transactions and customer filtering against sanctioned lists, KYC, etc., while, at the same time, striking the appropriate balance between privacy and transparency.

Current maturity of DLTs

DLT compliance with regulatory requirements remains, to a great extent, unexplored and considerable work is still required. Key questions such as who should be regulated, and by whom, are yet to be answered with the answer far from straightforward due to the decentralised and cross-border nature of distributed ledgers. Moreover, it is not yet clear whether existing regulations need to be adapted for distributed ledgers, or whether new regulation will need to be created. Two schools of thought are at play here: either we continue to work within the current regulatory constructs (messaging, roles, process, etc.) or we disintermediate and change all of the above. The former option would be much more straightforward in gaining regulatory approval. This is certainly an area to watch, since regulatory attention heightens as interest in the technology grows and production use cases start to emerge.

Future R&D

R&D related to regulatory compliance in a distributed ledger environment will need to come from both the industry and regulator bodies:

- Industry participants will need to clea understand how DLTs will impact thei ability to comply with regulatory repor and audit requirements. Another area to consider will be the level of data granularity to be reported versus curre regulatory mandates and how to prov appropriate levels of data detail witho violating privacy laws.
- Regulators will not mandate how the industry explores, develops, and considers options to DLT solutions, b instead will respond to initiatives from financial services providers. To this er there have been very positive comme recently from a number of regulatory authorities. For example, the US Commodity Futures Trading Commis (CFTC) recently encouraged distribut ledger exploration, warning regulator not to stifle innovation. Indeed, regula have started to explore how DLTs will impact the way they operate as this impacts on their technology requirem as well as the skill set of their workfo

ustry requirement

ndardisation is essential
ensure straight-through
cessing and interoperability
ween systems and
ticipants as well as the
rect interpretation of data
ng exchanged. In order to
arantee this, today's financial
ustry relies heavily on
ndards organisations such
SO, ISDA (responsible for
ML), FPL (responsible for
), etc.

Current maturity of DLTs

Today's distributed ledger landscape lacks
standardisation at all levels – from technical
protocols to ledger and transaction data
formats, to smart contracts. Moreover,
distributed ledger development is being
completed entirely in isolation from existing
business standards organisations such as
ISO, ISDA or FPL. The direct consequence of
this lack of standardisation is that the various
distributed ledgers are not interoperable and
information stored on the ledger is not aligned
to market standards and practices. Integrating
a distributed ledger environment with a legacy
system, if at all possible, may require extensive
conversion and data enrichment.

Most discussions around standardisation of
DLTs and smart contracts have focused on
technical protocols and much work remains
to be completed. As this work matures
we can expect attention to quickly turn to
business use cases and business automation
standards. Compliance with business market
practices will be required and, in order to
ensure backward compatibility with existing
legacy applications, DLT solutions will need to
integrate into the wider transaction automation
landscape which is rapidly evolving towards
ISO 20022.

Future R&D

There are a set of fundamental questions to be
addressed regarding standardisation:

- Is standardisation across distributed
  ledgers required or should DLTs
  have differing standards that are fully
  interoperable with each other and with
  those currently used in the industry?
  Requirements will need to be created as
  to how data/transactions can be passed
  between those solutions in order to
  optimise payment clearing speed, cost
  and reach.
- How can existing messaging and reference
  data standards such as ISO 20022 be best
  re-used in a DLT context?
- There will be a period of time when some
  financial services providers will have the
  ability to clear and settle transactions in
  a DLT environment, while others, who
  have not yet adopted the technology,
  will continue to transact on legacy
  infrastructure. Such a situation would
  potentially create a bifurcated market,
  distorting prices based on varying
  settlement times. Interoperability between
  these environments will need to be
  addressed both from an operational and
  regulatory perspective.
- Usage of smart contracts remains a key
  question in financial services owing to the
  nature of embedding business logic of a
  financial asset on the distributed ledger
  to be automatically executed. This is a
  very powerful concept and there are a
  number of potential use cases. Yet the
  need to understand what happens 'when
  it goes wrong', how to handle related
  errors and exceptions, the legal authority
  of smart versus traditional contracts, as
  well the standardisation of smart contract
  language, all will require serious time and
  effort on the part of financial services.

As mentioned above, to date DLT
development has occurred in complete
isolation from the current standards which
drive efficiency across financial services. This
creates potential challenges around integrating
current operational processes, aligning
assets that transact both in the current and
future DLT environment, and in ultimately
decommissioning legacy systems.

Industry requirement

A very strong identity framework is required to guarantee the identity of the parties involved in a particular business service, and to support non-repudiation of activities performed by the various participants. This is essential to provide trust in the system, ensure accountability and support any claims process. It is also a pre-requisite to be able to perform Know-Your-Customer and compliance checks.

Current maturity of DLTs

Linked to data privacy is the question of managing identities. In some existing distributed ledger implementations, participants remain pseudo-anonymous – a status not permitted to regulated businesses. The identities of both the participant organisation and those employees instructing the transactions will need to be traceable in a controlled fashion, that is to say, only by those who should have access. Indeed, following the 2008 crisis, the financial industry has invested heavily in legal entity identifiers and this needs to be an integral part of any solution.

Moreover, the key management system employed by DLTs to identify parties relies on self-signed keys supported by no recovery or revocation mechanism. This has the following implications:

- A key cannot be linked with certainty to an identity as there is no neutral third party certifying and guaranteeing that a particular key is associated with a particular individual or company.
- There is no facility to recover keys should they be lost, leading to assets being locked forever on the ledger should the ledger be used to track asset ownership.
- There is no facility to revoke a key should it be stolen or compromised. There is no way to indicate to other participants that a certain key should no longer be trusted and accepted by the system.

Future R&D

The question of key management, both in terms of issuance/identity and recovery, wil require close examination. In the current proposed environment, one option would be to use a central certification authority (CA) maintaining a certificate revocation list and providing key recovery facilities. This certification authority would need to be operated by a neutral trusted third party. Such solutions are widely used by financial institutions, supported by existing infrastructures and processes, compliant with security industry standards such as F level 2 or 3 and have a proven track recorc of performance, security and operat Leveraging this existing framework to add identity requirements is a natural solution, further R&D work is required to demonstra that when applied to DLTs they remain fit f purpose.

ustry requirement
:urity and cyber defence

ustry requirement

oer-crime is a very real and
ʒr increasing threat for the
ancial industry. Any DLT
ution must be designed with
 assumption that it will be
ɔject to cyber-attacks, and
s must be able to detect
ch attacks and protect itself;
reover, with attacks growing
ɹumber and sophistication,
ɪer defence mechanisms
st continuously be assessed,
ted and improved.

Current maturity of DLTs

Originally, DLTs were designed as open
systems, yet robust against cyber-threats,
thanks to fault-tolerant algorithms performing
transaction validation and ledger updates.
These have been designed with the underlying
assumption that a number of participants
are malicious. Security is ensured through
industry-standard cryptographic algorithms
which are used widely across the industry.
However, this high level of cyber resistance
and security comes at a cost. Indeed, open
distributed ledgers typically rely on a Proof-of-
Work algorithm guaranteeing a high security
level by ensuring that any ledger update has
been done by a participant who has spent
extensive computer resources in solving a
cryptographic problem. Attacking the system
would therefore require such computer power
and resources as to render it not economically
viable.

This model cannot, however, be translated to
the financial industry: the cost would outweigh
all the benefits. Hence alternative ways of
securing the system must be examined, not
to mention the scalability and latency issues.
The industry trend is to rely on a private and
permissioned ledger whereby participant
access is strictly controlled and reliant on
alternative consensus algorithms to perform
transaction validation. Combined with the
access control mechanisms, these algorithms
aim at ensuring a similar level of protection
whilst offering faster throughput and requiring
far less computer resources.

Future R&D

As the ledger is distributed amongst
participants, the protection of the non-
encrypted data is left to the responsibility of
each participant. This significantly increases
the risk of data leakage even in the case
of a private ledger where ledger access is
controlled. To address this risk, more work is
required to allow for partial or complete data
protection on the ledger through the use of
encryption or selective distribution.

The industry needs more R&D to understand
the impact of the following:

• How does the cyber threat matrix change
  in a distributed ledger environment?
• Does removing the single point of failure
  create multiple points of entry?
• Could an attacker create denial of service
  by bombarding the network with false
  transactions in order to slow or even
  spread confusion in the system?
• The question of attack prevention and
  detection in a distributed environment;
• Whether, and how, a node can be
  isolated to protect the system;
• In a permissioned environment, who is
  going to ensure malicious actors do not
  gain access to the system either through
  hacking or bypassing KYC provisions to
  create new nodes?

Industry requirement

Certain financial services are crucial in guaranteeing the financial stability of the global economy and hence need to operate with the highest level of service. The ability to support mission-critical applications, such as RTGS systems or CSDs, requires enterprise solutions engineered to guarantee extremely high availability and the means to be able to recover from catastrophic failure scenarios.

Current maturity of DLTs

Distributed systems are resilient constructs by nature and have a very strong ability to recover from failures without any loss of data. However, centralised systems already achieve record high-level service availability, with availability levels above 99% now common.

With no central infrastructure, service availability in a distributed system will depend on the availability of its participants' infrastructures, and therefore cannot be directly controlled by a central administrator. The obligation of availability therefore shifts to the participants of the distributed system and controls will need to be put in place to ensure that each participant meets pre-defined availability levels. This can only be achieved through very strict software development, qualification and release management as all software updates need to be applied by each participant. For example, weak cryptocurrency release qualification management cycles have already caused numerous issues, with emergency fixes required to recover from ledger inconsistencies (so called 'forks') resulting in interoperability and backward compatibility issues. This contrasts with a centralised system where an administrator can shield participants from a proportion of software upgrades which are applied only centrally.

In addition, the reliability of distributed systems has known limits. There is a maximum proportion of fraudulent participants that can be handled without compromising the integrity of a distributed system. Also, in the event of a network communication problem, distributed systems are susceptible to division, resulting in two or more groups of participants operating independently of each other (so-called 'partitions'). In such a situation, there is a maximum proportion of participants that can be isolated beyond which the system will not be able to restore a consistent ledger when the communication issue is resolved. Thus, the reliability limits of distributed systems need to be stated in clear service levels, understandable by business users in order that they are aware of, and can assess the business risks should these limits be exceeded and can also define the related business continuity plans.

Future R&D

To make a DLT-based solution fully reliable over multiple years or decades, R&D work still needs to be completed to define the rig software management and release policy principles in distributed environment, in line with best practice of the industry such as I

Additionally, some operational aspects nee to be examined considering the systemic r that failure of a critical financial system can represent. This encompasses areas such a how to enforce regular mandatory software upgrades, and apply emergency fixes to address bugs or security breaches; how to exclude non-compliant nodes; how to info participants should they become isolated; how to ensure data recovery from the ledg in case a local issue is fast enough to resu business operations as per defined service level agreements.

99,999%

ustry requirement	Current maturity of DLTs	Future R&D

ustry requirement

s not unusual for systems
he financial industry to
)port throughput in the order
several hundreds or even
usands of transactions
second. Therefore, any
T solution to be used by
financial industry must
guaranteed to cope with
scale of the use case it is
dressing.

Current maturity of DLTs

As a consequence of the 'Proof of Work' algorithm used by distributed ledger implementations deriving from Blockchain, those implementations are limited to a fairly modest number of transactions per second (TPS). This algorithm also introduces the possibility for the ledger to 'fork' into multiple ledger versions held by different participants, and, while forks are automatically corrected statistically after a few ledger updates, the whole process is lengthy with transaction "finality" reached after a considerable period of time (e.g., close to an hour in the case of some cryptocurrencies).

Using alternative consensus algorithms, described above, allows both problems to be solved. A number of current solution providers are experimenting with very high TPS and some have shown great promise. Such numbers should be treated with caution, however, as they have yet to be demonstrated in production-like environments with hundreds of participants geographically dispersed around the world submitting transactions simultaneously, which could significantly impact both the achievable throughput and the transaction latency. This is nonetheless a very encouraging and promising development which should be able to cater for a very large number of applications – although it may not be robust and scalable enough for extremely high throughputs and very low latency systems, such as those employed by trading platforms to support high frequency trading (HFT). Inherent to the concept of the distributed ledger is the fact that the information is stored forever. This may bring significant challenges from both a storage and network bandwidth point of view, as the volume of transactions increases.

Future R&D

R&D needs to be carried out in order to assess the various available consensus algorithms and validation methods against realistic and representative business throughput requirements. As such, tests need to be conducted in production conditions rather than lab environments to assess the robustness of the algorithms in exception scenarios and under stress. In particular, the following activities need to be conducted:

- Validation of the various systems against the CAP theorem ruling distributed systems in order to understand the practical limits beyond which consistency, availability and partition tolerance can no longer be guaranteed as well as how to recover in case such situations arise.
- Simulation of DLT behaviour in a WAN environment, prone to network disruption and where network latency between various participants can vary significantly based on physical location and available connectivity.

Conclusions of the technology assessment

As summarised in the following graphic, our assessment has demonstrated that, while there are promising developments in each of these requirements, significant extra R&D work is needed in all these domains before DLT can be applied at the scale required by the financial industry. Despite the emergence of new solution providers, and the natural maturation of existing software, there is no single mature DLT solution yet on the market that addresses all the requirements necessary for an enterprise grade implementation, with many questions remaining unanswered. As such, DLTs are at an early stage in their development. Further research, development and testing is needed to fully understand the capabilities of the technology and the business use cases best suited to it.

Moreover, additional research needs to be conducted regarding: the interoperability of DLT systems with legacy infrastructure; the interoperability between distributed ledgers across multiple counterparties, and the regulatory requirements to do so; as well as standardisation.

Equally, our assessment has highlighted that DLTs should not be viewed as a silver bullet to resolve all business issues; potential use cases should always be assessed to determine whether or not the key strengths of the technology could combine to resolve the business issue in question.

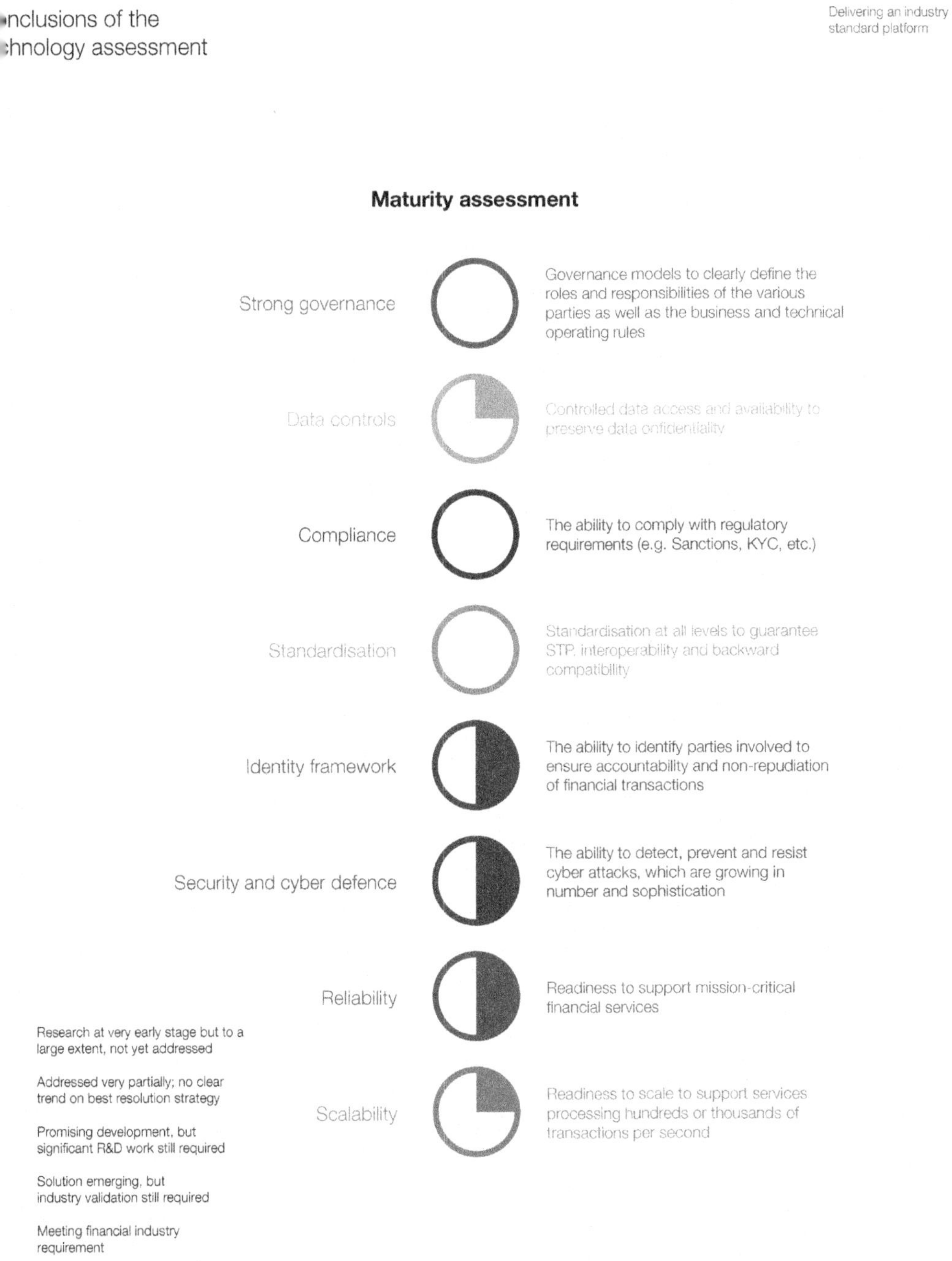
nclusions of the
chnology assessment
Delivering an industry standard platform
Maturity assessment
Strong governance
Governance models to clearly define the roles and responsibilities of the various parties as well as the business and technical operating rules
Data controls
Controlled data access and availability to preserve data onfidentiality
Compliance
The ability to comply with regulatory requirements (e.g. Sanctions, KYC, etc.)
Standardisation
Standardisation at all levels to guarantee STP, interoperability and backward compatibility
Identity framework
The ability to identify parties involved to ensure accountability and non-repudiation of financial transactions
Security and cyber defence
The ability to detect, prevent and resist cyber attacks, which are growing in number and sophistication
Reliability
Readiness to support mission-critical financial services
Scalability
Readiness to scale to support services processing hundreds or thousands of transactions per second
Research at very early stage but to a large extent, not yet addressed
Addressed very partially; no clear trend on best resolution strategy
Promising development, but significant R&D work still required
Solution emerging, but industry validation still required
Meeting financial industry requirement

**Leveraging SWIFT's
capabilities to deliver
industry-standard DLTs**

As a financial industry cooperative, SWIFT's focus is on building
technical, operational and business capabilities with a view to
evolving our platform such that DLT-based services could be
offered to our 11,000+ members, when the technology matures
and firm business use cases emerge. Our work is focused at
addressing the identified requirements to ensure that future
distributed ledger based services delivered by SWIFT are in
line with the needs and expectations of the financial industry,
guaranteeing end-to-end automation and backward compatibility
with legacy processes.

SWIFT has been delivering solutions for the financial industry
for the past 40+ years, and, in this context, has addressed
many of the challenges identified in its existing products and
services. Thanks to this, SWIFT holds a unique set of assets
and capabilities around strong governance, unrivalled standards
expertise, operational efficiency, security, reliability, and reach,
which we will leverage to develop DLT services that meet the
needs of our community.

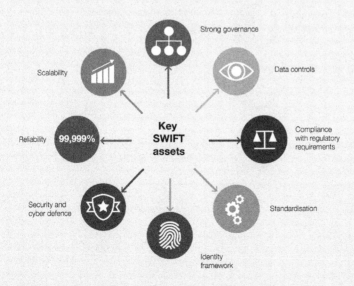

/eraging SWIFT's
pabilities to deliver
ustry-standard DLTs

Delivering an industry
standard platform

/ernance and access control

n industry cooperative, SWIFT has
ique governance model driven by its
munity to solve industry-wide issues. As
, SWIFT's governance has been designed
sure that we play a utility role, facilitating
cial transaction exchanges within the
stry, with the purpose of serving our
munity rather than maximising profit.
T governance is supported by a very
definition of roles and responsibilities and
very comprehensive framework allowing
ce administrators to offer their services via
T in order to control access, and define
orised participant interactions through
efinition of closed user groups or RMA
orisations.

a Controls

T systems and processes are
gned, built, operated and maintained to
antee the confidentiality of the data of
community. Data is being encrypted on
ole layers and very strict controls apply to
ct data access in line with a set of well-
mented policies. Our compliance with
policies is audited externally on a yearly
and details are made available to the
T community as part of the ISAE3000
t.

pliance with regulatory
irements

e request of its community, SWIFT
avily investing in building a complete
liance portfolio for its community.
liance is a challenge shared by all
ial institutions, and one that is best
ogether. Since investments in financial
compliance do not yield competitive
tage, it makes sense to collaborate to
ate costs and risks for all parties.

Standardisation

SWIFT Standards brings together a unique
and proven combination of capabilities for
defining business automation standards vital
for any industry application of DLTs. SWIFT's
work in ISO 20022 standards, its business
knowledge, and know-how of the various
financial markets – as well as its relationships
with the financial industry and ability to
convene and manage industry groups – have
all greatly contributed to the high level of
standardisation observed across today's
financial industry.

Identity framework

SWIFT services use advanced cryptographic
features to ensure identification, traceability
and accountability of all actions performed.
Financial institutions are identified through
their BIC and transactions are digitally signed
using PKI keys which are certified by SWIFT
certification authority allowing participants
to confidently trust that their counterparty
is genuine. Key management operations
are supported by very robust and secured
processes, allowing services to be operated
efficiently and situations in which keys are
either lost or compromised to be resolved via
certificate recovery and revocation facilities.

Security and cyber defence

Security has been part of the SWIFT DNA
from its inception; all the cyber defence
mechanisms protecting SWIFT's secure IP
network are equally relevant in a DLT context,
and can be leveraged to allow participants to
safely conduct their business on a protected
peer-to-peer private secured network.

Reliability

SWIFT is well known for its record high
availability[1], its extensive business continuity
plans, and for its ability to deliver mission
critical software for the financial industry.
It manages industry-wide migration
smoothly, with interoperability and
backward compatibility between versions
guaranteed. This know-how and expertise
can be leveraged in the DLT context, and is
undoubtedly an important quality required of
any credible solution provider.

Scalability

Today SWIFT supports very high volumes
of traffic on its various messaging services[2];
volume generated from a wide variety of
financial institutions located all around
the world, delivering services supporting
payments, securities, FX, and trade finance
business. SWIFT has scaled its systems in line
with its community requirement, while keeping
availability at the highest level.

Reach and integration with legacy systems

SWIFT's secure IP network has a very well
established presence within the financial
industry with more than 11,000 financial
institutions connected to date – making it the
natural choice for the provision of a secure
DLT-based service. Our messaging and
integration portfolio offers a wide range of
solutions designed to facilitate the connection
with customers' existing back-office systems,
and can be reused to bridge the new DLT-
based services with legacy systems inside a
financial institution.

Supporting industry transformation

The adoption of distributed ledger technology is
unlikely to happen through a big bang migration.
With the extensive set of legacy systems in
place today, adoption of distributed ledger
technology will not just require a technology
shift but would also imply a degree of business
transformation. Such processes take time, and
not all businesses and parties progress at the
same speed. Therefore, it will be necessary to
ensure that adoption takes place at a steady
pace to avoid the costs of running parallel
systems for an extensive period of time.

In this context, our experience in managing
community-wide transformation is valuable.
SWIFT has migrated its community
successfully on a number of occasions and
across multiple technology revolutions in a
smooth and timely fashion. This was achieved
through a combination of communication,
planning and execution skills; all leveraging
SWIFT's governance structures, and the
relationships developed over a considerable
period with our customer and vendor
community. The very same principles could
also be applied in a DLT context.

99% availability for SWIFTNet and FIN messaging
es in 2015
billion FIN messages in 2015

SWIFT's R&D on DLTs

As part of its R&D activities, SWIFT is actively experimenting with DLTs and is working on a number of initiatives, including:

Community engagement

SWIFT has dedicated significant resources to engage with its community, exploring business use cases in the securities, payments, trade finance and reference data areas, where DLTs could bring real business benefits over existing solutions. Principally, this has been done through bilateral discussions with dozens of financial institutions.

Linux Foundation's Hyperledger Project

SWIFT is both a Founding Member & Board Member of this open source project aimed at advancing DLTs. SWIFT is working in collaboration with this community to build the foundation of a production grade distributed ledger implementation which can address the known issues and limitations of current implementations. SWIFT is also actively experimenting with technologies in the Ethereum ecosystem of products.

Proofs of Concept

A number of DLT-related Proofs of Concept (PoC) are ongoing in SWIFT Innovation Labs to further increase our knowledge and expertise, and validate the SWIFT approach to building a platform which is agnostic of business use cases. The following PoCs are currently being worked on:

- **Identity and Access Management** – This PoC integrates a DLT solution with a SWIFTNet PKI solution and access control mechanism (such as a closed user group and RMA) to demonstrate how SWIFT can leverage its existing platform and assets to solve the identity and access management issues highlighted as part of our technology assessment.
- **Standing Settlement Instructions (SSIs)** – This aims at demonstrating the benefits of DLTs by building an SSI database for OTC markets in a reference data context in which there are no data confidentiality concerns. The PoC also explores interoperability and backward compatibility with existing SSI solutions such as the MT670/671.
- **ISO 20022** – This PoC aims at applying SWIFT standards expertise and the ISO 20022 methodology to the DLT context. It is assessing how interoperability with legacy systems can be achieved when not all stakeholders are on the distributed ledger. The bond lifecycle from issuance to asset service has been taken as an illustrative example, as a bond is a simple but relevant securities asset class to demonstrate SWIFT's capabilities.

More PoCs have been, or will be, launched in order to further develop SWIFT's capabilities to support DLT-based solutions on its platform. The areas covered in the PoCs should be considered as illustrative to prove the capabilities of the technology and support SWIFT's work to build a DLT platform which is standardised and use case agnostic.

/IFT's R&D on DLTs

ndards

SWIFT Standards team is investigating
 to understand how existing messaging
reference data standards can be re-used
DLT context. Re-use of existing standards
portant for two reasons:

First, to avoid 're-inventing the wheel':
existing standards such as ISO 20022
contain precise, industry-ratified
definitions of business concepts that can
be transposed to DLTs and accelerate
solution implementation.
Second, to facilitate end-to-end business
processes: it is unlikely that a complex
business process will be scoped to a
single DLT environment. Rather, DLTs
will interact with existing automation
mechanisms, including messaging
and APIs, and with other distributed
ledgers. For this to occur safely and
seamlessly, consistent, cross-referenced
definitions will be required between DLTs
and existing platforms where business
standards are already widely deployed.

SWIFT Standards team is also
dering what a business standard
ated to DLTs would look like. DLTs are
ent from messaging, and, although there
ch in existing standards that can be re-
 – from business content to governance
sses – DLTs bring a number of new
nges for formalising and standardising
ess automation.

SWIFT Innotribe

Our Innotribe programme has launched the
'Innotribe Industry Challenge', which brings
together SWIFT Member Institutions, FinTech
companies and SWIFT internal teams to
address obstacles and opportunities facing
the industry. The output of these Innotribe
Industry Challenges will be a number of
Proofs of Concept, which will enable us to
collaboratively explore, and design utility
solutions; the first Innotribe Industry Challenge
will investigate securities issuance and asset
servicing on DLTs.

The SWIFT Institute

The SWIFT Institute, which funds independent
financial industry research, is to publish
two academic research papers on DLTs in
2016; the first will focus on: "The Impact
and Potential of Blockchain on the Securities
Transaction Lifecycle".

The global payments innovation
initiative (gpii)

As part of the gpii, SWIFT is working
collaboratively with more than 50 of the
world's largest transaction banks to drive the
long-term vision for correspondent banking
and investigate their potential joint role in
deploying new technologies such as DLTs.
Throughout Q2/Q3 2016, 'Vision Workshops'
will be held with gpii initiative banks, as
well as SWIFT's banking and payments
board committee. The outcome will be a
draft 'vision' and roadmap for the future of
correspondent banking to be presented at
Sibos in September 2016 for wider debate in
the industry.

About SWIFT

SWIFT is a cooperative of and for the financial community – a trusted provider with our sights on serving the industry in new and ground-breaking ways.

To find out more about SWIFT's work on distributed ledger technologies, please contact DLT@swift.com

For more information about SWIFT, visit www.swift.com

 swiftcommunity   company/SWIFT

Copyright

Disclaimer

SWIFT supplies this publication for information purposes only. The information in this publication may change from time to time. You must always refer to the latest available version.

About Accenture

Accenture is a leading global professional services company, providing a broad range of services and solutions in strategy, consulting, digital, technology and operations. Accenture works at the intersection of business and technology to help clients improve their performance and create sustainable value for their stakeholders.

For more information about Accenture, visit www.accenture.com

 @Accenture   Accenture

Frédéric Le Borne
Managing Director
SWIFT Global Relationship Lead
frederic.le.borne@accenture.com

David Treat
Managing Director
Capital Markets Blockchain Global Practice Lead
david.b.treat@accenture.com

Fernand Dimidschstein
Managing Director
FinTech Innovation Lead
f.dimidschstein@accenture.com

Chris Brodersen
Accenture Research Principal
Capital Markets Blockchain Lead
c.brodersen@accenture.com

Disclaimer

Accenture's role in the paper has been limited to the provision of insights and expertise with regards to the current level of maturity of distributed ledger technology and its key functionality and strengths. While we take precautions to check that the source and the information we base our judgments on is reliable, we do not guarantee that this source and this information are accurate and/or complete and it should not be relied upon as such. The conclusions and recommendations provided in the paper represent the views of SWIFT and cannot be attributable to Accenture.

Glossary of Terms

30/360 Also 360/360, 30(E)/360 or Accrual Basis. A day/year count convention assuming 30 days in each calendar month and a "year" of 360 days; adjusted in America for certain periods ending on 31st day of the month (and then sometimes known as 30(A)/360).

AAA The highest credit rating given by Standard & Poors for a company or asset—the risk of default is negligible. Rating scale descends, that is, AA, A, BBB, BB.

Accrual Basis Basis for accruing, for example, interest income based on number of days See *30/360.*

Accrued Interest Interest due on a bond or other fixed income security from the issuer to the holder or that must be paid by the buyer of a security to its seller if purchase is between interest periods. Payment = coupon rate of interest multiplied by the number of elapsed days from the last interest payment date (ie, Coupon date) up to but not including settlement date for the trade.

Accruals Amounts recorded in the accounts that refer to future income or payments but form part of the current position. Important in the NAV of a fund.

Accumulation units/shares Unit or share where the income is reinvested in the fund.

ACD Authorized Corporate Director that is a corporate body and an authorized person given powers and duties under FCA regulations to operate an OEIC.

ACT/360 A day/year count convention taking the number of calendar days in a period and a "year" of 360 days.

ACT/365 Also ACT/365 Fixed or ACT/365-F. A day/year count convention taking the number of calendar days in a period and a "year" of 365 days. Under the ISDA definitions used for interest rate swap documentation, ACT/365 means the same as ACT/ACT.

ACT/ACT For an interest rate swap, a day/year count convention dividing the number of calendar days in the interest period that fall in a leap year by 366 and dividing the remainder by 365.

Actual Settlement Date Date the transaction effectively settles in the clearing house (exchange of securities eventually against cash).

Actual Settlement Date Accounting Date on which a custodian or other party will give value for the settlement.

Accumulation Fund A fund where the distribution of income is instead reinvested in the fund. Shares or units in a fund will be designated accordingly, that is, as income or accumulation shares or units.

Agent One who executes orders for or otherwise acts on behalf of another (the principal) and is subject to its control and authority. The agent takes no financial risk and may receive a fee or commission.

AGM Abbreviation for the statutory Annual General Meeting all companies must hold to report to shareholders.

AIFMD/Alternative Investment Fund Managers Directive A EU Directive, the Alternative Investment Fund Managers Directive (AIFMD) seeks a common EU approach to bringing hedge funds, private equity and other types of funds without a UCITS passport within the scope of regulatory supervision. It also aims to bringing transparency and stability to the way these funds operate.

Allotment The amount of a new issues (ie, number of bonds, shares) given to a syndicate member by the lead manager.

Also the amount of an issue allotted to a subscribing investor in an offering like an IPO or a rights issue or as a result of a capitalization.

Allotment Letter Formal letter or document (including in e-format) detailing the entitlement, terms and payment details of the holder of the existing shares or to an applicant for new shares.

ANNEXE IV Transparency reporting requirement for AIFMs and their AIFs under the AIFMD.

Alpha A term used in investment management to describe the amount by which an investment has exceeded its performance.

American Depository Receipt (ADR) A depository receipt issued by an American bank to promote trading in a foreign stock or share. The bank holds the underlying securities and an ADR is issued against them. The receipt entitles the holder to all dividends and capital gains in USD. ADR's allow investors to purchase foreign stock without having to involve themselves in foreign settlements and currency conversion.

American Style Option The holder of the long position can choose to exercise the position into the underlying instrument until the expiry day.

Amortization Accounting procedure that gradually reduces the cost value of a limited life asset or intangible asset through periodic charges to income. The purpose of amortization is to reflect the resale or redemption value. Amortization also refers to the reduction of debt by regular payments of interest and principal to pay off a loan by maturity.

Also the amortizing of expenses of an investment fund to avoid "spiking."

Amortizing CDO A collateralized debt obligation (CDO) where the principal investment is repaid at intervals during the life of the instrument.

Amortizing swap A swap where the notional principal decreases during the life of the swap.

Announcement In a new bond issue, the day on which a release is sent to prospective syndicate members describing the offering and inviting underwriters and selling group members to join the syndicate.

Annual General Meeting (AGM) Meeting of shareholders which a company must call every year. Main purposes are to receive the accounts, vote on dividends, and appoint directors.

Applies to investment companies and funds as well as commercial companies.

Arbitrage The simultaneous buying and selling of two different derivatives, or a derivative and its underlying, or two similar assets where the fair value and quoted prices are different but will converge at some point. The arbitrageur has a risk-less trade as the exposure is flat and the profit is the difference between the two prices traded.

Arbitrageur A trader or programmed dealing system which takes advantage of profitable opportunities arising from price anomalies between the same or similar products or instruments traded on different markets or systems.

Agent A third party who acts as an intermediary or broker in a transaction and who assumes no financial risk. For this service, the agent receives an agreed commission or fee.

Asset Allocation The process of structuring a portfolio by allocating capital to various asset classes.

Asset Backed Securities Debt obligations that pay principal and interest; principal only or interests only; deferred interest etc. which is backed off against some kind of asset rather than being a direct exposure to the issuer.

Asset Class A designated group of assets, for example, equities, debt, property, commodities, cash etc.

Asset Manager Person or sometimes refers to a company that makes investment decisions concerning the structure of investment portfolios.

These can be investments for any type of fund or structured product like a CDO and can be in respect of portfolios either owned by or outsourced to the asset manager.

Could also be referred to as investment manager or fund manager.

Asset swap An interest rate swap or currency swap used to change the interest rate exposure and/or the currency exposure of an investment. Also used to describe the package of the swap plus the investment itself.

Assets Everything of value that is owned or is due as a result of a purchase or entitlement: fixed assets (cash, buildings, and machinery) and intangible assets (patents and good will).

Assignment The process by which the holder of a position is matched against a holder of a similar but opposite position who has exercised his right attributable to the instrument held. For example, an *option buyer* exercises his right and the *option seller* is assigned or the *holder of a short* futures position tenders for delivery and a *holder of a long* position is assigned.

Can also refer to the assignment (passing) of the interest in a legal document or asset to another party.

Auction Method by which the issuer can offer securities to investors. Successful applicants pay the price that they have offered. Used for the issue of some types of government bonds.

Authentication agent A bank or suitably recognized party putting a signature on each physical bond to certify its genuineness prior to the distribution of the definitive bonds on the market.

Authorization Status required by the Financial Services Act 2012 for any firm or individual that wants to conduct investment business or provide financial advice.

Could also apply to the authorization by a regulator or other body to an institution such as an exchange, clearing house, central securities depository, or to an agent/ 3rd party.

Also an internal control over an instruction, that is, authorization of a payment.

Ballot A process that creates a random selection of applicants for something; for instance a new issue of shares.

Also a vote at a company meeting where a shareholder can utilize their voting right.

Ballot paper—formal document issued to those entitled to vote or, where appropriate, their proxy.

Bank–commercial Organization that takes deposits and makes loans as well as providing a variety of financial products to its customers.

Bank-investment Organization that combines corporate services, broking, trading, and investment management.

Bank–merchant Organization that specializes in advising on takeovers and corporate finance activities—also called corporate finance.

Bank of England (BOE) The UK's central bank which undertakes policy decided by the Treasury and determines interest rates as well as ensuring financial stability, managing inflation, and the value of the currency.

Nickname: "The Old Lady of Threadneedle Street"

Bank for International Settlements (BIS) Set up in the 1920's to administer debt repayments among European countries, it is now has an important role as the vocal point in organizing discussion on International finance.

Has been involved in the issuing of many important directives, for example, Basel II related to operational risk.

Bankers' acceptance Short term negotiable discount note, drawn on an endorsement by and accepted by banks which are obliged to pay the face value amount at maturity.

Base Currency Currency chosen for reporting purposes, for example, the base currency of a company's accounts or of an investment fund.

Also applies to an FX trade where one currency is the Base and the other the Quoted currency.

Basel II/Basel III An important directive related to operational risk that financial organizations face. The Directive is the work of the Bank for International Settlement and requires certain capital adequacy to maintain against possible loss as a result of operational risk events happening.

Basel III is now being structured and implemented.

Base Rate The rate of interest set by the banks as a basis for the rate on loans and deposits.

The central bank sets a base rate that other banks then work off.

Basis (Gross) The difference between the relevant cash instrument price and the futures price. Often used in the context of hedging the cash instrument.

Basis (Value or Net) The difference between the gross basis and the carry.

Basis Point (B.P.) A change in the interest rate of one hundredth of one percent (0.01%). One basis point is written as 0.01 when 1.0 represents 1%. That is, 0.01 = 1 basis point, so 0.10 = 10 basis points and 1.00 = 100 basis points.

Referred to as "bips".

Basis Risk The risk that the price or rate of one instrument or position might not move exactly in line with the price or rate of another instrument or position which is being used to hedge it.

Basis Swap An interest rate swap where the interest payments that are exchanged between each party are different types of floating rates.

Basis Trade A trade simultaneously of a future and the underlying; a facility offered by some exchanges.

BBA Abbreviation for British Bankers' Association.

Bear A nickname for an investor who believes prices will fall.

Bear Market A market in which prices are falling and sellers are more predominant than buyers. Usually refers to equity markets.

Bear Raid The selling of shares, generally in large volumes, to influence the price in order to acquire shares more cheaply. Strategy employed by some hedge funds involving selling short, that is, selling shares not yet owned.

Bear Squeeze Where an investor having gone "short" and sold shares they do not have in anticipation of either a share or the market as a whole falling, is squeezed by the rising price during the speculative period. The squeeze happens because the seller has sold short, borrowed shares to enable settlement of the trade and must at some point buy the shares to return the borrowed securities.

Bearer Document Documents which state on them that the person in physical possession (the bearer) rather than a named individual is the owner, example being currency.

Bearer Securities Unregistered securities where the holder of the document is deemed the owner. An example is a bearer bond. Income is usually paid on presentation of the coupon attached to the bond and redemption (return of original capital) also requires the presentation of the security.

Benchmark A performance comparator used to determine the relative rate of increase/decrease in a market or security, for example, index.

A benchmark is often a target against which investment performance is measured.

Can also be used to measure the performance of suppliers against for instance a service level agreement.

Benchmark Bond Likely to be the most recently issued and most liquid government bond.

Beneficial Owner The person entitled to all benefits of ownership even though a broker, bank custodian, nominee or 3rd party like a Central Securities Depository holds the security in their name.

Bermudan Option An option where the holder can choose to exercise on any of a series of predetermined dates between the purchase of the option and expiry. See also *American option, European option.*

Best-Efforts Basis Term describing how an instruction received by a broker or custodian will be managed. If due to factors beyond their control the instruction cannot be guaranteed to be completed it is carried out on a best efforts basis.

Best Execution The requirement for a broker to obtain the best market price when buying or selling a marketable investment on behalf of the client.

BIC Abbreviation for a Bank Identifier Code—used in payment instructions.

Bid 1. The price or yield at which a purchaser is willing to buy a given security.

2. To quote a price or yield at which a seller is able to sell a given security.

3. The investor's selling price of units in a unit linked policy.

The opposite to bid is "offer."

Bid/Offer spread The difference between the buying and selling price of units in a unit trust or a security. In the case of a unit trust, it includes any initial charges and investment costs.

Bilateral Netting A netting system in which all trades executed on the same date in the same security between the same counterparties are grouped and netted to one final delivery versus payment.

Bill of exchange A money market instrument, a written promise to pay a specified sum of money (usually postdated) that is similar to a cheque.

BIS Abbreviation for the Bank for International Settlements.

Bitcoin Bitcoin is a digital currency created in 2009. It follows the ideas set out in a white paper by the mysterious Satoshi Nakamoto, whose true identity has yet to be verified. Bitcoin offers the promise of lower transaction fees than traditional online payment mechanisms and is operated by a decentralized authority, unlike government issued currencies.

There are no physical Bitcoins, only balances associated with public and private keys. These balances are kept on a public ledger, along with all Bitcoin transactions, that is verified by a massive amount of computing power. Source: Investopedia

Black Days Prefix to a day where a market disaster occurs.

Blockchain A blockchain is a public ledger of all Bitcoin transactions that have ever been executed. It is constantly growing as "completed" blocks are added to it with a new set of recordings. The blocks are added to the blockchain in a linear, chronological order. Each node (computer connected to the Bitcoin network using a client that performs the task of validating and relaying transactions) gets a copy of the blockchain, which gets downloaded automatically upon joining the Bitcoin network. The blockchain has complete information about the addresses and their balances right from the genesis block to the most recently completed block. Source: Investopedia. The possible use of blockchain is being looked at in terms of the financial market infrastructure including clearing and settlement.

Block Trade A purchase or sale of a large number of securities normally much more than what constitutes a usual trade in the market in question. Many markets allow this type of trade.

Blue Chips Denotes the companies that in theory at least provide the safest equity investment potential. Companies listed in the FTSE 100 or S&P 500 index for instance are considered "Blue Chip."

Board Lot Standard unit of shares commonly traded in the market, often one share. Shares that are issued in fractions or multiples of a board lot are referred to as odd lots and jumbo lots respectively and may not be readily negotiable.

Bond An instrument often comprising a certificate of debt, generally long-term, under the terms of which an issuer contracts, inter alia, to pay the holder a fixed principal amount on a stated future date and, usually, a series of interest payments at predetermined times during its life.

Other types of bonds exist, that is, zero coupon bonds, convertible bonds etc.

Issued by both governments and corporate companies and sometimes municipal/local authorities.

Bonus Issue A free issue of shares to a company's existing shareholders. No capital is paid by shareholders and the share price falls pro rata. It is a cosmetic exercise to make the shares more marketable. Also known as a capitalization or scrip issue.

Could also be an issue of shares to investors, directors, or employees at the company's expense from shares held by the company.

Book Entry Transfer System of recording ownership of securities by computer where the owners do not receive a certificate. Records are kept (and altered) centrally in "the electronic book."

Books closed day Last date for the registration of shares or bonds for the payment of the next distribution of dividend or interest and also for other types of corporate action, subscription, offer etc.

Break A term used for any out-of-balance condition. A money break means that cash debits and credits are not equal. A trade break means that some information such as that from a contra broker is missing to complete that trade.

Bridge The electronic link enabling transactions between Clearstream and Euroclear participants to settle across the two CSDs.

Broker An agent, often a member of a stock exchange or an exchange member himself who acts as intermediary between buyer and seller. A commission is charged for this service.

Broker/Dealer Firm that operates in dual capacity in the securities marketplace: as principal trading for it's own account and as broker representing clients on the market.

Broken date A maturity date other than the standard ones normally quoted.

Broken period A period other than the standard ones normally quoted.

Broker Organization or individual who transacts business as an agent in return for a commission.

Broking The activity of a broker representing a client as agent and charging commission for doing so.

Bull Investor who believes prices or a market will rise.

Bull Market A market in which prices are rising and buyers are more predominant than sellers. Usually refers to equity markets.

Bulldog Bonds A sterling bond issued in London by an overseas government agency. The term is also used for debenture type issues from a commercial organization.

Bullet Maturity A bond that pays periodic interest and repays the principal on maturity.

Buying In (Buy In) The action taken by a broker failing to receive delivery of securities from a counterparty on settlement date to purchase these securities in the open market for immediate delivery. All costs are passed to the "failing" party.

BVIfsc BVI Financial Services Commission.

Calendar spread The simultaneous purchase (or sale) of a futures or option contract for one date and the sale (or purchase) of a similar futures contract for a different date. See *Spread*.

Call Deposits Deposits that can be called (or withdrawn) at the option of the lender (and in some cases the borrower) after a specified period. The period is short, usually one or two days, and interest is paid at prevailing short-term rates (call account).

Call Option An option that gives the seller the right, but not the obligation, to buy a specified quantity of the underlying asset at a fixed price, on or before a specified date. The buyer of a call option has the obligation (because they have bought the right) to make delivery of the underlying asset if the option is exercised by the seller.

Call Spread The purchase of a call option coupled with the sale of another call option at a different strike, expecting a limited rise or fall in the value of the underlying.

Callable Bond A bond where the issuer has the right to redeem all or some of the bond issue prior to maturity by paying some specified call price.

Cancellation price The lowest possible valuation of a unit in a unit trust under FSA regulations on any one day. The actual selling or bid price is usually higher.

Cap Also ceiling. A package of interest rate options whereby, at each of a series of future fixing dates, if an agreed reference rate such as LIBOR is higher than the strike rate, the option buyer receives the difference between them, calculated on an agreed notional principal amount for the period until the next fixing date.

Capital The value of an individual's savings and investments.
The capital showing in a firms accounts including investment funds.

Capital Adequacy Requirement for firms conducting banking or investment business to have sufficient funds to maintain a solvent business.

Capital Gain (or Loss) Profit (or loss) from the sale of a capital asset. Capital gains may be short-term (one year or less) or long-term (more than one year). Capital losses are used to offset capital gains to establish a net position for tax purposes.

Capital Adequacy Rules Regulations specifying minimum capital requirements for investment businesses and banks and how this must be met.

Capital Gains Tax (CGT) Tax payable by individuals on profit made on the disposal of assets.

Capital Markets A term used to describe the market where capital is invested and raised. Large amounts of money (capital) are raised by companies, governments, and other organizations for short, medium, and long-term use and involve the creation of financial instruments in which investors place excess capital, via cash deposits or invest through investment funds.

Capitalization The value of a limited company as determined by the par value, issue price, or market price (whichever is greatest) of its shares and the total number of shares in issue. The size of stock markets is often determined by the total aggregate of the capitalization of all the shares quoted on that market, for example, the FTSE 100 Index is made up of the 100 shares with the highest capitalisation based on the mid-price quoted on the London Stock Exchange times the shares in issue.

Capitalization Issue See *Bonus Issues.*

Carried Interest The amount of interest a fund promoter or manager has in the performance of the fund. A form of performance fee.

Carried Interest Partner The partner in a partnership that holds the carried interest.

CASCADE Clearstream CSD system accessed via Creation Connect.

Cash funds Another name for money market funds.

Cash Market Traditionally, this term has been used to denote the market in which commodities were traded for immediate delivery against cash. Since the inception of futures markets for T-bills and other debt securities, a distinction has been made between the cash markets in which these securities trade for immediate delivery and the futures markets in which they trade for future delivery.

Cash Sale A transaction for instance in a market which calls for delivery or exchange of the securities/goods for cash at the same time or during that same day.

Cash Settlement In the money market a transaction is said to be made for cash settlement if the securities purchased are delivered against payment on the same day the trade is made.

Can also describe the method of settlement by stipulating that only physical cash rather than by a cheque, electronic payment etc.

CCASS Clearing system for the Stock Exchange of Hong Kong (Central Clearing and Settlement System).

CCP A central clearing counterparty where positions novate for clearing and may be guaranteed for settlement. Can also be a clearing conduit where the parties to a trade remain responsible for settlement with each other via the CCP.

CDD An abbreviation for Client Due Diligence, carrying out checks like antimoney laundering etc.

CDS An abbreviation for the Canadian Depository for Securities.

Also an abbreviation for a credit default swap.

Ceiling See *Cap.*

Central Bank Influential institution at the core of a country's monetary and financial system, such as the Bank of England, the Federal Reserve in the United States of America or the European Central Bank. Its main aim is to ensure price stability in the economy through control of inflation and safeguard the financial industry.

Central Securities Depository (CSD) An organization authorized in a jurisdiction that holds records of securities positions and transfer of ownership in either immobilized or dematerialized form thereby enabling transactions to be processed by book entry transfer of ownership. Also holds physical securities.

Some CSDs also provide securities custody services.

Certificate Paper form of shares (or bonds), representing ownership of a company (or its debt).

Example—a share certificate.

Can also evidence ownership of units or shares in a fund.

Certificate of Deposit A money market instrument often in bearer form issued by a bank certifying a deposit made at the bank and which gives the purchaser a return.

CFD See *Contract for difference.*

CFMA Commodity Futures Modernization Act introduced in the United States to change the regulatory environment in derivatives markets.

CFTC The Commodities and Futures Commission, (United States)—a regulator.

CHAPS Clearing House Automated Payment System—clearing system for Sterling payments between member banks.

Chapter 11 Area of the US Bankruptcy Reform Act 1978 that protects companies from creditors.

Cheapest to Deliver The cash security that provides the lowest cost (largest profit) to the arbitrage trader; the cheapest to deliver instrument is used to price the futures contract.

CHESS Organization for holding shares in dematerialized form in Australia (Clearing House Electronic Sub Register System).

CIMA Cayman Islands Monetary Authority.

Chinese Walls Artificial barriers to the flow of information set up in large firms to prevent the movement of sensitive information between departments.

CHIPS Clearing House Interbank Payments System—clearing system for US dollar payments.

Chi –X Europe (BATS) A pan European multi trading facility (MTF) started in 2007 that combined with BATS Europe in 2011.

Churning A term used to describe dealing in a client's investments or advising a client to deal more frequently than is reasonable in the circumstances, thereby increasing commission revenue.

City Code Principles and rules written by Panel on Takeovers and Mergers to regulate conduct during a takeover.

Clean Price The total price of a bond less accrued interest.

Clearance The process of determining accountability for the exchange of money and securities between counterparties to a trade: clearance creates statements of obligation for securities and/or funds due.

Clearance Broker A broker who will handle the settlement of securities related transactions for himself or another broker. Sometimes, small brokerage firms may not clear for themselves and therefore employ the services of an outside clearing broker.

Clearing The centralized process whereby transacted business is recorded and positions are maintained, the preparation of a transaction for settlement. See also *Clearance*.

Positions are sometimes matched and or registered as genuine trades during the process of clearing.

It is a presettlement phase in securities and cash—hence clearing banks deal with cheques and cash payments and clearing houses/CCPs deal with securities etc.

Clearing Agent An institution that settles transaction for a large number of counterparties.

Clearing Broker Is the clearing agent for the trading broker in the market where the trade will be settled. It is usually the party with which the sub-custodian will actually settle the trade.

Clearing fee Fee charged by a clearing house or clearing broker, usually per trade or contract/ lot.

Clearing House Company or entity that acts as central counterparty for the settlement of stock exchange transactions sometimes becoming the counterparty to the trade through a process called novation. May also offer some type of guarantee of settlement it maintains the records of transactions and settles the transactions with members.

Most clearing houses are also very much involved in the risk management of the markets and the clearing house members.

Clearing House Funds Also known as next-day funds, where the proceeds of a trade are available on the day following the actual settlement date.

Clearing Organization Another name for the organization that acts as the guarantor of the performance and the settlement of contracts that are traded on an exchange.

Clearing Process System (CPS) Clearing system used by Euronext and NYSE-Liffe which has been replaced in 2012 by the *Universal Clearing Platform (UCP)*.

Clearing system Generic term used for a system established to clear transactions.

Clearstream International CSD and clearing house based in Luxembourg and Frankfurt and linked into Deutsche Borse through its merger with Deutsche Borse Clearing.

Closing day In a new bond issue, the day when securities are delivered against payment by syndicate members participating in the offering.

Closing Trade A bought or sold trade which is used to offset an open position, to reduce it or to fully offset it and close it.

Part of a "close out" of a position.

CME Abbreviation for the Chicago Mercantile Group. A commodity and financial derivative exchange now comprised of the Chicago Mercantile, Chicago Board of Trade, COMEX, Kansas City Board of Trade, and NYMEX exchanges.

CME ClearPort OTC trade capture and clearing system operated by the CME Group.

Collar Also cylinder, tunnel, fence, or corridor. The sale of a put (or call) option and purchase of a call (or put) at different strikes (typically both out-of-the-money) or the purchase of a cap combined with the sale of a floor in interest rates. See *Range forward*.

Collateral An acceptable asset used to cover a margin requirement or as security against a loan, obligation or debt. A risk management process

Collateralized Debt Obligations (CDOs) Type of structured product where a mix of some type of debt, that is, government bonds to junk bonds (Collateralized Bond Obligation) or loans (Collateralized Loan Obligation) is put together as a new product that is then issued in tranches to investors. Each tranche carries different levels of risk of default and a different return to the investor.

Collateralized Mortgage Obligations CMOs) A type of CDO, CMOs are backed by a pool of mortgages owned by the issuer. They usually reimburse capital at each coupon payment as per reimbursement of the underlying mortgages. Widely criticized as being the cause of the "crash of 2008" when defaults started to occur.

Commercial Book-Entry System (CBES) In the United States, the Commercial Book-Entry System (CBES) is a multitiered automated system for purchasing, holding, and transferring marketable securities. CBES exists as a delivery versus payment system that provides for the simultaneous transfer of securities against the settlement of funds.

At the top tier of CBES is the National Book-Entry System (NBES), which is operated by the Federal Reserve Banks. For Treasury securities, the Federal Reserve operates NBES in their capacity as the fiscal agent of the US Treasury. The Federal Reserve Banks maintain book-entry accounts for depository institutions, the US Treasury, foreign central banks, and most government sponsored enterprises (GSEs).

At the next tier in CBES, depository institutions hold book-entry accounts for their customers, which include brokers, dealers, institutional investors, and trusts. At the next tier, each broker, dealer, and financial institution maintains book-entry accounts for individual customers, corporations, and other entities.

Commercial paper Short-term obligations with maturities between 2 and 270 days issued by banks, corporations or other borrowers to investors with temporary idle cash. They are usually discounted although some are interest-bearing.

Commission Charge levied by a firm for agency broking or other services. Also known as brokerage.

Commodities The raw materials traded on specialist markets, that is, oil, coffee, copper (see also *Soft and Hard commodities*).

Commodity Futures These comprise five main categories; *agriculture* (Agri), for example, wheat and potatoes, *softs*, for example, coffee and cocoa, *precious metals*, for example, gold and silver, *non-ferrous metals*, for example, copper and lead, and *energy*, for example, oil and gas.

There are other categories like livestock, timber etc.

Commodity Swap A swap in which the rate of interest is linked to the price of a specific commodity such as cocoa or copper. Example change in the price of coffee versus Libor. Also an arrangement to exchange two commodities at some stage.

Common Stock Securities that represent ownership in for instance a US corporation. The two most important common stockholder rights are the voting right and dividend right. Common stockholder's claims on corporate assets are subordinate to those of bondholders preferred stockholders and general creditors. Called ordinary shares in the UK.

Compliance Officer Person appointed within an authorized firm to be responsible for ensuring compliance with the rules and regulations of the markets and jurisdictions where the firm does business as well as compliance with internal rules and controls.

Compound Annual Rate (CAR) The compounded annual rate of interest on a savings account taking into account the frequency of payment and assuming the re-investment of the interest.

Compound interest Interest calculated on the assumption that interest amounts will be received periodically and can be reinvested (usually at the same rate).

Conduct of Business Rules Rules created by a regulator such as the FSA in the UK related to how firms conduct their business. They deal mainly with the relationship between firm and client.

Conflicts of Interest Circumstances that arise where a firm including directors or senior management of investment funds has a situation which could encourage it not to treat its clients favorably. The more areas in which a firm or individual is involved in activity for both itself and clients the greater the number of potential conflicts.

Confirm (ation) A communication between two parties to a trade that seeks to match the details of the trade so that settlement can take place.

An agreement for individual OTC derivative transactions that details the specific terms of the trade often used in conjunction with the ISDA Master Agreement and Schedules.

Consideration The value of a transaction calculated as the price per share multiplied by the quantity being transferred.

Contingent Liability A position that has the potential for more than one settlement obligation for example variation margin on futures contracts

Continuous Net Settlement Extends multilateral netting to handle failing trades brought forward and to continue the process of trying to settle throughout a defined period—see *Multilateral netting.*

Contract The standard unit of trading for futures and options. It is also commonly referred to as a "lot."

Also an agreement between to parties for the supply of goods, services etc.

Contract for Difference (CFD) Contract designed to enable an exposure to an instrument, index or basket. Movement in the price creates a profit or loss that is subject to cash settlement only so the underlying is never exchanged.

Contract Note Legal documentation sent by securities house to clients providing details of a transaction completed on their behalf.

Can also apply to the document sent by a fund to an investor.

Contract Specification A derivative exchange designs its own products and publishes a contract specification setting out the details of the derivative contract. This will include the size or unit of trading and the underlying, maturity months, quotation and minimum price movement and value (see also *Tick*) together with trading times, methods and delivery conditions

Contractual Settlement Date Date on which seller and buyer are contractually obligated to settle the securities transaction.

Contractual Settlement Date Accounting Settlement value posted into a client's account by a custodian on an agreed (contractual) date irrespective of whether the transaction has actually settled.

Convergence The movement towards each other of the cash asset price and the futures or other derivatives price as the expiration date of the futures contract approaches.

Conversion premium The effective extra cost of buying shares through exercising a convertible bond (see *Below*) compared with buying the shares directly in the market. Usually expressed as percentage of the current market price of the shares.

Conversion price The normal value of one instrument or asset which may be exchanged for another instrument or asset.

Conversion ratio The number of shares into which a given amount (eg, £100 or $1000) of the nominal value of a convertible can be converted.

Convertible Bond/Convertible Securities Security (usually a bond or preferred stock) that can be exchanged for other securities, usually ordinary shares/common stock of the same issuer, at the option of the holder and under certain conditions.

Convertible Currency A currency that is freely convertible into another currency. Currencies for which domestic exchange control legislation specifically allows conversion into other currencies.

Convertible Term Assurance A term assurance policy that can be converted into a whole life or endowment policy.

Corporate Action One of many possible capital restructuring changes or similar actions taken by the company, which may have an impact on the market price of its securities, and which may require the shareholders to make certain decisions.

Corporate bonds Usually fixed interest securities issued by public and private companies.

Corporate Debt Securities Bonds or commercial paper issued by private corporations.

Corporate Finance General title that covers activities such as raising cash through new issues, creating solutions to funding requirements and utilizing a company's excess cash effectively.

Cost of carry The net running cost of holding a position (which may be negative), for example, the cost of borrowing cash to buy a bond, less the coupon earned on the bond while holding it.

Also used in the calculation of the fair value of a futures contract

Counterparty (ies) A trade can take place between two or more counter parties. Usually one party to a trade refers to its trading partners as counterparties.

Counterparty risk The risk that a counterparty fails to meet an obligation or fails to deliver services in accordance with a service level agreement.

Coupon A term used to describe the nominal rate of interest expressed as a percentage of the principal value. The interest is paid to the holder of, for example, a fixed income security by the borrower. The coupon is generally paid annually, semiannually or, in some cases quarterly depending on the type of security.

With physical (paper) instruments the coupon is attached and must be torn off and presented to the issuer's agent to obtain the interest.

Coupon Swap An interest rate swap in which one leg is fixed-rate and the other is floating rate. See also *Basis swap*.

Covered option A written option where the writer (seller) has sufficient underlying or cash to settle the option if the buyer exercises their right. See also *Naked option*.

Covered Writing The process of the sale of options where the seller owns the underlying which would be required to cover the delivery if the position is assigned.

Seller is known as a covered writer—opposite is a naked writer.

Creation Connect Clearstream communication system with access to CASCADE etc.

Creation price The highest possible buying price of units under FSA regulations before any initial charge. The actual price to the investor may be lower.

Credit Default Swap A swap where one side is a default event that results in the payment of the related loss and the other is the payment of a premium to secure the protection. If no event occurs then the seller of the protection keeps the premium.

Credit Derivatives Credit derivatives have as the underlying asset some kind of credit default. As with all derivatives, the credit derivative is designed to enable the risk related to a credit issue, such as non-payment of an interest coupon on a corporate or sovereign bond, or the non-repayment of a loan, to be transferred.

Credit risk The risk that a borrower, or counter-party to a deal, or the issuer of a security, will default on repayment or not deliver its side of the deal.

CREST/Euroclear The organization, known as a central securities depository (CSD), in the UK that holds UK and Irish company shares in dematerialized form and clears and settles trades in UK and Irish company shares. Now merged with Euroclear and called Euroclear United Kingdom and Ireland but still often referred to as "CREST."

Members like custodians have accounts within Euroclear where the positions and any transfer of ownership are recorded.

Cross Border Trading Trading which takes place between persons or entities from different countries.

Cross Currency Interest Rate Swap An interest rate swap where the interest payments are in two different currencies and the exchange rate, for the final settlement, is agreed at the outset of the transaction.

CSD Abbreviation for central securities depository (see *Central securities depository*).

CSSF Commission de Surveillance du Secteur Financier Luxembourg.

Cum-Dividend A security that is traded with the right to the current dividend.

Cum-Rights A term applied to a stock trading in the marketplace "with subscription rights attached" which is reflected in the price of that security.

Cumulative Dividend Dividend that is due but not yet paid on cumulative preferred shares. These must be paid before any ordinary dividends are paid.

Cumulative preference share A share that has preferential rights over ordinary shares. For example, if the company fails to pay a preference share dividend the entitlement to the dividend accumulates and the arrears of preference dividend must be paid before any ordinary dividend.

Currency Exposure Currency exposure exists if assets are held or income earned, in one currency while liabilities are denominated in another currency. The position is exposed to changes in the relative values of the two currencies such that the cost of the liabilities may be increased or the value of the assets or earning decreased.

Currency Futures Contracts calling for delivery of a specific amount of a foreign currency at a specified future date in return for a given amount of say US Dollars.

Currency Swap An agreement to exchange interest related payments in the same currency from fixed rate into floating rate (or vice versa) or from one type of floating rate to another. A currency swap is different to an interest rate swap as the principal amounts are also swapped.

CUSIP The Committee on Uniform Securities Identification Procedures, the body which established a consistent securities numbering system in the United States.

CUSIP Number Unique nine-digit number that identifies securities, US or non-US, which trade and settle in the United States (Committee on Uniform Security Identification Procedure).

Custodian Institution holding securities in safekeeping for a client. A custodian also offers other services to its clients such as settlement, portfolio services etc.

A custodian is an authorized/licensed entity, for example, a bank but can also be a securities depository such as Euroclear.

Customer—nonprivate An institutional or sometimes high net worth customer who is assumed to understand the workings of the capital markets and investment world and therefore receives little protection from the regulator.

Customer—private Customer who is assumed to be financially unsophisticated and therefore receives more protection from the regulator.

CySEC the Cyprus Securities and Exchange Commission the Cyprus regulator.

D.K. "Don't Know." Term that is used in operations teams and applies to a securities transaction pending settlement where fundamental data is missing which prevents the receiving party from accepting delivery.

Daily Official List London Stock Exchange produced document that provides record of prices at which all stocks were traded on the previous day.

Day Count The basis for the number of days that will be used in calculations. In the UK, this is usually 365 days whereas in the United States, it is 360 days in a year.

Day count fraction The proportion of a year by which an interest rate is multiplied in order to calculate the amount accrued or payable. Examples 30/360, Actual/365.

Day-Light Exposure The risk to the deliverer of securities or payer of the settlement value to the possibility of a counterparty defaulting on his obligations during the business day.

Dealer Individual or firm that acts as principal in all transactions, buying for their own account. Can also be called a trader.

Debenture Another name for a corporate bond—usually secured on assets of the company.

Debt Warrant An option to purchase more bonds on fixed terms at the time of the offering of the warrants.

Decompounded Rate Used primarily in the US dollar market. A scaled down rate used for a shorter period or "stub" in a swap.

Default Failure to perform on a futures contract, either cash settlement or physical settlement.

Deferred share A class of share where the holder is only entitled to a dividend if the ordinary shareholders have been paid a specified minimum dividend.

Can also describe a share where the dividend payment is deferred to some futures date by the payer or receiver.

Definitive Bond Any bond issued in final form. It is used particularly in reference to permanent bonds for which Temporary Bonds or Interim Certificates were issued.

Deflation Opposite of inflation and can be used as a method by governments to curtail rampant inflation, normally by reducing demand thereby lowering output and investment.

However severe deflation is as dangerous for an economy as high inflation.

Deliverable Basket or Deliverable List The list of securities that meets the delivery standards of futures contracts or other derivatives.

Delivery The delivery of an asset in settlement of a transaction.

A term used to describe the physical movement of the underlying asset on which the derivative is based from seller to buyer.

Delivery versus Payment (DVP) Settlement where transfer of the security and payment for that security occur simultaneously and also irrevocably. Also known as DVP.

Dematerialized (form) Circumstances where securities are held in a book entry transfer system with no certificates.

Department of Trade and Industry In the UK a department of government responsible for some commercial matters including monopolies and prosecution of insider dealing.

Deposit Account An account where interest is paid on the balance and in most cases, notice is required to make a withdrawal without penalty.

Deposit Protection Scheme A fund set up by the Banking Act of 1987 in the UK, which protects depositors in banks that go bust.

Depositary Organization similar to a custodian required for investment funds under the AIFMD and for funds such as UK OEICS

Depository Receipts Certificate issued by a bank in a country to represent shares of a foreign corporation issued in a foreign country. It entitles the holder to dividends and capital gains. They trade and pay dividend in the currency of the country of issuance of the certificate. For example, an American Depository Receipt (ADR).

Depository Trust Company (DTC) A US central securities depository through which members may arrange deliveries of securities between each other through electronic debit and credit entries without the physical delivery of the securities. DTC is industry owned with the NYSE as the majority owner. DTC is a member of the Federal Reserve System.

Depreciation The erosion of the value of something caused by a reduction in the value of a currency influenced by, for example, inflation and also the declining value created by a second hand sale of those goods, for example, a motor car.

Used in accounting to reflect the decline in the value of assets like equipment.

Derivative Generic term for a commodity, financial instrument or other type of product whose value is dependent upon the value of an underlying asset.

Derivative Instruments or Derivative Securities Financial or commodity instruments which are based on other underlying securities, for example, options or futures. Derivative securities do not directly raise finance or create wealth, rather they provide for the transfer of risk from hedgers to speculators which in turn can result in gains or losses for the speculator.

Deriv/SERV- MarkitSERV DTCC Deriv/SERV now called MarkitSERV is a provider of automation solutions for the global over-the-counter (OTC) derivatives market, offering a services for a range of credit, equity and interest rate products (see also *Markit*).

Designated account A unit holder or shareholder account with additional identification.

Deutsche Börse The German Stock and Derivatives Exchange Group that includes the derivatives exchange Eurex.

Dilution/Dilution Levy A situation where some investors interest in a portfolio is diluted by other investor's sales or purchase of units/shares in the fund. A dilution levy seeks to redress this situation

Direct Debit A method of payment where, on a regular basis, funds are extracted from the payer's account and paid into the recipient's account. A direct debit is variable and as such the amount debited can change.

Direct Market Participant A broker, broker/dealer or any direct member of an exchange.

Direct Placement Selling a new issue by placing it with one or several institutional investors rather than offering it for sale publicly. Also just referred to as placement.

Dirty Price The total price of a bond including accrued interest that will be used for settlement of a transaction.

Disclaimer A notice or statement intending to limit or avoid potential legal liability.

Discount The amount by which a future is priced below its theoretical price or fair value.

A money market instrument issued at a discount to the value received on redemption, for example, some treasury bills.

A bond issued at a discount to the value received on redemption, for example, a zero coupon bond.

Discount Factor The number by which a future cash flow must be multiplied in order to calculate its present value.

Discount Rate The rate of interest charged by the Federal Reserve in the United States to banks to whom money has been lent. Is also a term used for the same purpose by other central banks.

Discount Securities Noninterest bearing short-term securities that are issued at a discount and redeemed at maturity for full face value.

Distributions Income paid out from a unit trust or other fund that pays income.

Also the amount paid to each investor on the winding up of a fund such as a private equity fund.

The term distribution can also mean the sales/brokerage part of an investment bank

Dividend Distribution of profits made by a company to its shareholders if it chooses to do so.

Dividend Cover Dividends are paid out of a company's profits and dividend cover is the excess profits after the dividend has been calculated. For example, if a company has a profit of £60,000 and the total dividend is £10,000, the dividend is covered 6 times.

Dividend per share Indicated annual dividend based on the most recently announced quarterly dividend times four plus any additional dividends to be paid during the current fiscal year.

Dividend Yield The dividend expressed as a percentage of the share price.

Diversification Investment strategy of spreading risk by investing the total available in a range of investments.

Dodd-Frank The Dodd–Frank Act—a major us regulation affecting capital markets

Domestic Bond Bond issued in the country of the issuer, in the currency of the country and according to the regulations of that country.

Domicile Where an individual or a business including investment funds is legally deemed to be registered, based or living.

Don't Know (D.K.) Applies to a securities transaction on which fundamental data is missing or there is a discrepancy in the details of the transaction that prevents the receiver from accepting the delivery.

Double Taxation Treaty An agreement between two countries intended to avoid or limit the double taxation of income. Under the terms of the treaty an investor with tax liabilities in both countries can either apply for a reduction of taxed imposed by one country or can credit taxes paid in that country against tax liabilities in the other.

Dow Jones Index A main share index used in the United States of America.

Down-and-out option A knock-out option where the trigger is lower than the underlying rate at the start. There are also up-and-in option, down-and-in option, up-and-out option.

Drawdown A process of calling an amount from an account or available balance. In private equity funds it is the drawdown of the committed capital agreed by the investors

Drop-Lock A hybrid form of floating rate note that converts into a fixed rate bond once interest rates drop to a predetermined level.

DRP or (DRIP) Dividend Reinvestment Plan. Dividends are reinvested into shares rather than being distributed.

DTC Abbreviation for the Depository Trust Company—CSD for shares in the United States of America.

Dual Currency Bond A bond which pays interest in one currency and repays the principal in another currency.

Due Diligence The carrying out of duties with care and perseverance. Due diligence is generally referred to in connection with the investigations of a company, carried out by accountant's to ascertain the value of that company and also applies from a regulatory point of view that firms and key personnel should carry out their duties with due diligence to the regulatory environment.

An example is the client due diligence (CDD) when a firm or fund takes on a new client.

Dutch Auction A Dutch auction is where bids are made by an open-outcry or electronic system method and are accepted in descending order until the issue is completed.

ECB An abbreviation for the European Central Bank which is the central bank for countries using the Euro currency.

ECSDA An abbreviation for the European Central Securities Depository Association.

EUCLID Communications system operated by Euroclear.

EUREX German-Swiss derivatives exchange created by the merger of the German (DTB) and Swiss (SOFFEX) exchanges and part of the Deutsche Borse Group.

EURONEXT A pan-European securities and derivatives exchange listing Dutch, French, Portuguese, and Belgium securities and derivatives plus the derivative products traded on Euronext liffe. Joined with the New York Stock Exchange to create NYSE Euronext and NYSE-Liffe.

Earnings per share (EPS) The total profit of a company divided by the number of shares in issue.

Effective Date The date on which the interest period to which a FRA or swap relates, is to start which can be different from the date when the trade is agreed.

EIS Enterprise Investment Scheme in the UK aimed at early stage investment exposure for portfolios and tax efficient investment for individuals

Elective event Corporate action that requires a choice from the security owner.

Electronic Order Book The electronic order matching system used as the system for dealing in the shares that comprise the FTSE 100 stock.

Embedded option An option which is included as part of a product. Can be an option that the holder or the issuer can exercise, for example, callable and puttable bonds.

Emerging Market Often a non-limited or limited industrialized country with:

- low or middle per capita income, as published annually by the World Bank,
- Undeveloped capital market (ie, the market represents only a small portion of their GDP).

Can provide excellent investment opportunities but with often high risk.

EMIR An abbreviation for the European Markets Infrastructure Regulations which has led to the establishing of the clearing of OTC derivatives through CCPs.

Equilization A process for managing out inequalities, for example, in the share of performance fee each investor pays.

A process of showing the amount of capital and income involved in the subscription and redemption price of a debt fund.

Equity A common term to describe stocks or shares.

Equity/Stock Options Contracts based on individual equities or shares. On exercise of the option the specified amount of shares are usually exchanged between the buyer and the seller through the clearing organization.

Equity Index Swap An obligation between two parties to exchange cash flows based on the percentage change in one or more stock indices, for a specific period with previously agreed reset dates. The swap is cash settled and based on notional principal amounts. One side can involve a LIBOR reference.

Equity-Linked Bond A bond that can be converted into shares.

Escrow A bank account specifically designed to hold money independently, for example, during a dispute between two or more parties to prevent access to those funds until finalized.

ESMA European Securities Market Authority—European regulator.

E-T-C An abbreviation for an electronic trade confirmation system.

E-T-D This is the common term which is used to describe Exchange Traded Derivatives which are the standardized products. It also differentiates products which are ETD as opposed to those offered Over-The-Counter (OTC).

ETF Exchange-Traded Funds Passively managed basket of stocks that mirrors a particular index and that can be traded like ordinary shares. They trade intraday on stock exchanges, like securities, at market determined prices. In essence, ETFs are index funds that trade like stocks.

   Introduced in the United States in 1993 and in the UK in 2000, and based on the idea of gaining exposure to a stock index through a single tradable share (eg, iShares).

Ethical investments The investment in specific sectors and instruments through either personal conviction or the view that such companies have a higher potential, for example, investment in funds or companies supporting "green" issues, or the avoidance of so-called "unethical" areas such as animal experimentation, pollution etc.

EUCLID The Euroclear electronic communication system.

EURIBOR A measure of the average cost of funds over the whole euro area based on a panel of banks.

Euro The name of the single European currency used by several countries including Germany, France, Italy, Spain, the Benelux countries but not Switzerland, the UK, Denmark, and Sweden.

Euro-Commercial Paper Unsecured corporate debt with a short maturity structured to appeal to large financial institutions active in the Euro Market.

Eurobond An interest bearing security issued across national borders, usually issued in a currency other than that of the issuer's home country. Because there is no regulatory protection, only governments and top rated multinational corporations can issue Eurobonds that the market will accept.

   In order to avoid confusion with the Euro currency they are today sometimes called international bonds.

Euroclear A central securities depository, CSD, using book-entry clearing facility for most Eurocurrency and foreign securities. Is the CSD for Euronext and has links to other CSDs such as Clearstream through an electronic "bridge."

EuroMTS/MTS Group EuroMTS is part of the MTS Group that manages the pan-European electronic trading platform for government and quasi-government Eurobenchmark bonds as well as other areas of the capital markets.

   MTS Group is 100% owned by the London Stock Exchange.

European Style Option An option which can only be exercised on the expiry day.

Exception-based processing Transaction processing where straightforward items are processed automatically, allowing staff to concentrate on the items which are incorrect or not straightforward.

Exceptional In accounting, unexpected or one-off losses and gains are known as exceptional. They are part of a company's pretax profit and although irregular, they are derived from the company's normal business.

Execution and Clearing Agreement An agreement signed between the client and the clearing broker. This agreement sets out the terms by which the clearing broker will conduct business with the client.

Exchange A market place for trading that is authorized or licensed by a regulator. Has its own members who are subject to the rules of the exchange.

Exchange Delivery Settlement Price (EDSP) The price determined by the derivatives exchanges for physical delivery of the underlying instrument or cash settlement.

Exchange Owned Clearing Organization Exchange or member owned clearing organizations are structured so that the clearing members each guarantee each other with the use of a members default fund and additional funding like insurance.

Exchange Rate The rate at which one currency can be exchanged for another.

Excise Duties Type of tax levied on items such as alcohol, tobacco, and hydrocarbons.

Ex-Date Date on or after which a sale of securities is executed without the right to receive dividends or other entitlements.

Ex-dividend For example, after a stock has become "ex-dividend," a buyer of stock purchases it without the right to receive the pending interest or dividend payment.

Execute and eliminate order Type of order input into dealing systems like the LSE SETS. The amount that can be traded immediately against displayed orders is completed, with the remainder being rejected.

Execution The action of making transactions by trading in the relevant instruments and markets. Two parties "execute" the trade by being buyer and seller and a broker executes trades on behalf of their clients.

Execution and Clearing Agreement An agreement signed between the client and the clearing broker. This agreement sets out the terms by which the clearing broker will conduct business with the client.

Execution Only or Give-Up Agreement For derivatives the tripartite agreements that are signed by the executing broker, the clearing broker and the client. This agreement sets out the terms by which the clearing broker will accept business on behalf of the client.

Exercise The process by which the holder of an option or a warrant, may take up their right to buy or sell the underlying asset.

The process of carrying out a benefit or entitlement, that is, conversion of a convertible bond.

Exercise price (or Strike price) The fixed price, per share or unit, at which an option or warrant conveys the right to call (purchase) or put (sell) the underlying shares or units.

Exit charges Instead of or as well as making an initial charge, some investment funds make a charge if investors sell or redeem their holding within, say, five years.

Exotic Options More complex structured options including look-backs, barriers, baskets, ladders, etc. They have different terms to standardized traded options.

Expenses The broker's or fund's costs incurred in buying and selling shares. Also costs associated with sales, marketing, client services, legal expertise etc.

Expiry date The last date on which a holder can exercise their right related to options. After this date an option is deemed to lapse or be abandoned.

The date at which a contract or agreement matures or ceases to apply.

Extraordinary General Meeting (EGM) Any meeting of a company's shareholders other than its AGM.

Ex-Warrants The buyer will not be entitled to warrants that will be distributed to owners/holders of securities after the security goes "ex."

Face Value The value of a bond, note, mortgage or other security that appears on the face of the issue (if paper), unless the value is otherwise specified by the issuing company. Face value is ordinarily the amount the issuing company promises to pay at maturity. Face value is also referred to as *par value* or *nominal value*.

Failed transaction A transaction that does not settle on time, that is, the securities and/or cash are not exchanged as agreed on the settlement date. Also known as a "settlement fail.'

FATCA The US Foreign Account Tax Compliance Act which requires Foreign Financial Institutions (FFIs) to provide details investments held by them in accounts for US citizens.

FATF Financial Action Task Force on Money Laundering.

FCA Abbreviation for the newly created Financial Conduct Authority, a UK regulator (see also *FSA*).

Federal Reserve Book Entry System CSD for US government securities.

FIA Abbreviation for the Futures Industry Association based in the United States.

Fill or Kill order Type of order input into a market or trading system. It is either completed in full against displayed orders or cancelled.

Final Settlement The completion of a transaction when the delivery of all components of a trade is performed.

Financial Futures/Options contracts Financial futures is a term used to describe a legally binding contract based on financial instruments like currencies, debt instruments and financial indices.

Financial Services Act 2012 The legislation that created the UK Regulators, the Financial Conduct Authority and the Prudential Regulation Authority.

Financial Transaction Tax (FTT) Proposed EU tax on a wide range of financial transactions.

First notice day The first day that the holders of short futures positions can give notification to the exchange/clearing house that they wish to effect delivery.

Fiscal Agent A commercial bank appointed by the borrower to undertake certain duties related to the new issue, such as assisting the payment of interest and principal, redeeming bonds or coupons, handling taxes, replacement of lost or damaged securities, destruction of coupons and bonds once payments have been made.

Fiscal Years In the UK these run from 6 April to 5 April and are the periods of assessment for both income tax and capital gains tax.

Fit and Proper Under UK regulation everyone conducting investment business must be a "fit and proper person." The Act does not define the term, a function which is left to the regulators such as FSA.

The Financial Information eXchange (FIX) Protocol The Financial Information eXchange (FIX) Protocol is a technical specification for electronic communication of trade-related messages. The FIX Protocol is a series of messaging specifications developed through the collaboration of banks, broker-dealers, exchanges, industry utilities and associations, institutional investors, and information technology providers from around the world. FIX is open and free, but is not software. FIX is integral to many order management and trading systems.

Fixed Income Interest on a security that is calculated as a constant specified percentage of the principal amount and paid at the end of specified interest periods, usually annually or semiannually, until maturity.

Fixed interest securities Another term for "bond," or a security/instrument carrying a fixed rate of interest.

Fixed leg In a swap, the flow of say a fixed-rate interest payment from one party to the other.

Fixed-rate A borrowing or investment where the interest or coupon paid is fixed throughout the arrangement.

Fixed-rate cont'd In a FRA or coupon swap, the fixed-rate is the fixed interest rate paid by one party to the other, in return for a floating-rate receipt (ie, an interest rate that is to be refixed at some future time or times).

Fixed Rate Borrowing A fixed rate borrowing establishing the interest rate that will be paid throughout the life of the loan.

Fixed rate payer In a swap, the party that pays the fixed-rate.

Fixed rate receiver In a swap, the party that receives the fixed rate.

Flat Position A position which has been fully closed out and no liability to make or take delivery exists.

Flat Yield The yield of a bond calculated as $\dfrac{\text{Annual Coupon}}{\text{Current market price}} \times 100\%$ *Also called the income yield.*

Flex Options Contracts which are a cross between OTCs and exchange traded products. The advantage of flex options is that participants can choose various parts of the contract specification such as the expiry date and exercise price.

Flotation When a company has its shares first quoted on the stock market it is said to have "floated" its shares.

Floating leg In a coupon swap, the flow of a floating-rate interest payment from one party to the other.

Floating-rate A borrowing or investment where the interest or coupon paid changes throughout the arrangement in line with some reference rate such as LIBOR.

Floating-rate cont'd In a FRA or coupon swap, the floating-rate is the floating interest rate (ie, an interest rate that is to be refixed at some future time or times) paid by one party to the other, in return for a fixed-rate receipt.

Floating Rate Note (FRN) Bond where each interest payment is made at the current or average market levels, often by reference to LIBOR.

Floating Rate Payer Payer of floating rate in a coupon swap.

Floating Rate Receiver Receiver of floating rate in a coupon swap.

Floor A package of interest rate options whereby, at each of a series of future fixing dates, if an agreed reference rate such as LIBOR is lower that the strike rate, the option buyer received the difference between them, calculated on an agreed notional principal amount for the period until the next fixing date. See *cap, collar.*

Floor brokerage The process of delegating the execution of futures and options to another counterparty.

Foreign Bond Bond issued in a domestic market in the domestic currency and under the domestic rules of issuance by a foreign issuer (for example, Samurai bonds are bonds issued by issuers of other countries on the Japanese market).

Foreign Currency Fund A mutual fund investing in foreign currencies.

Foreign Exchange Exchange of one currency into another one.

Forex Abbreviation for foreign exchange (currency trading).

Forward Market/Contract Where a price is agreed now for delivery of goods in the future. Used in currency, securities and commodities markets, often in conjunction with dealing in immediate delivery (see *Spot Market*) as a safety net.

Forward contracts in currencies are a fixed rate for buying and selling at a date forward in time. Also known as an outright forward

Forward Rate Agreements (FRAs) An agreement where the client can fix the rate of interest that will be applied to a notional loan or deposit, drawn or placed on an agreed date in the future, for a specified term.

Forward Delivery Transactions that involve a delivery date in the future.

Forward Swap A swap agreed today that starts at some point in the future.

Forwardation Where a dealer purchases goods on the Spot Market to meet his future obligations, especially when those goods are cheaper now than quoted on the Forward Market.

Forwards Are very similar to futures contracts but they are not usually traded on an exchange. They are not marked to market daily but settled only on the delivery date.

Franked Income Where tax has already been paid on income.

Free of Payment Refers to the movement of currencies where there is no associated countervalue at the time of settlement due to timing differences in the payment systems or is a situation which is not dependent on the simultaneous payment of the cash value during the movement of assets, for example, in a stock loan or collateral movement.

Movement of securities with no corresponding payment, for example, switching assets between custodians.

Front End Loading The deduction of costs from the initial contributions to savings vehicles such as investment funds, endowment policies or personal pension plans. Also applies to mortgages and loans where although spread throughout the term, in the early years the bulk of the repayment is of interest with very little reduction in the capital content. Toward the end of the term, the interest diminishes and virtually all the repayment is of capital.

Front Running The illicit utilizing by brokers and market-makers of advance warning or information about orders or trades for personal or corporate profit.

FSA Financial Services Agency (Japan).

Previously the mnemonic for the Financial Services Authority the UK regulator now replaced by the FCA and PRA.

FSA Seychelles The Seychelles Financial Services Authority.

FSC Mauritius Financial Services Commission Mauritius.

FT Index The Financial Times Ordinary Share Index consists of 30 large companies across a broad field and gives an indication of share price trends. The larger Index, the FTSE 100 (known as the "Footsie") provides a wider indication of 100 leading companies on the Stock Market. All stock markets have an index, for example, The Dow Jones in the US, the DAX in Germany or the Nikkei in Japan.

FTSE 100 index Main UK share index based on 100 leading shares.

FTSE Mid 250 UK share index based on the 250 shares immediately below the top 100.

Fund Administrator Internal team or an organization appointed to administer a fund. Responsibilities can include calculating the NAV, maintaining records of the funds activities and dealing with investors in the fund.

Associated terms are Fund Support, Fund Operations, Fund Accounting, and Transfer Agency.

Fund Administration Agreement Sets out the legal basis and terms and conditions with a third party administrator.

Fund Manager Individuals or specialists companies responsible for investing the assets of a fund in such a way as to maximize its value. They do this by following a strategy to buy and sell equities and other financial instruments.

See also *asset manager and investment manager*.

Funds General term for mutual funds, unit trusts and OEIC's (open ended investment companies) and other collective investment schemes.

Fund of Funds A fund that specialises in buying shares in other funds rather than individual securities.

Common example is a Fund of Hedge Funds which invests in the shares of Hedge Funds and is in turn invested in by institutions like pension funds.

Fungible Contract A futures or other contract with identical administration in more than one financial center which can be settled in one center against another.

Futures A derivative product traded on an exchange which is a contract in the form of an agreement to buy or sell an asset at a certain time in the future for a certain price that is agreed today.

Future Value The amount of money which can be achieved at a given date in the future by investing (or borrowing) a given sum of money now at a given interest rate, assuming compound reinvestment (or refunding) of any interest payments received (or paid) before the end.

Futures and Options Fund (FOF) Type of authorized unit trust that can invest partially in derivatives.

Futures Strip A series or stream of short-term futures contracts which when grossed up will generate a return for a term equal to the length of the strip.

GABRIEL The FCA online regulatory reporting system for the collection, validation, and storage of regulatory data.

Geared Futures and Options Fund (GFOF) Type of authorized unit trust that can invest in derivatives.

Gearing The characteristic of for example derivatives which enables a far greater reward for the same, or much smaller, initial outlay. It is the ratio of exposure to investment outlay, and is also known as leverage.

Generic Swap A generic swap is one for a standard period, against a standard fixing benchmark such as LIBOR. Also known as a "plain vanilla" swap.

GFSC Guernsey Financial Services Commission.

Gilt Long standing term used to describe a domestic sterling-denominated long-term bond backed by the full faith and credit of the United Kingdom and issued by the Treasury.

Gilt Edged Market Makers (GEMMs) A firm that is a market maker in gilts. Also known as a primary dealer.

Gilt Edged Security UK government borrowing.

Give-Up The process of giving a trade to a third party who will undertake the clearing and settlement of the trade.

Global Bond A (temporary) certificate representing the whole of a bond issue.

Global Certificate Certificate held at the Central Depository recording the total issue of a bond.

Global Clearing The channeling of the settlement of all futures and options trades through a single counterparty or a number of counterparties geographically located.

Global Custodian Institution that safekeeps, settles, and performs processing of income collection, tax reclaim, multicurrency reporting, cash management, foreign exchange, corporate action, and proxy monitoring etc. for clients' securities in all required marketplaces.

Does so by utilizing subcustodians in each jurisdiction.

Global Depository Receipt (GDR) A security representing shares held in custody sold to investors in various countries.

Gold Widely used commodity and regarded as a safe haven in times of uncertainty.

Good Delivery Proper delivery of certificates that is negotiable and complete in terms of documentation or information.

GRA The Gibraltar Regulatory Authority.

Granter Another term for a person who has sold an option position to a buyer.

"Greeks" A collective term for delta, gamma, theta, and vega, which relate to the movement in price of an option as a result of the movement in the underlying price, the rate of that movement and time erosion.

Grey Market Generally speaking it is a market for a new issue before the securities have been distributed to subscribers.

Gross A position which is held with both the bought and sold trades kept open.

Gross Domestic Product (GDP) A measure of the country's entire output.

Gross Redemption Yield (GRY) The annual return on owning a bond, allowing both for interest and profit on redemption.

Grossing Up The process of calculating the gross income from a figure net of taxation.

Growth Stock Companies with or with the expectation of a rapid rise in expansion and subsequent share value.

GSCC Government Securities Clearing Corporation—clearing organization for US Treasury securities.

Guaranteed Bond Bonds on which the principal or income or both are guaranteed by another corporation or parent company in case of default by the issuing corporation.

Haircut Amount by which an asset being used as collateral is discounted. Can also be called margin.

Hard Commodities Commodities such as tin or zinc. Futures on them are traded on the London Metal Exchange.

Hedge Fund Vary enormously but essentially funds that are investing in a wide variety of instruments and strategies often designed to generate exceptionally high return but with higher risk of loss. Can gear the fund, short sell and invest in credit risk and other types of investments that retail funds cannot use. Sales limited to high net worth individuals and other funds.

Hedge Ratio Determining the ratio of the futures to the cash position so as to reduce price risk.

Hedging A trading method which is designed to reduce or mitigate risk. Reducing the risk of a cash position in the futures instrument to offset the price movement of the cash asset. A broader definition of hedging includes using futures as a temporary substitute for the cash position.

High risk Volatile investments that rise and fall sharply in value.

High Water Mark A benchmark used in the calculation of performance fees for investment managers.

HKEC/HKE/HKEx The Hong Kong Exchanges and Clearing comprised of the Hong Kong Futures Exchange, The Stock Exchange of Hong Kong Ltd and The Hong Kong Securities Clearing Company Ltd.

   The Central Clearing & Settlement System (CCASS) is used for securities and *the Derivatives Clearing & Settlement System (DCASS)* is used for derivatives. There is also the *SEOCH, the Stock Exchange of Hong Kong Options Clearing House.*

Holder A person who has bought an open derivatives contract.

Holder of Record The party whose name appears on a company's stockholder register at the close of business on record date. That party will receive a dividend or other distribution from the company in the near future.

Holding Company A company which owns more than 50% of the shares of another company as its holding company.

Home State Regulation Under the EU regulations an investment business is authorized in the place of its head office and registered office. This home state authorization entitles it to conduct business in any member state of the European Union.

Host State Regulation Any European investment business operating outside its home basis is regulated by its host for its Conduct of business.

Hurdle Rate A benchmark used in the calculation of performance fees for investment managers.

ICE/ICE Clear See *Intercontinental Exchange*.

ICSD An International Central Securities Depository which clears and settles international securities or cross-border transactions through local CSD's, for example, Clearstream, Euroclear, DTC.

IFSRA Irish Financial Services Regulatory Authority.

Immobilization The storage of securities certificates in a vault in order to eliminate physical movement of certificates/documents in transfer of ownership.

Implied Repo Rate The rate of return before financing costs implied by a transaction where a longer-term cash security is purchased and a futures contract is sold (or vice versa).

In-the-money A call option where the exercise price is below the underlying share price or a put option where the exercise price is above the underlying share price.

Income Enhancement Strategy that uses written call options to generate premium against underlying assets held.

Income Fund A fund that concentrates on finding companies whose dividends are likely to be above average or bonds with good yields so that income can be periodically distributed to investors.

Income Tax An annual tax on the income of an individual.

Independent Clearing Organization The independent clearing organization is quite separate from the actual exchange or market that it clears. Increasingly clearing organizations are becoming part of the exchange or owned by exchanges, for example, ICE, LSE acquiring LCH.Clearnet etc.

Index funds Funds that invest to perform in line with a stock market index, for example, the FTSE 100. Also known as "tracker" funds.

Index linked bond Bond whose interest payment and redemption value are linked to the retail prices index.

Index Swap A swap where payments on one or both of the legs are based on the value of an index, such as an equity index. See *Equity Index Swap*.

Indexation Where investments, wages, contributions etc. are linked to a benchmark such as inflation. For example, a contribution to a pension scheme may increase by 3% or the retail price index, whichever is the higher.

Indirect Market Participation Nonbroker/dealers, such as institutional investors, who are active investors/traders but who access markets via an intermediary like a broker.

Individual Savings Account A UK savings vehicle where the individual can save either on a regular monthly or lump sum basis with exposure to varying degrees of risk but with tax free concessions. An ISA is a "wrapper" into which cash, unit trusts and mutual funds are placed to get the tax benefit.

Inflation A period of generally rising prices and devaluation of money through a number of causes such as rises in fuel, manufacturing and labor costs. For example, high salary or wage demands not covered by productivity.

Inflation Accounting The allowing for the impact of inflation in preparing company accounts.

Initial charge/Fee A charge—typically 0.5–5%—that is paid to cover an investment manager's expenses, such as commission, advertising, administration, and dealing costs.

Initial Margin or Deposit The deposit that the clearing house calls as protection against a default of a contract. It is returnable to the clearing member once the position is closed. The level is subject to changes in line with market conditions. Clearing brokers in turn call initial margin from their clients.

Inland Revenue/HMRC The government department responsible for the administration and collection of tax in the UK now called Her Majesty's Revenue and Customs.

Inside Information Information relating to a security which is not publicly known and which would affect the price of the security if it was public.

Insider Directors, employees, shareholders, and other persons having inside information.

Insider Dealing The criminal offence whereby those with unpublished price sensitive information deal, advise others to deal or pass the information on. Maximum penalty is seven years jail and an unlimited fine.

Institutional Investor An institution which is usually investing money on behalf of others. Examples are mutual funds and pension funds.

Integration The third stage of money laundering, in which the money is finally integrated into the legitimate economy. See *placement, layering*.

Interbank Market A market for transactions exclusively or predominantly within the banking system. In most countries, the market for short-term money is an Interbank market since banks borrow and lend amongst one and another in order to balance their books on a daily basis. Nonbank entities may or may not be permitted to participate.

Interbank Rates The bid and offered rates at which international banks place deposits with each other.

Intercontinental Exchange (ICE)/ICE Clear Intercontinental Exchange® operates global commodity and financial products market places and also runs ICE Clear United States, Europe, and Canada plus ICE Clear Credit for credit derivatives clearing. Owns the NYSE Euronext market.

Inter Dealer Broker (IDB) Member of the London Stock Exchange that acts as a link between firms to enable them to trade with each other anonymously.

Interest Rate Futures Can be based on a debt instrument such as a Government Bond or a Treasury Bill or Note as the underlying product and require the delivery of a bond or will be cash settled to fulfil the contract.

Contracts based on interest rates, for example, 3month Sterling Interest Rate.

Interest Rate Cap An option product where the holder (buyer) is guaranteed a maximum borrowing cost over a specified term at a rate of his choosing. A premium is required.

Interest Rate Collar An option product where the holder (buyer) is guaranteed a maximum and minimum borrowing cost over a specified term at rates of his choosing. A premium may be required, but may net to zero. Involves the simultaneous trading of caps and floors.

Interest Rate Floor An option product where the holder (buyer) is guaranteed a minimum yield on a deposit over a specified term at a rate of his choosing. A premium is required.

Interest Rate Guarantee Also IRG. Effectively an option on a forward rate agreement. An IRG can be either a borrower's option (ie, a call on an FRA0 or a lender's option (ie, a put on an FRA).

Interest Rate Swap An agreement to exchange interest related payments in the same currency from fixed rate into floating rate (or vice versa) or from one type of floating rate to another.

Interim dividend Dividend paid part way through a year in advance of the final dividend.

Intermediary A bank, broker or financial institution which accesses markets on behalf of a client or puts two counterparties together for a fee usually called a commission.

International Capital Markets Association ICMA/IPMA/ISMA The International Primary Markets Association merged with the International Securities Market Association to create the *International Capital Markets Association*.

International Equity An equity of a company based outside the UK but traded internationally

International Financial Centre A designated "territory" or location sometimes with very low tax rates and a different type of regulation (*an "offshore center" like the Cayman Islands or Dublin*) to the rest of the location which is home to domestic investors and companies. Also offers international banking, investment and other financial services.

In general terms financial center also means locations such as New York, London, Frankfurt, and Tokyo.

International Monetary Fund Set up by the Bretton Woods agreement into which member countries contribute to provide assistance during periods of economic instability, thereby smoothing out the world trade cycle and avoiding a major plunge into depression as seen in the 1930s.

International Securities Identification (ISIN) A coding system developed by the ISO for identifying securities. ISINs are designated to create one unique worldwide number for any security. It is a 12 digit alpha/numeric code.

International Standards Organization (ISO) An international federation of organizations of various industries which seeks to set common international standards in a variety of fields.

Interoperability Ability of diverse systems, teams or organizations to work together.

Interpolation The estimation of a price or rate, usually for a broken date in a swap, from two other rates or prices, each of which is for a date either side of the required date.

In-the-money An option whose strike is more advantageous to the option buyer than the current market rate. See *at-the-money, out-of-the-money*.

Intervention The process whereby the Bank of England acts to influence the exchange rate for sterling by buying it to support its value or selling it to weaken it.

Intra-Day Margin Additional margins calls over and above the initial margin which the clearing organization can call during the day when there is a very large movement up or down in the price of the contract.

Intrinsic Value The amount by which an option is in-the-money.

IRS See *Interest Rate Swap*. Also the Internal Revenue System, tax system, in the United States.

Investment Banks A bank that has multiple activities, that is, Banking, principal trading, brokerage, asset management etc.

Originally "investment banking" was about providing services to key corporate and other institutional clients including financing, advisory, and other such activities.

Investment Business Dealing, advising or managing investments. Those doing so need to be authorized.

Investment funds General term for unit trusts and OEIC's (open ended investment companies) and their equivalents in other countries like SICAVS, Investment Companies with Variable Capital (ICVCs) and mutual funds as well as nonretail funds like hedge funds and private equity funds.

Investment Services Directive (ISD/MiFID) European Union Directive imposing common standards on investment business. Is now part of the Markets in Financial Instruments Directive (MiFID).

Investments Items defined by regulators and covered by their regulations used in the investment process. Can include shares, bonds, options, futures, life assurance, investment funds and pensions, as well as commodities, and alternative investments.

Investment Grade A grading level that is used by certain types of funds for determining assets that are suitable for investment in by the fund. Can be based on grading issues by organizations such as S & P, Fitch, or Moodys.

Investment Manager Either a person or a firm that manages assets and makes investment decisions.

See also *fund manager and asset manager.*

Investment Trust (Company) Company quoted on an Exchange which has a fixed number of shares. The value of these shares is determined by supply and demand. The shares do not therefore normally reflect the value of its underlying assets and can be at a premium or discount on net asset value. Basically a trading investment company, it can borrow to provide gearing, can invest in a very wide range of securities, both listed and unlisted, and can hedge any currency risks.

Invoice Amount The amount calculated under the formula specified by the futures exchange, which will be paid in settlement of the delivery of the underlying asset.

IOSCO Abbreviation for the International Organization of Securities Commissions.

Irredeemable Gilt/Bond A gilt or bond with no fixed date for redemption. Investors receive interest indefinitely. Can also called a perpetual bond.

ISDA Abbreviation for the *International Swaps and Derivatives Association*, previously known as the International Swap Dealers Association. Many market participants use ISDA documentation across many products when trading over the counter.

ISSA An abbreviation for The International Securities Services Association.

Issue/Issuers Stocks or bonds sold (issued) by a corporation or government entity at a particular time. They are referred to as issuers.

Issue Price The price at which new securities or other financial instruments are offered in the primary market, that is, the offer price in an initial public offering.

Issuer Legal entity that issues and distributed securities and other instruments.

Issuing Agent Agent (eg, bank) who puts original issues out for sale.

Issuing House Institutions that issue shares for companies wishing to raise capital by underwriting shares issued direct to the public through the company or by buying and selling the shares itself.

"J" Curve A term used to describe the change in an investors capital from negative to positive during the duration from capital drawdown to distribution of return of a private equity fund.

JASDEC Japan Securities Depository Centre—the CSD for Japan.

JFSC The Jersey Financial Services Commission.

JSE TradeElect The Johannesburg Electronic Trading system.

JSCC Abbreviation for Japan Securities Clearing Corporation—clearing organization in Japan.

JSE Abbreviation for the Johannesburg Stock Exchange.

Junk Bonds High-risk bonds that have low ratings or are in default, where there is a risk of nonpayment of obligations such as interest or bond redemption.

Knock-in-option An option that is activated if a trigger level is reached. See *barrier option, knock-out option.*

Knock-out option An option that is cancelled if a trigger level is reached. See *barrier option, knock-in option.*

Know Your Customer (KYC) The conduct of business rule requiring investment advisers to take steps, before giving investment advice, to determine the financial position and investment objectives of the client.

Korea Securities Depository (KSD) CSD and clearing organization for the Korean Stock Exchange.

Large caps The shares of big companies like the "Blue Chips" or those with large market capitalization which is the number of shares issued multiplied by the current share price.

Last notice day The final day that notification of delivery of a futures contract will be possible. On most exchanges all outstanding short futures contracts will be automatically delivered to open long positions.

Last trading day Often the day preceding last notice day which is the final opportunity for holders of long positions to trade out of their positions and avoid ultimate delivery.

Layering The second stage of money laundering, in which the money is passed through a series of transaction to obscure its origin. See *placement, integration.*

LCH/LCH.Clearnet London Clearing House now merged with Clearnet to create LCH. Clearnet. The London Stock Exchange has a major stake in the firm.

Lead Managers In the securities markets the description given to the investment bank/broker appointed to handle a new issue.

Also used to identify the lead party in a syndication.

LEI Legal Entity Identifier—important tool for client due diligence.

Legal Title or Ownership Legal title to property is held by the person who controls the property and in whose name the property is registered.

Leverage The magnification of gains and losses by only paying for part of the underlying value of the instrument or asset; the smaller the amount of funds invested, the greater the leverage. It is also known as gearing.

In funds the term can apply to the borrowing of large amounts of capital over and above the subscription capital, which then creates a liability in the fund. If the strategy does not work the investors could lose all their capital as the fund clears the liabilities first. Example would be a Leveraged Buy Out Fund (LBO).

Liability Swap A swap which is coupled with for instance a bond in order to change the structure of the bond. The bond may already have been issued by the borrower or it may be issued together with the swap as a package.

LIBID The London inter-bank bid rate. The rate at which one bank will lend to another.

LIBOR The London inter-bank offered rate. It is the rate used when one bank borrows from another bank. It is the benchmark used to price many capital market and derivative transactions. Following a major rigging scandal changes to the way LIBOR is calculated have been made.

LIBOR-in-arrears swap A swap in which LIBOR is set usually two days prior to the payment date.

LIFFE The London International Financial Futures and Options Exchange, now part of NYSE Euronext and referred to as *NYSE Liffe.*

LIFFE Connect (Connect) Electronic dealing system developed by LIFFE and now used to trade derivatives on Euronext.

Limit Order Type of order input into the LSE SETS. If not completed immediately the balance is displayed on the screen and forms the Order Book.

Limit Order cont'd An order in which a customer sets the maximum price he is willing to pay as a buyer or the minimum price he is willing to accept as a seller.

Limited Partner The investor in a partnership.

Line of Credit A commitment by a bank to make loans to a borrower up to a specified maximum during a specified period.

Linked Forex When the currency is purchased via a fx trade to cover the local cost of a securities trade.

Liquidation Term used to describe the closing of open positions or the winding up of a fund or company.

Liquidator Person appointed to sell the corporate assets of a company in receivership, distributing the proceeds among the creditors.

Liquidity A liquid asset is one that can be bought or sold at any time or converted easily and rapidly into cash without a substantial loss of value. In the markets, a security is said to be liquid if the spread between bid and asked price is narrow and reasonable size can be done at those quotes.

Liquidity risk The risk that a party may not be able to close out a position because the market is illiquid.

Listed company Company which has been admitted to listing on a stock exchange and whose shares can then be dealt on that exchange.

Listed Securities Securities Listed on a stock exchange that can be traded on this exchange. Called the secondary market.

Listing Status applied for by companies whose securities are then listed on a stock exchange and available to be traded. The listing was a capital raising event in the primary market.

Listing Particulars Detailed Information that must be published by a company applying to be listed. This is typically via a Prospectus or Offering Document.

Listing Rules Rule book for listed companies which governs their behavior. Commonly known as the Yellow Book.

LLC Limited Liability Company, many investment funds are set ups a LLC's.

LLP Limited Liability Partnerships, some private funds are set up as LLP's with a General Partner who makes the investment decisions and limited partners provide the monies for investment. Tax is sometimes a factor in using an LLP.

Lloyds of London World's largest insurance market.

Loan Stock See *bonds.*

Local An individual member of an exchange who trades solely for their own account.

Local Currency Currency of the country of settlement.

Lombard Rate The rate of interest at which the German Bundesbank lends to commercial banks when the loans are against Treasury Bills or bills of exchange.

London Inter Bank Offer Rate (LIBOR) Rate at which banks lend to each other which is often used as the benchmark for floating rate loans (FRNs).

London Metal Exchange (LME) Market for trading in derivatives of metals such as copper, tin, zinc etc., as well as plastics. Is merging with the HKEC.

London Stock Exchange (LSE) Market for trading in securities. Formerly known as the International Stock Exchange of the United Kingdom and Republic of Ireland or ISE.

Long/Long position A bought position in a derivative or security that is held as an open position, that is, an investors buys BP shares and is termed as being "long" of BP.

Long Coupons 1. Bonds or notes with a long current maturity;

2. A coupon on which the period is longer than the others or the standard coupon period.

Long-dated Gilts with more than 15 years until redemption.

Long Position Refers to an investor's account in which he has more shares of a specific security than he needs to meet his settlement obligations.

Long/Short Fund A hedge fund strategy involving being long and simultaneously short of different assets with the possibility of positive returns on both positions.

Look Back Option An option that gives the holder the right to exercise the option at the most advantageous price reached by the underlying asset during the look back period. This is often the life of the option.

Lot A term used to describe the standard unit of trading for futures and options. The term "contract" is also used.

Low risk Where the value of an investment is unlikely to fall, although there is no guarantee.

Managed Fund A collective investment scheme with an active manager.

A fund for individual investors but managed collectively often using futures contracts.

Management Expense Ratio (MER) A measurement of the expenses associated with the management of an investment fund.

Manager of Managers Unlike a fund of funds where the fund manager selects funds to buy, the owner/sponsor of a fund appoints several managers to run the portfolios (Multi Manager Fund). The Manager of Managers is responsible, not just for identifying competitive managers, but for monitoring the overall portfolios at a stock-by-stock, manager-by-manager level. The emphasis is on a clear and consistent investment process.

Manager's report Available periodically and at least annually, it details the exact position of the fund, for example, its investments, the manager's investment commentary, the performance of the portfolio etc.

Mandate Document that sets out the terms under which the investments of a fund must be managed. Will detail investments that are not permitted etc.

Managers face penalties for breaching a fund's mandate.

Mandatory event (Corporate Action) A corporate action which affects or changes the structure of the securities without giving any choice to the security holder.

Mandatory Quote Period Time of day during which market makers in equities are obliged to quote prices under London Stock Exchange rules.

Margin *Initial* margin is collateral placed by one party with a counterparty or clearing house at the time of a deal, against the possibility that the market price will move against the first party, thereby leaving the counterparty with a credit risk.

Margin cont'd *Variation* margin is a payment made, or collateral transferred, from one party to the other because the market price of the transaction or of collateral has changed. Variation margin payment is either in effect a settlement of profit/loss (eg, in the case of a futures contract) or the reduction of credit exposure.

Margin cont'd In a loan, margin is the extra interest above a benchmark such as LIBOR required by a lender to compensate for the credit risk of that particular borrower.

Margin cont'd Money or assets that must be deposited by participants in securities lending, repo's or OTC derivatives markets as a guarantee that they will be able to meet their commitments at the due date.

Margin (trading on) Facility provide to hedge funds by a prime broker.

Marginal Rate of Tax The rate of tax which will apply to the next unit of income.

Mark-To-Market The process of revaluing the position in an OTC or exchange traded product each day.

It is the using the difference between the closing price on the previous day versus the current closing price. For exchange traded products this is referred to as variation margin.

Market Description of any organization or facility through which items are traded. All exchanges are markets.

Market Counterparty A person dealing as agent or principal with the broker and involved in the same nature of investment business as the broker. This also includes fellow members of the SFA or trading members of an investment exchange, for those products only where they are members.

Market Forces This is supply and demand allowing buyers and sellers to fix the price without external interference.

Market Maker A trader who works for an organization such as an investment bank. They quote bids and offers in the market and are normally under an obligation to make a price in a certain number of contracts. They create liquidity in the contract by offering to buy or sell.

Market Price In the case of a security, the market price is usually considered as the last reported price at which the stock or bond has been sold.

Market risk Also position risk. The risk that the market value of a position falls or that it becomes illiquid and cannot be acquired/disposed of.

Market Value The price at which a security is trading and could presumably be purchased or sold.

Markit Markit is a leading, global financial information services company. The company provides independent data, valuations and trade processing across all asset classes in order to enhance transparency, reduce risk and improve operational efficiency. Worked in collaboration with DTC to create MarkitSERV.

Master Agreement This agreement is part of the ISDA documentation for OTC transactions and is signed between the client and the broker. It covers the basic terms under which the client and broker wish to transact business. Each individual trade has a separate individual agreement with specific terms known as a confirmation.

Matching (Comparison) Another term for comparison (or checking); can be via a matching system to compare trades and ensure that both sides of trade correspond. Is a clearing process.

Maturity The date on which the principal or nominal value of a bond becomes due and payable in full to the holder.

The time at which a derivative ceases to exist.

MCSD The Misr for Clearing, Settlement, and Depository, clearing house and depository for the Egyptian Stock Exchange.

Medium Dated Bond or Note with a time to maturity typically somewhere between 1 and 15 years. Varies from country to country but in the UK, Gilts due to be redeemed within the next seven to fifteen years.

Medium risk Where the value of an investment may rise as well as fall in the short term but total loss of value is unlikely.

Merchant Banks Often relatively small but prestigious financial institutions, who deal mainly with companies and wealthy individuals in providing a range of financial services including, among others, corporate finance and portfolio management.

Mergers and Acquisition (M&A) Divisions of investment banks or merchant banks responsible for advising on takeover and merger activity. Usually work with the corporate finance department and is often kept as a single unit.

MFSA Malta Financial Services Authority.

MiFID In Europe the *Markets in Financial Instruments Directive (MiFID)* has replaced the Investment Services Directive (ISD). MiFID extended the coverage of the ISD regime and introduced new and more extensive requirements to which firms will have to adapt, in particular in relation to their conduct of business and internal organisation. Reform of the regulation introduced MiFID II and now MiFID III is in process.

Mismatch Risk The risk that arises in a swap portfolio when the terms of two off-setting swaps do not exactly match, for example, a mismatch between 3- and 6-month LIBOR.

Model risk The risk that the computer model used by a bank for valuation or risk assessment is incorrect or misinterpreted.

Model Code for Securities Dealing In the UK relates to directors dealing in their own company's securities. Prohibits them from doing so during the two months before results are announced.

Modified following The convention that if a settlement date in the future falls on a nonbusiness day, the settlement date will be moved to the next following business day, unless this moves it to the next month, in which case the settlement date is moved back to the last previous business day.

Monetary Authority of Singapore (MAS) The overall investment regulatory body in Singapore.

Monetary Interest Rate The actual interest rate received in money terms.

Money Laundering The process where criminals attempt to conceal the true origin and ownership of the proceeds of their criminal activities and to legitimize these proceeds by introducing them into the mainstream of financial activities.

Money Market The market for the purchase and sale of short-term financial instruments. Short term is usually defined as less than one year to maturity of the instrument.

Money Market Fund An open-end mutual fund that invests in commercial paper, banker's acceptances, repurchase agreements, government securities, and other highly liquid and safe securities. The fund pays money market rates of interest. Many money market funds are part of fund families; investors can switch their money from one fund to another and back again without charge.

Money Rate of Return Annual return as a percentage of asset value.

Money Supply Measure of the money available in the economy.

Monti Titoli CSD for Italian Securities that is owned by the London Stock Exchange Group.

Moody's Investment Service Moody's is one of the two most popular bond rating agencies in the United States. The other agency is Standard and Poor's.

Mortgage A form of security on borrowing commonly associated with home borrowing.

Mortgage-Backed Security Security backed by an investment company that raises money from shareholders and invests it in stocks, bonds or other instruments (unit trust, investment fund, SICAV—BEVEK).

Multilateral Trade Facility (MTF) Electronic trading platforms set up as alternatives to established bourses and exchanges often citing speed and cheapness as advantages
   Examples: Chi-X, Turqouise.

Multilateral netting Trade between several counterparties in the same security are netted such that a counter-party makes only one transfer of cash or securities to another party or to a central clearing system. Applies only to transactions due for settlement on the same day.

Mutual collateralization The deposit of collateral by both counterparties to a transaction.

Mutual Fund Term used particularly in the United States to describe a fund operated by an investment company that raises money from shareholders (investors) and invests it in stocks, bonds, or other instruments (examples unit trust, investment fund, SICAV).

Naked Option An option bought or sold for speculation, with no offsetting existing position in the underlying behind it.

Naked Short Selling A strategy where an investor or fund manager believes that a security will fall in price and sells the security, which they do not own, with the expectation of buying back at a lower price.

Naked Writing Where the seller does not own the stock corresponding to the call option which he has sold and would be forced to pay the prevailing market price for the stock to meet delivery obligations, if called.

Names Individuals of Lloyds of London who join together in syndicates to write insurance business. Their liability is unlimited and therefore all their personal wealth is at risk.

NASDAQ National Association of Securities Dealers Automated Quotation system, an electronic market in the United States, Dubai, and Europe.

National Securities Depository Depository for the National Stock Exchange in India.

Net Asset Value (NAV) In investment funds, the market value of the fund share or unit. It is common practice for an investment trust to compute its assets daily, or even twice a day, by totaling the closing market value of all securities and assets (ie, cash) owned. All income, liabilities and expenses are deducted, and the balance is divided by the number of shares outstanding. The resulting figure is the net asset value per share.

Hedge funds, property funds, and closed end funds will calculate the NAV periodically.

Net Present Value (NPV) The net total of several present values (arising from cash flows at different future dates) added together, some of which may be positive and some negative.

Netting Trading partners offset their positions thereby reducing the number of positions for settlement and also the counterparty risk. Netting can be on a *bilateral, multilateral,* or *continuous net settlement* basis.

Used by clearing houses who net members trades for settlement.

New Issues Companies raise capital by issuing new securities. New issue is the name given to the bonds or stocks offered to investors for the first time.

Nikkei Dow Index Main share index in Japan.

Nikkei Futures Futures contracts traded on the Tokyo Stock Exchange, SGX, and OSAKA exchange.

Nil paid rights price Ex-rights price less the subscription price of a rights issue.

No-Par Value (NPV) Stock with no cash value assigned on the issuance of certificates. Note: NPV is also an abbreviation for net present value.

Nominal Amount Monetary value stated on the face of a security (principal value, par value). Securities processing: number of securities to deliver/receive.

Nominal value of a bond The value at which the capital, or principal, of a bond will be redeemed by the issuer. Also called par value or face value.

Nominal value of a share The minimum price at which a share can be issued. Also called par value. A share where the minimum price or more has been paid on issue is known as "fully paid."

Nominated Advisor Firm appointed to advise directors of companies looking to list on the LSE's Alternative Investment Market on their responsibilities. Role can be combined with that of nominated broker.

Nominate Broker Firm appointed to assist dealing in AIM listed securities.

Nominee An organization that acts as the named owner of securities on behalf of a different beneficial owner who remains anonymous to the company.

Noncallable Cannot be redeemed by the issuer for a stated period of time from date of issue.

Nonclearing member A member of an exchange who does not undertake to settle their business. This type of member must appoint a clearing member to register all their trades at the clearing organization.

Noncompetitive bid In an auction, bidding for a specific amount of securities without mentioning a price. Usually, the price paid will be equal to the average of the accepted competitive bids.

Noncumulative preference share If the company fails to pay a preference dividend the entitlement to the dividend is simply lost. There is no accumulation.

Nondeliverable forward(NDF) A forward contract that is cash settled.

Example: A foreign exchange forward outright where, instead of each party delivering the full amount of currency at settlement, there is a single net cash payment to reflect the change in value between the forward rates transacted and the spot rate two working days before settlement.

Nonprivate Customer A person who is not a Private Customer or who has requested to be treated as a Nonprivate Customer.

Nonprofit Policy An endowment or whole life policy where the benefit is a guaranteed sum only.

Nonvoting shares Some companies have two types of shares. In such cases, for example, an investment fund, voting shares are restricted to owners and directors to maintain control, whereas nonvoting shares are held by investors.

Where a corporate has issued nonvoting shares they generally are priced lower than the voting ordinary shares as they have less shareholder rights.

Normal Bonus The annual bonus paid on a with profits policy.

Normal Market Size (NMS) Minimum size in which market makers must quote bids and offers on LSE. Also the minimum shares that can be transferred, on most markets this is one share.

Nostro A bank's nostro account is its currency account held with a foreign bank.

Nostro reconciliation Checking the entries shown on the bank's nostro account statement with the bank's internal records (the accounting ledgers) to ensure that they correspond exactly.

Note Bonds issued with a relatively short to medium maturity are often called notes.

Notional The notional amount of a transaction where the value itself is not transferred in settlement. For example, contracts for differences require a notional principal amount on which settlement can be calculated but that notional amount is not settled. An interest rate swap would be another example.

Novation The process where registered trades are cancelled with the clearing members and substituted by two new ones—one between the clearing house and the clearing member seller, the other between the clearing house and the clearing member buyer.

The legal transference of an interest or obligation to another party that replaces the original party.

NSCC National Securities Clearing Corporation—clearing organization for US shares.

NYMEX New York Mercantile Exchange; the largest energy derivative exchange and part of the Chicago Exchanges Group.

NYSE New York Stock Exchange which acquired Euronext but is now part of ICE

OASYS Trade Confirmation system for US brokers operated by Thomson Financial Services.

OATs Obligations Assimilables du Tresor—a 7–10 year French Treasury bond.

Obligation netting An arrangement to transfer only the net amount (of cash or a security) due between two or more parties, rather than transfer all amounts between the parties on a gross basis.

OEICs A style of investment funds similar to unit trusts and common in European countries.

Abbreviation for Open Ended Investment Company. OEICs are investment funds that "pool" investor's money.

ICVC (Investment Company with Variable Capital) is a newer name for the well-established OEIC structure.

In Europe a common product that is an open ended investment structure is a SICAV.

Unit trusts differ from OEICs & ICVCs, in that they often have dual pricing, with a bid to offer price spread. OEICs/ICVCs have a single price for buying and selling, based on the daily valuation of the underlying investments carried out at their mid-market price.

While technically speaking the structure of the three types of funds are different, from an investor's perspective they are all collective investments.

Off-balance sheet A transaction whose principal amount is not shown on the balance sheet because it is a contingent liability or settled as a contract for differences. It is not an asset.

Off-Market Coupon Swap A swap in which the coupon is above or below the current market value.

Offer for Sale Historically, the most popular form of new issue in the UK for companies bringing their securities to the stock market for the first time. The company offers its shares to the general public. Often called an IPO, initial public offering and is made via the issuing of a Prospectus or Offering Document.

Offering Memorandum An offering document or letter which sets out the terms of the offer of shares in a company or fund.

Offer Price The price at which a trader or market maker is willing to sell a contract.

Office of Fair Trading (OFT) Government department which advises the Secretary of State for Trade and Industry on whether or not a proposed takeover should be referred to the MMC for full investigation.

Offshore Relates to locations outside the regulation, tax, and legislative authorities of the investor. Popular offshore locations are Channel Isles, Cayman, BVI, Isle of Man, Bermuda etc.

Offshore may not necessarily be outside the national boundaries of a country. In some countries, certain banks or other institutions may be granted offshore status and thus be exempt from all or specific controls or legislation. In others, areas are designated as benefiting from different tax and or regulatory regimes, for example, Luxembourg, Dublin.

Offshore locations allow investors to have a different tax and or regulatory regime applied to their investments while in that location however should the money be brought back "onshore," that is, from the Bermuda to the UK then it would become subject to the tax and regulation of that jurisdiction.

Offshore Financial Centre Another name for an international financial center located in a recognized offshore location. May be certain tax and regulatory advantages.

Omnibus Account Account containing the holdings of more than one client.

On-balance sheet A transaction whose principal amount or value is shown on the balance sheet.

On-line Processing which is executed via an interactive input onto a PC or stationary terminal connected to a processing center.

Open Economy A country where there are no restrictions on trading with other countries.

Open Ended Fund Type of investment such as Unit Trusts or OEICs, which can expand by issuing more units or shares usually without limit. Can of course also reduce in size by cancelling shares or units upon redemption by investors.

Open Ended Investment Company (OEIC) New corporate structure introduced in 1997. It is a form of collective investment vehicle. See *OEICS*.

Open Order A purchase or sale order at a stated price that is good until cancelled or executed.

Open Outcry The style of trading whereby traders face each other in a designated area such as a pit and shout or call their respective bids and offers. Hand signals are also used to communicate. It is governed by exchange rules.

Opening Trade A bought or sold trade that is held open to create a position.

Open Interest In derivatives exchanges the number of contracts both bought and sold which remain open for delivery on an exchange. Important indicator of liquidity.

Open Position The number of contracts or shares which have not been offset. The resultant position will be held in the clearing organization, firm, or custodian records at the close of business.

Operational risk The risk of losses resulting from inadequate systems and control, human errors, or management failings.

Option An option is in the case of the *buyer*; the right, but not the obligation, to take (call) or make (put) for delivery of the underlying product and in the case of the *seller;* the obligation to make or take delivery of the underlying product.

Option Premium The sum of money paid by the buyer, for acquiring the right of the option. It is the sum of money received by the seller for incurring the obligation, having sold the rights, of the option.

    Note: It is the sum of the intrinsic value and the time value that makes the price of the option.

Optional Dividend Dividend that can be paid either in cash or in stock. The shareholders entitled to the dividend make the choice when the option is offered by the issuer.

Options On Futures These have the same characteristics as an option, the difference being that the underlying product is either a long or short futures contract. Premium is not exchanged as the contracts are marked to market each day.

Order driven market A stock market where brokers acting on behalf of clients match trades with each other either on the trading floor of the exchange or through a central computer system.

Ordinary Shares Known as common stock in the United States and equities in the UK. Shareholders are the owners of a company and are protected so the maximum loss is the value of their shares and not the full debt of the company. In addition to ordinary shares there can also be preferred and deferred shares.

Oversubscribed Circumstances where people have applied for more shares than are available in a new issue.

Out-of-the-money A call option whose exercise price is above the current underlying share price or a put option whose exercise price is below the current underlying share price. This option has no intrinsic value.

Out of Pocket Expenses Expenses and costs which are charged to the client without taking any profit.

Outperformance Term used to describe a fund/fund manager that beats a stock market index or an average of competing funds.

Out-Trade A trade which has been incorrectly matched on the floor of an exchange.

Over-The-Counter (OTC) A one-to-one agreement between two counterparties where the specifications of the product are completely flexible and nonstandardized. A bilaterally negotiated transaction.

Overdraft Use of a financial facility where there is withdrawal of more money than is in a bank account at a given time.

Overnight Money Money placed on the money market for repayment for the next day.

Oversold Where a rush of selling shares has depressed the market for no justifiable reason. Can also be a term used to describe a dealing error, that is, sold 100 instead of 10.

Panel on Takeovers and Mergers (PTM) A nonstatutory body comprising City institution which regulates takeover activities.

Par Value See *Nominal Value.*

Par Yield Curve A curve which measures yield over time.

Pair Off Back-to-back trade between two parties where settlement occurs only by exchanging the cash difference between the two parties.

Pari Passu Without partiality. Securities that rank pari passu, rank equally with each other.

Participation Swap A transaction which operates as a cap on a full notional principal if LIBOR is set above the agreed interest rate and operates as a swap on a portion of the notional principal if LIBOR is set below the agreed interest rate.

Passive Manager A fund or manager where the fund is invested in such a way that it replicates all or a large part of a market. An example is a tracker fund where the fund is invested proportionally to an index it tracks.

Payer The payer in a swap is the counterparty which pays the fixed rate and receives the floating rate. The other party is the payer of floating and receiver of fixed.

Paying agent A bank which handles payment of interest and dividends on behalf of the issuer of a security.

Payment Date Date on which a dividend or an interest payment is scheduled to be paid.

Pension Fund Fund set up by a corporation, labor union, governmental entity, or other organization to pay the pension benefits of retired workers. Pension funds invest billions of dollars annually in the securities markets and are therefore major market players.

Performance Fees Fees payable to a fund manager when the value of a portfolio has risen above a previous level (high water mark) and or has met a benchmark over a period (hurdle rate). Usually a percentage of the growth in the period. Common in hedge funds.

Perpetual bond A bond which has no redemption date.

Physical Delivery Used to describe a derivative contract that on delivery will result in the asset being delivered, for example, bond futures, stock options, commodities.

Also the delivery of a security in paper rather than electronic form.

PICs Term used for property index certificates, a type of bond.

PIFs Term used for forward contracts based on a property index, that is, property index forwards.

Pit The designated area on the market floor where a particular contract is traded. In the LME it is termed the ring.

Placement The first stage of money laundering, in which the money is passed placed in the banking system. See *layering, integration. Note:* not to be confused with the placement of new securities directly with the clients of an investment bank rather than being offered publicly or the placing of shares in a hedge fund.

Placement Memorandum Offering document for a hedge fund.

Placing Another term for the procedure used for new issues where a securities house contracts its own clients to offer them stock. It is almost always used for new issues of international/ eurobonds and sometimes for equities.

Plain Vanilla or Vanilla Swap A swap which has a very basic structure.

Portfolio List of investments held by an individual, fund portfolio or company, or list of loans made by a bank or financial institution.

Power of Attorney The legal authority for one party to sign for and act on behalf of another party.

Preemption Rights The right of existing shareholders purchase shares in a new issue to maintain their percentage holding. Normally happens either when a company is trying to raise cash or as a result of a takeover for paper which the seller does not want.

Preference Shares Shares that have preferential rights to dividends, usually a fixed sum, before dividends are paid out to ordinary shareholders. They usually carry no voting rights. The rights of preference shareholders are established in a company's articles of association and may differ between companies in a variety of ways.

Premium An option premium is the amount paid up-front by the purchaser of the option to the writer.

Also the amount of a price above the fair value of the instrument.

Prepayments An accounting process to reflect a payment in one accounting period that is for services in a different period.

Present value The amount of money which needs to be invested (or borrowed) now at a given interest rate in order to achieve exactly a given cash flow in the future, assuming compound reinvestment (or refunding) of any interest payments received (or paid) before the end. See *future value*.

Presettlement Checks and procedures undertaken immediately after execution of a trade prior to settlement. Can be part of clearing. Often carried out in the Middle Office.

Price/earnings ratio The share price of a company divided by its earnings per share. A high p/e ratio implies that the company is well thought of for its future prospects.

Price (Conversion) Factor The price at which a bond would trade, per 1 nominal, to yield the notional coupon of the futures contract on the delivery day (or the first day in the deliverable month if this applies).

Price/Pricing Policy The method of establishing a price for the valuation process associated with assets. Used by fund administrators to value a portfolio and by middle office to value traders position. Assets can be "easy" or "difficult" to value and most firms will have a pricing policy that sets out the methodology to used in the process.

Primary Dealer A dealer in the primary market for securities and other instruments.

Primary Market Market for the offer or placement of new securities such as international, domestic, and foreign bond issues or equities. Any subsequent resale or purchase is handled on the secondary market.

Prime Broker Usually a major investment bank that offers hedge funds (and others) a broad range of services including execution, stock lending, loans, sales, custody services etc.

Prime Broker Agreement Key agreement between the customer (ie, hedge fund) and the PB, can also cover Custody services offered by the PB.

Prime Rate Term used in US banks for the rate at which they lend to prime or first class customers. Similar to the base rate in the UK.

Principal protected product An investment whose maturity value is guaranteed to be at least the principal amount invested initially.

Principal Trading When a firm buys from or sells to another firm for its own account. Trades result in a profit or loss for the firm.

Principal-To-Principal Market A market where the clearing-house only recognizes the clearing member as the entity it will deal with and hold liable to settle transactions, and not the underlying clients of the clearing member.

Principal Value That amount inscribed on the face of a security and exclusive of interest or premium. The amount is the one used in the computation of interest due on such a security.

Private Customer An individual person who is a client of a broker.

Private Equity Shares in nonquoted (unlisted) companies, that is, privately owned companies.

Private Equity Fund A type of investment fund that invests in private companies often with a definitive life of the fund, typically ten years. Capital is committed to the fund by investors and drawn down over a period as the investments are made. The sponsor of the fund is often a private equity firm which uses investment advisers to identify the companies the fund will invest in. Can be established as a limited liability partnership (LLP) or limited liability company (LLC).

Private placement Issue of securities that is offered to a limited number of investor.

Privatization Process whereby the government puts state owned industries into the private sector, for example, water, electricity. Usually involves an offer for sale of the shares in the newly created company. The government may continue to hold some shares.

Property Derivatives A market in derivatives traded OTC and based mainly on swaps utilizing the Investment Property Databank (IPD) indices versus Libor or index versus index.

Property Management Company (PMC) A management company that deals with the day to day operation of physical property owned by another party, for example, a property fund.

Proprietary Trader A trader who deals for an organization such as an investment bank taking advantage of short term price movements as well as taking long term views on whether the market will move up or down. See also *principal trading*.

Prospectus A document that sets out the terms of the offer to subscribe for shares in a company or investment fund.

Protected Funds Funds other than money market (cash) funds which aim to provide a return of a set amount of capital back to the investor, with the potential for some growth.

Proxy Appointee of a shareholder who votes on his behalf at company meetings.

Proxy Statement Material information to be given to a corporation's stockholders prior to solicitation of votes.

Public Offering Offer of securities to the general public.

Public Placement An issue of securities that is offered through a securities house to institutional and individual clients.

Put Option An option that gives the buyer the right, but not the obligation, to sell a specified quantity of the underlying asset at a fixed price, on or before a specified date. The seller of a put option has the obligation (because they have sold the right) to take delivery of the underlying asset if the option is exercised by the buyer.

Putable In the case of a bond, it is the right of the investor to sell the bond back to the issuer. In the case of a swap, it is the right of the fixed rate receiver to cancel the swap.

Quoted Colloquial term for a security that is traded on the Stock Exchange.

Quote Driven Dealing system where some firms accept the responsibility to quote buying and selling prices.

Ramp A method employed to inflate a share price with the intention of selling before the price drops back again.

Also the period associated with a CDO where there is no return to the investors while the value "ramps up."

Range forward A forward outright with two forward rates, where settlement tales place at the higher forward rate if the spot rate at maturity is higher than that, at the lower forward rate if the spot rate at maturity is lower than that, or at the spot rate at maturity otherwise. See *collar*.

Rating Evaluation of risk by rating services such as Moody's or Standard and Poor's on companies, governments, countries, and financial products.

RCH Abbreviation for Recognized Clearing House under the UK Financial Services Act.

Real Interest Rate The rate of interest after taking inflation into account.

Real Time Gross Settlement Gross settlement system where trades are settled continuously through the processing day—abbreviate to RTGS.

Realized profit/loss Profit or loss which has arisen from a purchase and sale of an asset.

Receiver Person, usually an accountant, appointed by creditors in an attempt to rescue an ailing company through tighter financial controls than were already in place. Generally, they succeed only in utilizing the company assets to reimburse secured creditors after which any remaining creditors can appoint a liquidator.

Also applicable in swaps as the opposite of the payer.

Recession Temporary reduction in trade that creates a downturn in the economy. A number of causes can create this situation such as falling share and property prices, lack of consumer confidence, unemployment etc.

Usually two successive months or periods of no or negative growth in an economy is considered a recession.

Recognized Investment Exchange (RIE) Status given by a regulatory body to an approved exchange.

Reconciliation The comparison of a person's, a fund's or firms records of cash and securities positions with records held by another party and the investigation and resolution of any discrepancies between the two sets of records.

For example, a fund portfolio to assets held by a custodian or a cash position to a bank account.

Record Date The date on which a securities holder must hold the securities in order to receive an income or entitlement.

Redemption The purchase and cancellation of outstanding securities including shares or units in a fund through a cash payment to the holder by the issuer.

Redemption Price A price at which bonds may be redeemed, or called, at the issuer's option, prior to maturity (often with a slight premium).

The redemption (sale) of units or shares in a fund.

Reference Term used in OTC derivatives to determine the entity or price or source that will in turn determine value, settlement etc., for example, Libor as the reference entity in an interest rate swap.

Referral A proposed takeover is investigated thoroughly and if there are concerns that it is not good for the market, that is, it may create a monopoly, it may be referred to a government department for a decision on whether to allow the offer to proceed.

Reflate The opposite of deflation is reflation and is used by governments to increase consumer spending.

REGIS-TR Clearstream operated trade repository for OTC derivatives.

Registered Bond A bond whose owner is registered with the issuer or its registrar.

Registered Title Form of ownership of securities where the owner's name appears on a register maintained by the company.

Registrar An official of a company who maintains its share register.

Registrar of Companies Government department, in the UK Companies House, responsible for keeping records of all companies.

Relative Return A fund's performance relative to the rest of its sector, or an index.

Reorganization Generally any event where the equity, debt, or capital structure of a company is changed.

Replacement cost The mark-to-market loss which would be incurred if it were necessary to undertake a new transaction to replace an existing one, because the counterparty to the existing transaction defaulted.

Repurchase Agreement (Repo) Borrowing funds by providing a government security for collateral and promising to "repurchase" the security at the end of the agreed upon time period. The associated interest rate is the "repo-rate."

Reputational risk The risk that an organization's reputation will be damaged.

Reserve Currency The trading balance of a country, normally held in readily convertible currencies such as sterling, dollars, Yen etc.

Reserves The assets of a country are made up of in part, its financial reserves such as gold, convertible currency, International Monetary Fund credits and special drawing rights. Other assets include property, overseas investments etc.

Reset Date The date when periodic payment terms are established, that is, floating rate on a swap. See also *rollover*.

Resettable Coupon A bond that allows the issuer to reset the coupon midway through the life of the bond.

Residence The status determining the extent to which a person is taxed in a country with a global system of taxation. Residence is determined according to periods of physical presence in the country.

Resolution Proposal on which shareholders vote, put them at a meeting.

REIT Real Estate Investment Trust.

Retail Fund An investment fund authorized by a regulator that can be marketed to almost any kind of investor including those with limited understanding of capital markets. There is a correspondingly high level of protection for investors through the regulations.

Retail Price Index (RPI) Index that shows the movement of a basket of prices, in the UK used as a measure of inflation.

Retractable Coupon A bond that allows the investor to sell the bonds back to the issuer at par if the new fixed rate on a resettable coupon bond is unacceptable.

Return The amount by which savings may increase due to a combination of interest or dividend income and capital growth.

Reverse Repo Purchase of gilt where the price and date for its resale is fixed at the same time.

Reverse Takeover The acquisition of a company by a smaller concern. Can also apply where a large organization takes over a smaller one but the overall running of the amalgamated company would be by the latter.

Reverse Yield Gap Usually equities produce a higher yield than bonds. When the converse applies it is known as the Reverse Yield Gap.

Rights Issue Offer of new shares made to existing shareholders under a preemptive right where the shares are first offered to existing shareholders but they have no obligation to buy them.

Right Of Offset Where positions and cash held by the Clearing Organization in different accounts for a member are allowed to be netted.

Risk A measure of the probability that the value of savings and the income from them will fall as well as rise.

Risk Warning Document that must be dispatched and signed by private customers before they deal in traded options.

Risk-weighted assets See *capital adequacy ratio*.

Roller coaster swap A swap in which the notional principal amount varies up and down over the life of the swap.

Rollover A rollover can be when the next leg of a swap is calculated or when a futures position in an expiring month is "rolled" to the next maturity. For example, the position in the Mar. expiry is closed out and reopened in the next available maturity, say the Jun. expiry.

Rolling Settlement System used in most countries including England. Trades are settled a set number of days after being transacted.

Rouble Currency of Russia

Round Lots The minimum amounts for which dealer's quotes are good.

Round Tripping The combined commission or fees for both the opening and closing leg of a trade.

Running a Book Firms who are buying and selling stock for themselves hoping to profit from price differences are said to run a book in that stock.

Safekeeping Holding of securities on behalf of clients. They are free to sell at any time. Part of the services offered by custodians.

Sale of rights nil paid The sale of the entitlement to take up a rights issue—see also *nil paid price*.

Same Day Funds Refers to the availability of funds on the same day as they are deposited.

Samurai Bond A bond denominated in JPY and issued in the Japanese capital market by a foreign borrower.

Savings Account An interest bearing account with a bank or other savings institution which normally does not provide cheque and other transaction facilities.

Sawtooth risk A swap in which the notional principal amount varies up and down over the life of the swap, with an overall upward or downward trend.

Scaling Down When a new issue is oversubscribed, the procedure whereby applicants receive a proportion of the number of shares for which they applied.

Scheme Particulars Offering document associated with Unit Trusts.

Scrip Dividends Scrip dividends options provide shareholders with the choice of receiving dividend entitlements in the form of cash, share, or a combination or both. The amount of stocks to be distributed under a scrip option is calculated by dividing the cash dividend amount by the average market price over a recent period of time.

Scrip Issue See *Bonus Issue*.

SD Indeval Clearing House and Depository for the Mexican market.

SEATS Plus An order-driven system used on the London Stock Exchange for securities which do not attract at least two firms of market makers and for all AIM listed securities.

Secondary Market Market place for trading in existing securities. The price at which they are trading has no direct effect on the company's fortunes but is a reflection of investors' perceptions of the company.

Sectors Investment funds are divided into a variety of categories to keep together funds of a similar type, for example, "cash," North American, European. The areas they operate in are called sectors.

  Stock markets are also divided into sectors, for example, financials, energy, transport etc.

Secured A debt issued by a company that is charged against an asset, or a private transaction like a mortgage, where the property is charged against the loan to purchase it.

Securitization The use of securities and other assets to guarantee the repayment of a debt. An example would be using the rents from a property to guarantee a bond that is issued to raise capital to purchase more property.

Securities Can mean any instrument in the markets but generally refers to bonds and equities.

Securities House General term covering any type of organization involved in securities although usually reserved for the larger firms.

Securities Lending Loan of securities for a fee by an investor to another (usually a broker-dealer), usually to cover a short sale or to enable settlement of a trade. Collateral is required see also *stock lending*.

Securities and Exchange Commission (SEC) The overall securities and equity derivatives regulatory body in the United States of America.

SEDOL Stock Exchange Daily Official List, a securities numbering system assigned by the International Stock Exchange in London.

Segregated account Account in which there is only the holdings of one client.

Segregation Of Funds Regulatory requirement where the client assets are held separately from those assets belonging to the broker, custodian or other firm operating for the client.

SEHK Stock Exchange of Hong Kong.

Selective Marketing See *Placing*.

SEPA Single Euro Payments Area—integrated payment process for euro denominated transactions for EU and EFTA countries.

Service Level Agreement An agreement between the service supplier and the customer for instance a custodian and the customer will have a SLA covering their relationship.

Can also apply internally within a firm particularly in the area of IT and the business units.

SETS Abbreviation for the London Stock Exchange Trading System.

Settlement The fulfilment of the contractual commitments of transacted business.

Settlement Date The date on which a trade is cleared by delivery of securities against funds (actual settlement date, contractual settlement date).

Share Futures Based on individual shares. Delivery is fulfilled by the payment or receipt of cash against the exchange calculated delivery settlement price.

Share Option A right sold to an investor conferring the option to buy or sell shares of a particular company at a predetermined price and within a specified time limit.

Shell Company A company in name only but quoted on the stock exchange. Shells are used when setting up a new business avoiding the sometimes long and expensive process.

Shogun Bond Straight bond denominated in foreign currency, other than JPY, issued by a foreign issuer on the Japanese capital market.

Short/Short Position A sold position in a derivative or security that is held as an open position.

Short Coupons Bonds or notes with a short current maturity.

Short Cover The purchase of a security that has been previously sold short. The purpose is to return securities that were borrowed to make a delivery.

Short-dated Gilt Gilts due to be redeemed within the next seven years, according to the LSE, (FT states up to 5 years).

Short Position Position created by the selling of securities, commodities etc. which are not owned.

Short Sale The sale of securities not owned by the seller in the expectation that the price of these securities will fall and can be bought later at a lower price or as part of an arbitrage.

Short Selling Selling stock that you do not own. Requires the borrowing of securities to settle the trade.

Short-term Security Generally an obligation maturing in less than one year.

Short Termism An investment view that assumes a quick realization of profits.

SGX The merged central Stock Exchange of Singapore and the derivatives exchange SIMEX.

SICAV Abbreviation for the French: Societes d'Investissement a Capital Variable. A UCIT domiciled in Luxembourg or France.

SICOVAM CSD for French corporate securities and OATs (now merged with Euroclear).

Simple interest Interest calculated on the assumption that there is no opportunity to reinvest the interest payments during the life of an investment and thereby earn extra income.

Single Currency Interest Rate Swap An interest rate swap where the interest payments are exchanged in the same currency.

Sinking Fund In the case of a loan repaid by instalments, each instalment can be considered to consist of two parts. One portion of each instalment represents the interest payable on the loan, the other portion, which represents the repayment of capital, is known as the "sinking fund."

SIS SEGA Inter Settle—CSD for Switzerland.

Slump An excessive long-term recession with disastrous economic implications.

Soft Commodities Description given to commodities such as sugar, coffee, and cocoa, traded through exchanges such as the NYSE Liffe.

Sovereign Debt Securities Bonds issued by the government of a country.

Sovereign Wealth Funds Investment management operated on behalf of a country, for example, the Abu Dhabi Investment Authority.

SPAN Abbreviation for Standardized Portfolio Analysis of Risk. A form of margin calculation which is used by various clearing organizations.

Speculation A deal undertaken because the trader or investor expects prices to move in his favor and thereby realize a profit.

Speculator The speculator is a trader or investor who wants to assume risk for potentially much higher rewards.

Sponsored Member Type of CREST member whose name appears on the register but has no computer link with CREST.

Spot delivery A delivery or settlement of currencies on the value date, two business days later.

Spot market Market for immediate as opposed to future delivery. In the spot market for foreign exchange, settlement is in two business days ahead.

Spot Month The first month for which futures contracts are available.

Spot Rate The price prevailing in the spot market.

Spread 1. The difference between bid and asked price on a security.

2. Difference between yield on or prices of two securities of different types or maturities.

3. In underwriting, difference between price realized by an issuer and price paid by the investor.

4. Difference between two prices or two rates. What commodities traders would refer to as the basis.

Spread cont'd A trading strategy in which a trader buys one instrument and sells another, related instrument with a view to profiting from a change in the price difference between the two. A futures spread is the purchase of one futures contract and the sale of another; an option spread is the purchase of one call (or put) and the sale of another.

Spread cont'd The difference between the bid and offer prices in a quotation.

Spread cont'd The difference between one price or rate and another, for example, the extent to which a swap fixed-rate is higher than a benchmark Treasury bond yield, or the extent to which the floating-rate in a swap is above or below LIBOR.

Splitting Rights This is where an investors using a formula work out how many rights to sell to take up the rest of their entitlement for no cost.

SSRC/CSCCRC The China Securities Central Clearing & Registration Corporation (CSC-CRC) is responsible for the central depository, registration, and clearing of securities. It carries out the T + 1 settlement for A shares and T + 3 for B shares.

Stamp duty Tax on purchase of property including shares in the UK.

Stamp Duty Reserve Tax (SDRT) (UK) Tax payable on the purchase of UK equities in uncertificated form (ie, those held within the Euroclear system).

Standard and Poors US indices on which futures and options contracts are based. CME introduced S&P 500 index futures as the first index based derivative.

Standard Settlement Instructions Instructions for settlement with a particular counterparty which are always followed for a particular kind of deal and, once in place, are therefore not repeated at the time of each transaction.

Standing Instruction Default instruction, for example, provided to an agent processing payments or clearing securities trades; provided by shareholder on how to vote shares (eg, vote for all management recommended candidates).

Standing Order An instruction to a bank to pay regular agreed amounts on specified dates. These cannot be altered by the bank.

Stepped A stepped coupon is one that rises or falls in a predetermined way over the life of an arrangement.

Stock In some countries (eg, the United States..), the term applies to ordinary share capital of a company. In other countries (eg, UK), stock may mean share capital that is issued in variable amount instead of in fixed specified amounts, or it can describe government loans, for example, "gilt edged stocks."

Can also form part of the balance sheet of a company being the amount of assets held

Stock Dividend Dividends paid by a company in stock instead of cash. Also called scrip dividend.

Stock Exchange Electronic Trading System (SETS) Electronic dealing system for some stocks on the London Stock Exchange. It is an order book system.

Stock Market Indices They show how a specified portfolio of share prices are moving in order to give an indication of market trades. Each stock market of the world is represented by at least one index. The FTSE 100 Index, for example, reflects the movements of the share prices of the UK's largest 100 quoted companies.

Stock market Term used to describe where securities are/have been traded, that is, "today on the stock market shares closed higher."

Stock Index Futures/Options Based on the value of an underlying stock index like the FTSE 100 in the UK, the S&P 500 index in the United States and the Nikkei 225 and 300 in Japan. Delivery is fulfilled by the payment or receipt of cash against the exchange calculated delivery settlement price.

These are referred to as both indices and indexes.

Stock Lending Process of lending, for a fee, securities against collateral.

Stock Lending Agreement The terms under which the lender and borrower enter into the loan and which carries important information about early termination of the loan, substitution of collateral etc. A Global Master Securities Lending Agreement has been created by the International Securities Lending Association (ISLA).

Stock (or Bond) Power A legal document, either on the back of registered stocks and bonds or attached to them, by which the owner assigns his interest in the corporation to a third party, allowing that party the right to substitute another name on the company records instead of the originals owner's.

Stock Split When an issuer splits its equity, it divides existing shares on a ratio, for example, 1×50 p nominal share becomes 5×10 p nominal shares or 1 share with a price of €50 becomes 4 shares with a price of €12.50. There is no change to the overall value of the investors holding.

STP See *Straight through Processing*.

Stop (Order) An owner of a physical security that has been mutilated, lost or stolen will request the issuer to place a stop (transfer) on the security and to cancel and replace the security.

Also used when placing a deal, that is, "stop loss" sell or buy if a certain price is hit after I have traded.

Straight Debt A standard bond issue, without right to convert into the common shares of the issuer.

STRATE Electronic settlement and depository organization for the Johannesburg Stock Exchange (Share Transactions Totally Electronic).

Straddle The purchase (or sale) of a call combined with the purchase (or sale) of a put at the same strike (generally purchased with both at-the-money).

Straight-through processing (STP) Computer transmission of the details of a trade, without manual intervention, from their original input by the trader to all other relevant areas—position keeping, risk control, accounts, settlement, and reconciliation.

Street Name Securities held in street name are held in the name of a broker or another nominee such as a custodian.

Strike price The fixed price, per share at which an option (or warrant) conveys the right to call (purchase) or put (sell) the underlying shares.

Strike price/rate Also exercise price. The price or rate at which the holder of an option can insist on the underlying transaction being fulfilled.

Strip The purchase or sale of a series of consecutive interest rate futures contracts or forward rate agreements.

Stripped Bonds (Strips) Bonds where the rights to the interest payments and eventual repayment of the nominal value have been separated from each other and trade independently. Facility introduced in the UK for gilts in Dec. 1997.

Structured Product A package of products, often but not always derivatives, created to meet the needs of a specific investor or group of investors. Can be designed in response to a request from a client or by a bank and then marketed to clients.

Stump period A calculation period, usually at the beginning or end of a swap, other than the standard ones normally quoted.

Subcustodian A firm in a foreign country that acts on behalf of the global custodian as its custody agent.

Subscription Price Price at which shareholders of a corporation are entitled to purchase common shares in a rights offering or at which subscription warrants are exercisable.

Subscriptions In a bond issue, the buying orders from the lead manager, comanagers, underwriters and selling group members for the securities being offered.

The amount payable by investors to acquire units or shares in a fund or new securities being offered by way of an offering or corporate action.

Subsidiary A company, at least 50% of which is owned by another company. See *Holding Company.*

Surrender Value The value for which a life assurance policy can be cashed in for prior to maturity.

Swap A transaction where two parties agree directly or through an intermediary to exchange flows and sometimes assets. Examples are interest rate swaps where interest flows based on a notional amount and a benchmark floating rate against a fixed rate are exchanged and currency swaps where the currencies and interest rates are exchanged at the beginning and end of the swap. Traditionally traded over the counter but some swaps are now being standardized and traded on exchanges.

Swap Spread The difference between the bid and offered side of a swap. Can also refer to the spread over treasuries—that is, the difference between the yield on the treasury note and the bid or offer on the swap.

SwapClear A clearing-house and central counterparty for swaps operated by LCH Clearnet.

Swaption An option convertible into a predetermined swap transaction. Options can be payers or receivers, American or European.

SWIFT Society for Worldwide Interbank Financial Telecommunications—secure electronic communications network between banks and other financial market institutions.

Switching The facility to move the money invested in a unit-linked policy or other type of investment from one fund to another.

Syndicate A group of bond houses which act together in underwriting and distributing a new securities issue or a group of insurers who operate as a syndicate each taking some of the exposure to the risk.

Takeover When one company obtains more than 50% of another company's shares.

Tap Stocks A portion of Gilt-edged securities that are held over after the day of issue and made available by the government broker to satisfy demand and to control interest rates, market prices, and liquidity.

   Tap issues are so called because amounts of the total issue can be issued as and when, that is, by turning on or off the "tap."

TARGET(2) Trans European Automated Real time Gross settlement Express Transfer—system linking the real-time gross settlements for euros in the 15 European Union countries. Now superseded by TARGET2.

TARGET2 Securities (T2S) A project to create a single securities and payment system in Europe to replace the current country by country systems.

Tax Avoidance The legitimate arrangement of a taxpayer's affairs so that he receives income or gains in such a way that takes him out of the tax regime altogether or reduces his tax liability. Tax avoidance is not illegal.

Tax Evasion Tax evasion means ignoring or concealing a tax liability which has already arisen, Tax evasion is a criminal offence.

Tax Haven Another name for an international financial center where favorable tax laws apply.

Tax Reclaim The process that a global custodian and/or a holder of securities performs, in accordance with local government filing requirements, in order to recapture an allowable percentage of taxed withheld.

Tender Short futures positions that will, depending on the specific exchange, be tendered for delivery on expiry of the contracts or during a defined delivery period.

Tender Offer Formal offer to buy made to holders of a particular issue by a third party. Detailed offer is made by public announcement in newspapers and sometimes by personal letter of transmittal to each stockholder.

TER Abbreviation for Total Expense Ratio.

Terms For a new securities issue, the characteristics of the securities on offer: coupon, amount, maturity.

Termination The cancellation of a swap or other derivative, agreement or contract. The terms and conditions under which termination can and will take place is set out in the documentation agreed between the parties to the trade or the agreement or contract.

Termination date The end date of a swap.

Tier Capital Capital adequacy related capital of a bank. Tier 1 is core capital Tier 2 is other undisclosed reserves, subordinated loan etc.

Theoretical Spot Rate The rate used as a discount factor to derive the zero-coupon yield curve.

Theoretical Value Another term for fair value of a futures or options contract.

Thin Market A period of sparse trade on the stock market that can affect prices and the ability to trade.

Tick Size The value of a one point movement in the contract price of a future.

Tied Agent An individual or business which only sells one company's products (such as life assurance) making no pretext of offering independent advice on all the products available.

Time Deposit Deposit on an account held with a financial institution for a fixed term or with the understanding that the depositor can withdraw only by giving notice.

Time Value The amount by which an option's premium exceeds its intrinsic value. Where an option has no intrinsic value the premium consists entirely of time value.

The element in the price of something that relates to the time to maturity, for instance it is part of the "fair value" of a futures contract.

Tom-Next Money placed on the money market from tomorrow for repayment the day after.

Tom/Spot Week Money placed on the money market from tomorrow for repayment one week after (Tom/Spot Month).

Total Expense Ratio (TER) A measurement of the expenses of an investment fund against the return of the fund.

Total Return Swap A total return swap is a derivative where one party, the ratepayer, makes periodic fixed or floating rate payments to another, the total return payer, and receives from the other the total return on some reference asset. Used in relation to credit and is therefore a term sometimes used in relation to credit derivatives.

Touch The best prices available for a stock on the stock market, looking at all market makers or other prices available.

Tracking Error The difference in returns between a fund and its benchmark; also the extent to which a tracker fund tracks its benchmark.

Trade Date The date on which a trade is made.

Trade Guarantees Guarantees in place in a market which ensure that all compared or netted trades will be settled as compared regardless of a counterparty default.

Trade Repository An organization that records and reports to regulators noncentrally cleared OTC transactions.

Traded Option An option which is traded on an exchange.

Trader An individual who buys and sells securities with the objective of making short-term gains.

Transfer Change of ownership of securities or other assets. Final process of settlement of a trade or the movement of collateral.

Transfer Agent(Agency) Agent appointed by a corporation to maintain records of stock and bond owners, to cancel and issue certificates and to resolve problems arising from lost, destroyed or stolen certificates.

Maintains the record of subscriptions, redemptions, and the register of ownership of units and shares in an investment fund. Also responsible for carrying out CDD and communicating with investors. Is an element of the fund administration process.

Transfer Form Document which owners of registered documents must sign when they sell the security. Not required where a book entry transfer system is in use.

Transparency The degree to which a market is characterized by prompt availability of accurate price and volume information which gives participants full knowledge of the details of transactions being executed on the exchange.

TRAX See *Xtrakter*.

Treasury Arm of Government responsible for all financial decisions and regulation of the financial services sector, for example, HM Treasury in the UK.

Also Division within a firm dealing with funding, capital liquidity and cash flow management.

Treasury Bill Money market instrument issued with a life of less than one year issued by the United States and UK governments.

Treasury Bonds (US) US government bond issued usually with a 30 year maturity. (also known as the "long" bond.

Treasury Note A government obligation usually with maturities of 1–10 years, carrying a fixed rate of interest.

Treasury Notes (US) US government bond issued with 2-, 3-, 5-, and 7-year maturity.

Treasury Operations The management of excess cash and funding requirements through purchasing and issuing financial instruments and the depositing and taking of cash deposits.

Treasury Operations teams support this process by recording and settlement of the transactions.

Tri-party Repo Repo which utilizes an intermediary custodian to oversee the exchange of securities and cash.

Triple A—rating The highest credit rating for a bond or company by Standard & Poors—the risk of default (or nonpayment) is negligible.

Trust A legal arrangement where one person (the trustee) holds property (the trust property) on behalf of one or more other persons (the beneficiaries).

Trust Property The property put into trust by the settlor.

Trustee A trustee is appointed to oversee the management of certain funds. They are responsible for ensuring that the fund is managed correctly and that the interests of the investor are protected and that all relevant regulations and legislation are complied with including the trust deed, offering documents, prospectus etc.

The trustee owns the assets of the fund on behalf of the investors and only the trustee can create or cancel units in a unit trust.

Turn See *Spread.*

Turnaround Securities bought and sold for settlement on the same day.

Turnaround Time The time available or needed to settle a turnaround trade.

Turquoise Turquoise is a multilateral trading facility established by nine leading European investment banks, It is a competitor to exchanges but is now owned by the London Stock Exchange.

Two-way Price Simultaneous prices in a stock quoted by a market maker, the lower at which he is willing to buy and the higher at which he is willing to sell.

Some unit trusts are quoted on a two or dual pricing basis being the price at which the manager is prepared to buy or liquidate units or sell or create new units. The pricing mechanism is controlled by regulations.

UCITS A European Union Directive for a retail fund template when authorized in a member state and complied with can then be marketed in all EU countries without need for further authorization. It stands for *"Undertaking for Collective Investments in Transferable Securities"* and it is currently operating under its 4th version with UCITS V already in process.

Uncovered Dividends A dividend that is not paid out of profits and therefore means that the organization has had to liquidate assets to make the payments.

Underlying Asset or Underlying The asset or product from which the future or option's price is derived and which may be deliverable. Another term used is reference entity

Undersubscribed Circumstance when people have applied for fewer shares than are available in a new issue.

Underwrite Accept financial responsibility for (a commercial project); sign and issue (an insurance policy), thus accepting liability.

Underwriter(s) As part of a syndicate, a dealer who purchases new issues from the issuer and distributes them to investors.

Also the structurer of a CDO.

Institutions which agree to take up shares in a new issue if it is undersubscribed. They will charge an underwriting fee.

Insurance underwriters take on the risk of the insurance usually through syndication.

Unit Investment Trust A closed end fund used by small investors to spread investment risk.

Unit Linked Policy An endowment or whole life policy which invests in a unitized fund and the value of the policy is the value of the units purchased.

Unit Trust A system whereby money from a number of investors is pooled together and invested collectively on their behalf under trust law. Each owns a unit (or number of them) the value of which depends on the value of those items owned by the trust.

Unrealized profit Profit that has not arisen from a sale or purchase that offsets the original transaction—an increase in value of an asset for long position and a decrease in value for a short position. There can also be an unrealized loss on a position.

Up-and-in option A knock-in option where the trigger is higher than the underlying rate at the start. See *down-and-in option, up-and-out option, down-and-out option*.

Up-and-out option A knock-out option where the trigger is higher than the underlying rate at the start. See *up-and-in option, down-and-in option, down-and-out option*.

Value Added Tax A type of sales tax used in Europe.

Value at Risk (VaR) The maximum amount which a bank expects to lose, with a given confidence level, over a given time period.

Variance/Volatility Swap Swaps based on the volatility of an underlying index not the price or value.

Variation Margin The process of revaluing an exchange traded product each day. It is the value created by recalculating the position using the closing price on the previous day versus the current closing price. It is physically paid or received each day by the clearing organization to members and by members with their clients, although in the latter case a cash position in the client account is updated. The calculation is done on a mark-to-market basis.

Vega Another part of the "Greeks" and is a measure of the rate of change in an option's price caused by changes in volatility.

Venture Capital Funds Funds that are designed to raise capital from investors and to then invest the capital in newly formed unquoted or private equity companies.

Venture Capital Trusts Trusts set up to encourage investment in small to medium size businesses by investing in a range of companies thereby reducing some of the risk.

Volatility The degree of scatter of the underlying price or market when compared to the mean average rate. A volatile market experiences high degrees of scatter whereas a price or market lacking volatility is experiencing little movement away from the average

Volatility trades like volatility swaps or option straddles use the degree of volatility change during a period.

Vostro A vostro account is another bank's account held at our bank in our currency.

VPC Swedish Central Securities Depository (Värdepappercentralen).

Wall Street Term used to describe the financial center around the New York Stock Exchange, which is situated on the corner of Wall Street. Much the same as the Square Mile in London also known as the "City."

Warehouse A swap portfolio held by a market-maker. The market-maker may enter into a swap and put it in the warehouse until a suitable counterparty can be found.

Used for storage of commodities during the delivery.

Warehouse cont'd "Warehousing" may also be a term used when a large order for securities or derivatives is being completed over a period of time. The trades done are "warehoused" until the order is completed and allocated to the client or accounts within a client.

Warrants An option style product which can be listed on an exchange and raise money for the issuer, with a lifetime of generally more than one year.

Warrants are also issued for some commodities like for instance copper and these warrants entitle the holder to delivery of a certain amount of the metal, for example, Copper warrants on the LME in London.

Warrant agent A bank appointed by the issuer as an intermediary between the issuing company and the (physical) warrant holders, interacting when the latter want to exercise the warrants.

Waterfall A term given to the order of the distribution of return in a private equity fund.

Withholding Tax In the securities industry, a tax imposed by a government's tax authorities on dividends and interest paid to a person or entity outside of that country, which may be reclaimed if a tax treaty exists between the jurisdiction and the investor's jurisdiction.

World Bank Survivor along with the International Monetary Fund of the 1944 Bretton Woods agreement. Officially the International Bank for Reconstruction and Development, its aim is to lend or guarantee loans to poorer countries by utilizing aid from member countries.

Writer A person who has sold an open derivatives contract and is obliged to deliver or take delivery upon notification of exercise from the buyer.

Writer cont'd In the insurance market the company, person, or syndicate that is issuing the insurance, that is, the "writer" of insurance.

See also "*underwriter.*"

XETRA Dealing system of the Deutsche Börse.

Xtrakter MarketAxess operated trade repository for OTC derivatives and owner of the TRAX trade matching, transaction reporting, market and reference data system.

Yankee bond A US dollar bond issued in the United States of America by a non-USA issuer.

Yield Internal rate of return expressed as a percentage.

Yield Curve For securities that expose the investor to the same credit risk, a graph showing the relationship at a given point in the time between yield and current maturity. Yield curves are typically drawn using yields on government bonds, corporate bonds, swaps etc. of various maturities.

In effect a forecast of future returns that can be then used to present value instruments like IRS etc.

Yield to Maturity The rate of return yielded by a debt security held to maturity when both interest payments and the investor's capital gain or loss on the security is taken into account.

Zero coupon Bond A bond issued with no coupon but at a price substantially below par (discount) so that only capital is accrued over the life of the loan, and yield is comparable to coupon bearing instruments.

Zero-Coupon Yield Curve When the theoretical spot rates are constructed as a curve to show yield over time.

Zloty Polish currency.

Important Note:

The contents of this glossary of terms have been compiled from reliable sources and are believed to be correct, however The DSC Portfolio Ltd, Loader Associates Limited, and Computer Based Learning Limited can take no responsibility whatsoever for any loss, claim, or damages caused in whatever manner as a result of the reader using information taken from this work.

Useful Websites and Links

1. Association of Mutual Funds in India—https://www.amfiindia.com/
2. The Investment Company Institute—https://www.ici.org
3. The Investment Association (formerly the Investment Management Association) http://www.theinvestmentassociation.org/
4. Thomson Reuters—www.thomsonreuters.com
5. Alternative Investment Management Association (AIMA)—www.aima.org
6. The Jersey Funds Association—www.jerseyfunds.org
7. Jersey Finance—https://www.jerseyfinance.je
8. US Securities & Exchange Commission—https://www.sec.gov
9. The Association of the Luxembourg Fund Industry—www.alfi.lu
10. www.issanet.org (International Securities Services Association)
11. www.fca.gov.uk (Financial Conduct Authority UK)
12. www.isma.co.uk (International Securities Markets Association)
13. www.bis.org (Bank for International Settlement)
14. www.cls-group.com (CLS Bank)
15. www.isda.org (International Swaps and Derivatives Association)
16. www.isla.co.uk (International Securities Lending Association)
17. www.bba.org.uk (British Bankers Association)

Qualification and Training

1. The Advanced Certificate and Diploma in Fund Administration—http://onlinelearning.cltint.com/
2. IFF Fundamentals of Fund Administration and Clearing Settlement and Custody—www.iff-training.com
3. Euromoney—Investment Fund Operations- www.euromoney.com/Euromoney-Financial-Training
4. OneStudy Jersey—Fundamentals of Fund Administration—www.onestudy-training.co.uk

Suggested Reading

1. *Clearing Settlement & Custody*—David Loader published by Elsevier
2. *FundsEurope magazine*—www.fundseurope.com
3. *Global Custody*—www.globalcustody.net
4. *FIA SmartBrief*—www2.smartbrief.com/news

5. *Measuring and Managing Operational Risks in Financial Institutions*—Christopher Marshall published by Wiley
6. *Controls, Procedures and Risk*—David Loader published by Butterworth Heinemann
7. Operations Management and Advanced Operations Management—David Loader published by Wiley/CISI
8. Regulation and Compliance in Operations—David Loader published by Butterworth Heinemann
9. *Against The Gods –The Remarkable Story of Risk*—Peter L Bernstein published by Wiley

Index

Printed in the United States
By Bookmasters